DIALECTICAL LEFTISM'S ASSAULT ON CANADA

THE PROPHETS, POLICE AND POLITICOS

MAVROS WHISSELL

DIALECTICAL LEFTISM'S ASSAULT ON CANADA
Copyright © 2024 by Mavros Isaac Whissell

All rights reserved. Neither this publication nor any part of this publication may be reproduced or transmitted in any form or by any means, electronic or mechanical, including photocopying, recording or any information storage and retrieval system, without permission in writing from the author.

Scripture quotations taken from The ESV® Bible (The Holy Bible, English Standard Version®). ESV® Text Edition: 2016. Copyright © 2001 by Crossway, a publishing ministry of Good News Publishers. The ESV® text has been reproduced in cooperation with and by permission of Good News Publishers. Unauthorized reproduction of this publication is prohibited. All rights reserved.

The views and opinions expressed in this publication belong solely to the author and do not reflect those of Word Alive Press or any of its employees.

ISBN: 978-1-4866-2562-8
eBook ISBN: 978-1-4866-2563-5

Word Alive Press
119 De Baets Street Winnipeg, MB R2J 3R9
www.wordalivepress.ca

Cataloguing in Publication information can be obtained from Library and Archives Canada.

To my parents, Robert and Cynthia, for showing me there was a path
To Pastors David and Richard, for reminding me of the path
To those along the way and in the distance

ACKNOWLEDGEMENTS

I'D LIKE TO thank all the people who have helped me create this book in various capacities. Thank you first and foremost to my wonderful and faithful daughters, Ellie and Liza, for their patience and support during all my hours spent writing away on my laptop. Thank you to my mother, Cynthia, for love and support, and for the many hours of proofreading and invaluable suggestions. This book would not have been possible without you!

Thank you to Pastor David for providing me with so much insight and inspiration in the many avenues covered in the book. Your wisdom and guidance made this effort possible. Thank you to the unflappable William D. Gairdner for reviewing an early version of the manuscript and setting me on the right course. Thank you to Francine for the hours of proofreading and informal editing, and for fine tuning my work with your God-given talent. Thank you to Paul, whose gift to me of Haidt's book set this ball rolling! Thank you to Alison for your feedback on the early version of some chapters that provided important adjustments.

Thank you to Word Alive Press and especially Ariana, Kerry, and Crystal for your professionalism and care.

Thank you most of all to my friends on Woken Promises Facebook page, especially Michael M, Remo W, Bill W, Jim W, Marie K, Brad F, Brad M, Lain E, John M, Tony C, Patricia S, Jamie D, Pierre P, Deborah B, Mary NB, Rob D Sr, John C, Steve P, Frank R, Daniel F, Terry C, Paul L, Jim P, Joe A, Hermes L, Vicky BA, John R, Happy W, Jim R, Lauren S, Orling W, Peter C, Dan C, Keyser S, Marlene L, Sue ST, Sue C, Lucasi K, Evan M, Henry F, Ed G, William S, Granny A, Brent W, Ruth C, Gordon C, Barry S, Linda R, Beisel B, John S, Zuzana S, Tanya H, Jose B, Chris Y, Rob B, Paul H, Paul E, Nyla B, Don P, Jeremy H, Alex R, Mateusz W, Casey B, Bernadette M, Jim B, Hyphen P, Rick

M, Stephen D, Andre W, Mircea P, Clifford Y, Casey T, Kevin Y, Audrey YB, Peter T, Michelle BK, Richard Z, Velma C, Joe F, Dan S, Donna G, Mike L, and Larry D. You have all been supportive, and this effort is really for you guys! If I left anyone out, don't worry. I will include you in my next endeavour!

CONTENTS

ACKNOWLEDGEMENTS — v
PREFACE — ix

PART I: INTRODUCTION — 1
CHAPTER ONE: WHAT IS DIALECTICAL LEFTISM? — 3
CHAPTER TWO: LIES UNLIMITED — 15

PART II: THE SEED IS DEVOURED — 21
CHAPTER THREE: THE NEW LEFT — 23
CHAPTER FOUR: THE SOCIAL GOSPEL — 35
CHAPTER FIVE: EDUCATION, THE STATE ... AND RELIGION? — 47
CHAPTER SIX: SIGNS OF A TRAJECTORY — 63

PART III: THE VINE SUFFOCATES — 79
CHAPTER SEVEN: ORTHODOX AND CULTURAL MARXISM — 81
CHAPTER EIGHT: NEO-MARXISM — 107
CHAPTER NINE: MARXISM IS A THREAT TO PUBLIC SAFETY — 121
CHAPTER TEN: CO-OPTING THE CIVIL RIGHTS MOVEMENT — 137
CHAPTER ELEVEN: CRITICAL LEGAL STUDIES VS. POSTMODERNISM — 149
CHAPTER TWELVE: WOKE IDEOLOGY — 159

PART IV: THE WHEAT AND THE TARES — 179
CHAPTER THIRTEEN: THE CBC'S LEFT-LEANING BIAS — 181
CHAPTER FOURTEEN: STATISM AND MILITANT ATHEISM — 201
CHAPTER FIFTEEN: MODERN MARXIST METHODOLOGY — 217
CHAPTER SIXTEEN: POLICE AND IDENTITY POLITICS — 229

PART V: THE HARVEST — 247
CHAPTER SEVENTEEN: THE ATTACK ON CIVIL SOCIETY AND THE STATE — 249
CHAPTER EIGHTEEN: CONCLUSION — 265

BIBLIOGRAPHY — 273
AUTHOR BIO — 275

PREFACE

Why do people want to play victim when they could be so much more?

WHAT YOU ARE about to embark upon, dear reader, is a recorded search for truth, conducted over many years. A single question sparking a series of questions carefully addressed to answer (in some part) the chaos rising around us in Canada today. The question can't be solved utilizing left or right political ideologies either, because it has too much to do with the human condition. Our ephemeral and fragile existence is invariably punctuated by hardship and suffering. The government has proven incapable of sufficiently addressing such trials. Throughout history, political ideologies have foundered in their attempt to play saviour to humanity, whether left, centre, or right.

Despite our inherent condition, we appear more capable creatures than ever. We're better-educated, richer, and healthier human beings than at any time in history. The average lifespan has increased from a stout thirty-three years during the medieval period in Europe to over eighty in Canada today. We've seen incredible advancements in science and medicine that help to propel us toward whatever the ultimate human capacity will reveal itself to be. Concomitantly, technology is pushing the boundaries of reality itself while also making once arduous tasks into effortless button-clicks.

So why aren't we generally purposeful, satiable people?

Why is there so much depression and anxiety? Can all the progress we've achieved genuinely be called progress if it has done so little to alleviate human suffering? You can live for one thousand years, but if they're all miserable, what kind of a life is that? What has science and technology bought us? I'm left wondering that if even the widespread disappearance of poverty has done little to alleviate the human condition, how little chance other advancements have at delivering.

So maybe, just maybe, humans are still suffering, despite progress, because we're still human. Progress, wealth, longevity, and health have done little to change our passions, which still centre on material gain, money, sex, fame, and power. Just as they did in ancient times. Some say we damage ourselves by chasing these sorts of things, for which sacrifice is often necessary payment.

But wait—maybe it's not our fault. Maybe suffering is the fault of a few miserable despots who are ruining it for the rest of us. Or even a secret elite that confab in secluded antechambers, puffing away on Cuban cigars, chortling to themselves about how to make the next big world crisis.

It's easy to point fingers at tyrants like Xi Jinping, Chairman Mao, Pol Pot, Fidel Castro and the like. It's a little bit harder to call out their underlings in communist and socialist parties, whose power and responsibilities are never quite as clear. It's harder still to understand the millions of people who have acquiesced to or adopted socialist and communist beliefs, because that great number has generally done so out of belief (sometimes desperate belief) that the state could solve the human condition.

There are many causes for suffering in the world, and they are invariably linked to that condition. My question focused on those who sought a genuine solution to human suffering within the ideology of Marxism. How did these socialists and communists—few evil and despotic, but innumerable genuinely concerned citizens—fall for this?

My question was designed to discover why this ideology of playing the victim continues to survive, despite the suffering it has caused (and continues to cause). The short answer is captured in three distinct reasons. The first is that it's a way to accumulate power. Many people are drawn by this, but few possess both the rank evil disposition and the extensive social connections required to achieve such power.

The second is that ideologies are robust, multigenerational viruses that last so long people simply forget about them. Our ancestors may have seen and "defeated" it, but the same virus can still come back against the next generation and attack. If our descendants have forgotten how to deal with it, an entirely novel war will befall them.

The final reason is that ideologies mutate over time, just as viruses do, and this is particularly the case for the ideological path of *dialectical leftism*, which contains that Marxist ideology. It's responsible for a great deal of the deadliest mind viruses we face today. Herein we examine the evolution, proliferation, and survival of dialectical leftism, the most concrete answer to why people want to play victim today.

Mavros Whissell
Sudbury, ON
October 2023

PART I
INTRODUCTION

CHAPTER ONE
WHAT IS DIALECTICAL LEFTISM?

BEFORE WE GET to the "what," we must first answer the "why." Why call it *dialectical* leftism? Why not call it *radical* leftism, leftist *extremism,* or even simply the *far* left? While some consider all these terms interchangeable, discernment is added when using the qualifier "dialectical" before the word "leftism." It tells us that we're dealing with a creature that changes appearance over time as it adds new parts (and sometimes removes others), that it's a leftist ideology that doesn't stay entirely the same because it changes according to something called a *dialectical process,* which will be described thoroughly herein. Despite this, the creature also retains specific characteristics no matter how much it appears to have changed—parts it has had since the beginning that, like vital organs, can't be removed. Those people who prefer the other terms mentioned above aren't wrong either. Dialectical leftism is a far-reaching, radical, extremist ideology, best identified by its unchanging characteristics. It has also revealed itself to be something entirely unexpected.

Throughout this book, a repeated assertion is that dialectical leftism is a faith, and this may upset some people. Progressive believers like to claim that theirs is a scientific path, often while reminding the rest of us plebs that we need to "trust the science." Unfortunately for them, all that begging to "trust the science" doesn't support dialectical leftism, the chief ideology of the radical left. It's a faith because it's based neither on reason nor the scientific method but rather on the unproven assumption that there's an absolute truth hiding within existing ideology, waiting to be discovered. That is why it's a faith. And like many faiths, it has mutated significantly over time.

Let's look briefly at the evolution of dialectical leftism. It will be fully explained later and throughout the book to solidify our understanding. **Chapter references for these detailed explanations are written in bold below.** For now, it will suffice to have an overview of how the beliefs of many of the most radical progressives have changed over time. Here is a very abridged history of dialectical leftism, presented in three stages, summarized in Table 1 below:

Table 1: Three Stages of Dialectical Leftism[1]

	Stage	Name	Approx. Active Time Range
Dialectical Leftism	1	Orthodox Marxism	1848–today[2]
	2	Neo-Marxism	1924–today[3]
	3	woke ideology	1985–today

STAGE 1: ORTHODOX MARXISM

Dialectical leftism began as the ideology known as Orthodox Marxism (or just Marxism can suffice) from the 1850s onward, roughly from around the time Karl Marx and Friedrich Engels' *Manifesto of the Communist Party* was released. Marx hoped to follow in the footsteps of Napoleon and overturn the existing establishment, except now it was rich industrialists and not the dying monarchies who needed to be slaughtered to free the people. Marx's revolutionary ideas slowly spread for the next seventy years, contributing to unrest in Europe and a violent overthrow of the Russian monarchy near the end of WWI. Around that same time, Germany came very close to falling under its own communist revolution, although Marx would be rolling over in his grave to learn it failed. A more detailed history of this is covered in **Chapter Seven: Orthodox and Cultural Marxism**.

STAGE 2: NEO-MARXISM

Left-leaning academics noted both the success of Orthodox Marxism in Russia and its failure in Germany. The contradiction left them puzzled. If Orthodox Marxism didn't work in an industrial society like Germany, why had it succeeded in pre-industrial Russia? After all, Marxism specifically presented the idea of

---

[1] In this book, we argue that Cultural Marxism is not a distinct step forward in the ideology of dialectical leftism but is instead a methodological side-step that occurred beginning in the early 1900s. Cultural Marxism was heavily incorporated into Neo-Marxism, as it was one of the first attempts to address the failure of Orthodox Marxism.

[2] Orthodox Marxism typically exists today as the dominant component in Marxism-Leninism.

[3] Neo-Marxism typically exists today as a component in woke ideology, synthesized with postmodernism.

overthrowing industrial capitalist society. A change was needed to address this failure. Beginning in the 1920s, dialectical leftism combined with aspects of modern science and empirical research to form the ideology known as Neo-Marxism, meaning simply "new Marxism." The idea was that a scientific focus would correct for Marxism's early failures. This was roughly the time when the so-called Frankfurt School coalesced at the University of Goethe in Frankfurt, Germany. If you've never heard of the Frankfurt School or its official name, The Institute for Social Research, don't worry. This will be covered in ample detail in **Chapter Eight: Neo-Marxism.**

While Neo-Marxism was being developed in the 1920s, the older Orthodox Marxism spread virulently to the far East and overtook China, Mongolia, and Korea. Within the next sixty years it would also claim Vietnam and Cambodia. Cuba fell to Orthodox Marxism in 1959 under Castro. After the end of WWII, Orthodox Marxism (combined with Leninism) became the default ideology in all the countries Russia occupied after Germany was defeated. It's a strange irony that while Neo-Marxism was in its infancy, Orthodox Marxism, its parent, took over a great deal of the world. Neo-Marxism would do its own (lesser) spreading beginning in the 1960s. But after a failed coup in France in 1968, the world became much more aware of Neo-Marxism's potential to destroy industrial society, and countermeasures were enacted.

STAGE 3: WOKE IDEOLOGY

By the 1980s, Neo-Marxism was tired out and needed a boost. The dreams of Marxists everywhere were facing a stark reality. They claimed to have abandoned Orthodox Marxism by leaving the violent nightmare of Stalinist Russia behind. But the secret was out. Neo-Marxism was just as violent and totalitarian as its predecessor. It also failed to bring about tangible results. This began to drive many peace-loving leftists away, especially those who protested the Vietnam War.

As disappointed academics watched Neo-Marxism begin to wane, it became clear that yet another change was needed to reinvigorate the path of dialectical leftism. In the 1980s, Neo-Marxism began to combine with a rapidly rising leftist ideology known as "postmodernism" and became today's woke ideology. While transitioning into woke ideology, dialectical leftism usurped the *Civil Rights Movement* for the purpose of fomenting a revolution in the United States. This shocking turn of events, and what happened in its wake, will be explained in **Chapter Ten: Co-opting the Civil Rights Movement, Chapter Eleven: Critical Legal Studies Vs. Postmodernism**, and in **Chapter Twelve: Woke Ideology**. In this form, it has begun to bend the United States and Canada to its will, though it has not yet brought about collapse.

To understand more about why it should be considered a faith, let's examine what disciples of the dialectical leftist faith believe today, within the blurred lines of woke ideology. Their beliefs include some tenets approaching two hundred years of existence, while also including much newer contributions brought within the last forty years. It's a kind of Frankenstein's monster.

Orthodox Marxism and woke ideology are similar but different. On the surface, it seems like there is no way the Orthodox Marxism of 1850 can possibly be related to the woke ideology from the 1980s onward. But hold on for a moment! Despite all these different parts added together over time in the monster, there are some ways in which these two ideologies reveal a clear connection, namely unchanged parts since the beginning in Orthodox Marxism that can be found in today's woke ideology. Tenets that dialectical leftism has maintained since its beginning include:

1. the goal of revolution
2. the necessity for violence and deception
3. the worldview of determinism focused on identity (oppressor vs. oppressed)
4. the threat of forced redistribution (of money and property)
5. the faith that a utopia awaits at the end of the dialectical process

These are as true for the woke ideology of today as they were when Marx first published them in the *Manifesto of the Communist Party* in 1848. They are vital organs that cannot be removed.

From its original form, the key difference in dialectical leftism today is that instead of capitalists exploiting the working-class (as postulated in Orthodox Marxism), woke ideology regards the ultimate oppressor as the straight, White, cisgender male. This bogeyman is guilty in perpetuity of subconsciously promoting transphobia, homophobia, misogyny, racism, and White supremacy, regardless of what he believes he is doing. In the mind of woke ideologues, because the oppressor's hatred toward marginalized communities is unconscious, he can't control it, nor can he legitimately deny it.

Even as it demonizes the newest oppressors based on immutable identity characteristics (Whites, males, cisgenders, etc.), the woke ideology also redefines who the oppressed people are. It does this by asserting a new value-scale to be used in society. In the new woke value-scale replacing meritocracy, an individual's oppressed identity will be the replacement for hard work, success, or talent. To the disciples of dialectical leftism, those are beholden to White supremacy and thus maintain the power of the oppressors (again: Whites, males, cisgenders, etc.). The woke ideology postulates that the state, the law, and the police all work together in a conspiracy to keep down marginalized communities in the name of White supremacy. The White male is conflated with the fascist menace that threatened to take over the entirety of Europe in WWII.

DIALECTICAL LEFTISM INVADES CANADA'S FREE SOCIETY
Now that we have a cursory definition of what dialectical leftism is and how it's changed over time, we'll begin to look at its application to Canadian society. We'll look at institutions belonging to the Canadian government, including the executive branch of the federal government (the state), the dominantly state-subsidized Canadian Broadcasting Corporation (the media), and the enforcement arm of the state (the police).

We'll also look at primary, secondary, and post-secondary public schools in Canada (education). Primary and secondary schools are almost entirely funded by municipal and provincial taxes in Canada. Their curricula are determined by provincial and territorial governments, so they fall in line as a part of the state despite belonging to civil society. They could be called state-sponsored equivalents. Post-secondary schools, like universities, can be up to 50 per cent government subsidized, with the rest of their funding coming from tuition fees and donations. Universities could be considered a state-influenced equivalent operating within civil society because of their heavy monetary dependence.

Finally, in this work we'll examine an institute of civil society—an organization not belonging in any way to the state—known as the Christian Church (the Church). Although there are clearly many other religions practised in Canada, our nation boasts over 22 million citizens who identify as Christian, and in past years, the proportion of Christians to non-Christians was much higher than it is now.

The State
Canada's federal Liberal government demonstrates a strong ideological connection to dialectical leftism and, as such, may well be putting us on the path toward the kernel of truth they believe exists. They have accepted that it's necessary to force the state, civil society, and the citizenry forward through revolutions such as the industrial revolutions of the past. In fact, Deputy Prime Minister Chrystia

Freeland discussed this "reality" at a World Economic Forum conference in 2019 called Tackling the Growth Paradox.[4] Such ideologues believe these revolutions will eventually lead to better conditions for the average human. They believe that with each step forward, there will eventually be a greater and more equitable distribution of misery and suffering, and that all of it, piloted by the state, will lead to the best possible life on earth a person can receive. That is the progressive mindset of dialectical leftism. It is a faith by its very nature.

As we wait for the utopia to be reached, we the citizens of Canada are expected to accept a miserable transition period as a necessary evil, for the good of all "peoplekind."[5]

In this ugly interim, the absence of the feeling of freedom is a lament of many Canadians, wondering when or even *if* they will return to a condition where their way of life seemed a great deal less regulated. That tangible increase in regulation has required a substantial growth in government.

According to the Treasury Board of Canada, by the summer of 2023, under the Trudeau Liberals, the number of federal public workers had increased by 40 per cent since 2015.[6] Trudeau has added a staggering 98,000 new federal public service employees, equivalent to the population of Red Deer, Alberta. As of today, approximately 1 per cent of all Canadians work for the federal public service.

The Canadian state has ideologically shifted to the left, attempting to adopt woke, Marxist, and even technocratic ideologies under the Trudeau government, even in economic terms, to create a bigger "nanny state" than ever. The effectiveness of this approach seems to be in serious question, as only so much failure can be blamed on previous governments or the pandemic. Many signs point to a state that is thoroughly indoctrinated with dialectical leftism to the detriment of civil society and the citizens of Canada. We will discuss this in **Chapter Fourteen: Statism and Militant Atheism**, and in **Chapter Seventeen: The Attack on Civil Society and the State**.

---

[4] World Economic Forum, "Davos 2019—Tackling the Growth Paradox," YouTube Video, 1:00:25, February 19, 2019, https://www.youtube.com/watch?v=STpNXut3zic.

[5] Although peoplekind is not a word, it was famously used by Prime Minister Justin Trudeau. See: CTV News, "Trudeau Tells Woman to Say 'Peoplekind' Not 'Mankind,'" YouTube Video, 0:45, February 7, 2018, https://www.youtube.com/watch?v=Uln6ULsPQno.

[6] B. Passifiume, "Trudeau Government Increased Federal Employees 40% Since Election in 2015," *National Post*, July 10, 2023, https://nationalpost.com/news/canada/trudeau-government-increased-federal-employees-since-2015.

CHAPTER ONE: WHAT IS DIALECTICAL LEFTISM?

The Media

In Canada, the most powerful and influential media institution remains the Canadian Broadcasting Corporation (CBC). Whether from its historical coverage of all things Canadian or its modern social justice focus, the CBC has legions of fans dedicated to its television, radio, and internet productions.

Where there is a potential problem for the CBC is in its being beholden to the Canadian state (which is responsible for endorsing their paycheques) to the tune of 69 per cent of their overall funding. The salaries and bonuses being doled out since 2015, revealed through request by the Canadian Taxpayers Federation, have raised serious concerns.[7] The bonuses received by CBC employees in 2022 averaged $14,000 per employee. The CBC's funding for the 2021–2022 fiscal year reached 1.2 billion dollars.

These numbers would be a lot less concerning if they were distributed to an institution that conducted reporting in a fair and balanced manner. However, the CBC has of late adopted a great deal of the woke ideological stances common among radical left activists. Some time was spent by the author looking into their promotion of Marxism itself as an ideology, and it was found that, at least leading up to 2020, they had given a lot of airtime and interviews to Marxist academics.[8] An informal evaluation of these academics who teach from a Marxist perspective (based on their publications and publicly expressed opinions) was conducted. The CBC even published a radio episode titled "Reclaiming Marxism in an Age of Meaningless Work" in 2019, promoting anti-capitalist ideas of US professors arguing for the viability of the Marxist perspective in combating nihilism.[9]

In **Chapter Thirteen: The CBC's Left-Leaning Bias**, we'll examine the author's experiences with the CBC while managing the Facebook site called "Woken Promises." The conclusion is that the CBC demonstrates a clear left-leaning bias, unsurprisingly very similar to the executive branch of the federal government when occupied by the Liberal Party of Canada.

---

[7] R. Thorpe, "CBC Doles out $16 million in Bonuses in 2022," Canadian Taxpayers Federation, March 9, 2023, retrieved August 5, 2023, https://www.taxpayer.com/newsroom/cbc-doles-out-16-million-in-bonuses-in-2022.

[8] These Marxist academics include Dr. Kevin Walby, criminologist, University of Winnipeg; Dr. Jeffrey Monaghan, criminologist, Carleton University; Vanier Scholar and BLM member Robyn Maynard, University of Toronto; and Dr. Liam Kennedy, criminologist, King's University College.

[9] "Reclaiming Marxism in an Age of Meaningless Work," CBC: Ideas, June 14, 2019, https://www.cbc.ca/radio/ideas/reclaiming-marxism-in-an-age-of-meaningless-work-1.5175707.

PART I: INTRODUCTION

The Police

A concerning sign that society is unstable is the sudden explosion of the number of police officers murdered in the line of duty, as happened in Canada from September 2022 to May 2023. Over that nine-month span, nine officers were murdered,[10] a total not anywhere near approached since 1962—it's the highest total in sixty years. Some have argued that it's due in part to the erosion of trust between police and the public, as a report in the *Ottawa Citizen* suggested:

> Police are more accountable than ever, and yet trust in the police has declined. According to Statistics Canada in 2019, about 40 per cent of Canadians who reported a recent encounter with police were likely to say that they had a great deal of confidence in the police. But only a quarter of those who said they came into contact with the police in the previous year for emotional problems, mental health, or alcohol or drug use felt a great deal of confidence.
>
> The distrust is more pronounced in racialized communities. As of 2020, 21 per cent of Black people and 22 per cent of Indigenous people had little or no confidence in the police.[11]

Herein we shall argue that there are two key groups actively pushing for mistrust between the police and the citizenry. The first and most important group are Marxist-based agitators, including the No Pride in Policing Coalition, and the much larger organizations Black Lives Matter (BLM), and Antifa.[12] They seek to defame police and promote exclusively negative (and sometimes outright false) narratives about police encounters. We will discuss the techniques these groups use in **Chapter Nine: Marxism Is a Threat to Public Safety** and **Chapter Fifteen: Modern Marxist Methodology**. These groups are frequently directed by academic activists who reinforce *direct action* from positions of power and relative safety in their colleges and universities.

The second group creating mistrust in police includes all the individuals who decide to submit to claims of systemic racism in policing despite the

---

[10] J. Laucius, "Nine Police Officers in Canada Have Been Slain Since Last September. The Big Question Is Why Now?" *Ottawa Citizen*, May 19, 2023, https://ottawacitizen.com/news/local-news/nine-police-officers-in-canada-have-been-slain-since-last-september-the-big-question-is-why-now.

[11] Ibid.

[12] The website for the No Pride in Policing Coalition (Toronto) can be found at https://www.noprideinpolicing.ca/.

fact that they previously didn't accept or acknowledge those claims. These are individuals who virtue signal with actions like taking a knee or writing public confessions.

An example of this exists in the Liberals' Minister of Defence, Bill Blair. Back in 2014, as Chief of the Toronto Police Service (TPS), Blair made it clear he didn't believe the police were systemically racist, or even racist at all, for that matter, when he wrote the following in the *Toronto Star*: "We are not racist but we are all human. The science of bias teaches us that even the best-intentioned, most decent and honourable people can be influenced by the implicit bias all people have."[13]

But in 2020, after his subordinate, RCMP Commissioner Brenda Lucki, made the mistake of saying that she too believed the police weren't systemically racist, Blair, then Minister of Public Safety, chastised her for it. Lucki then publicly confessed to the RCMP's systemic racism, and Blair released a confession of his own, claiming that, unlike in 2014, he (suddenly) believed in systemic racism: "Blair, a former Toronto police chief, acknowledged in a statement Wednesday that 'Indigenous people, Black Canadians and other racialized people … experience systemic racism and disparate outcomes within the criminal justice system.'"[14]

Most recently, Blair claimed that under his leadership, the TPS became the most diverse police force in Canada.[15] To many people, such confessions and virtue signalling create the image of solidarity with radical left extremist groups, and this reinforces disenfranchisement between the state and civil society. We've seen such actions by Prime Minister Justin Trudeau, former RCMP Commissioner Brenda Lucki, and many other high-ranking police officers and politicians who sign on to keep themselves (or their subordinates) from being labelled as racist. We'll examine the problems associated with this modus operandi of *confessor behaviour* in **Chapter Sixteen: Police and Identity Politics**.

---

[13] W. Blair, "Chief Blair: Racial Profiling Not Tolerated in Toronto Police Force," Toronto Star, July 28, 2014, https://www.thestar.com/opinion/contributors/chief-blair-racial-profiling-not-tolerated-in-toronto-police-force/article_97f41a9f-a23f-55a6-a4ab-65bfe3b5bb09.html.

[14] R. Patel, "Public Safety Minister Broached Systemic Racism with RCMP Head before Course Reversal," CBC News: Politics, June 13, 2020, https://www.cbc.ca/news/politics/public-safety-minister-broached-systemic-racism-with-rcmp-head-before-course-reversal-1.5611339.

[15] S. Ritchie, "Bill Blair Says He Oversaw Culture Change at Toronto Police, Not Everyone Agrees," *National Post*, August 25, 2023, https://nationalpost.com/news/canada/bill-blair-says-he-oversaw-culture-change-at-toronto-police-not-everyone-agrees.

PART I: INTRODUCTION

The Church

At the beginning of the twentieth century, the left-leaning Christian church, including the Methodist, Presbyterian, and Congregationalist Protestant denominations, were coming to a crisis of faith. They had to face the new wave of Charles Darwin's ideas, a new higher criticism against the Bible, and the general expansion of science. As a left-leaning church, they were determined to reconcile their belief system with the social clime. These factors, when combined with their witnessing of widespread human suffering in Canada around the turn of the century, led to a movement known as the Social Gospel. The Social Gospel diminished acknowledgement of the divinity of Christ and promoted a doctrine of earthly works. Despite the earthly benefits of good works to aid the suffering, the line between faith in Christ's all-atoning sacrifice and the work of the people began to blur.

There were several problems with this approach, which sometimes confused humanity with its Saviour, and they would eventually become evident in characters like Albert Edward Smith, a Methodist minister who found it easy to adapt his Social Gospel beliefs to his later decision to join the Communist Party of Canada. Other radical social gospelers, like William Ivens, would choose to form their own church to promote socialist policies and represent the working class through the façade of a church. These Marxist co-optations of the church, and what they led to, will be discussed in **Chapter Four: The Social Gospel**.

The Education System

A unique relationship exists between dialectical leftism and education, the explanation of which can only be revealed properly through a historical review of the Western education system, beginning at the fall of Rome and extending into today's modern universities. The institution of public education in the Western world began throughout Europe as small classes inside monasteries, called monastic schools.

Many monastic schools and their later descendants, cathedral schools, would be used as the birthplace of the medieval university. These universities began forming around 1100. The medieval universities had theological affiliations that had to be declared by students, and many universities had a theology faculty. The Word of God featured prominently in medieval universities. In **Chapter Five: Education, the State ... and Religion?** we'll examine the history of the rudimentary Western education system, demonstrating how it was clearly focused on Christianity.

After the Protestant Reformation, however (and then, following that, the liberal wave secularizing Europe under Napoleon), Christianity fell into disrepute in the institutions of education. The belief was that this new liberalism (now referred to as Classical Liberalism) would be able to hold universities to rationally-based, scientific perspectives—that is, ones based solely on the scientific method. That turned out to be wrong. Concomitant with the decrease of Christian influence in Western universities, the rise of the new faith of dialectical leftism would occur to fill the void. We'll discuss the events leading up to the inception of dialectical leftism in Western education in **Chapter Six: Signs of a Trajectory**.

Before we get to these more concerning and in-depth avenues of dialectical leftism, we'll take a brief look at the more recent history of Marxism by analyzing early twentieth-century communism, the practical application of Orthodox Marxism, in **Chapter Two: Lies Unlimited**. From there, we'll go on to examine the more recent practical attempt by the dialectical left to revise Marxism and reject Stalinism in **Chapter Three: The New Left**.

CHAPTER TWO
LIES UNLIMITED

THE MINDSETS AND ideologies around the globe are nearly infinitely varied, mixed, and difficult to demarcate. Yet they all contain one identifiable factor that ties them together: lies. Dialectical leftism, throughout history, has relied upon suppression of truth to maintain itself. This is because dialectical leftism is often confronted by evidence contrary to its assertions, and instead of addressing such realities, it attempts to construct its own reality—a kind of accelerated moral relativity.

The weight of ideological lies and the destruction they cause can be best seen throughout the history of the ideology of Marxism and the corresponding practice of communism. Only one other ideology can be as clearly linked to a trajectory of death as this belief promotes and, as we shall see, there were hints from its very inception that communism was a similar kind of one-way ticket.[1]

In this chapter, the key point is that even though an ideology may not be falsifiable, what really counts is if it requires deception to be sustainable. This is a truth that dialectical leftism has been unable to escape throughout its history. Every time it has run into contradictions that have stopped it dead in its tracks, a new ideology is created to overcome the reality stopping it. As we shall see in Chapter Eight on Neo-Marxism, there was a distinct failure of Orthodox Marxism to predict class revolution in industrial capitalist societies, as there were none. Ever. But the shocking continuation is that Neo-Marxism was also unable to predict cultural revolution,

---

[1] Of course, fascism is a very dangerous ideology that has also killed in the tens of millions, but it has neither killed as many people nor is it as widely popular as communism throughout history. Communism remains the greater of the two totalitarian threats throughout history, likely due to its more universal appeal.

despite new ideas like *false consciousness* and the use of empirical data. So Neo-Marxism added a postmodern component to escape its failure, as we'll see in Chapters Eleven and Twelve.

The current chapter includes a list of all the communist regimes past and present in Table 2, the most important of which to remember (in addition to Soviet Russia) are the four that currently remain on the planet: China, Laos, Vietnam, and Cuba. Note that North Korea is now only nominally communist. It officially follows the *Juche* ideology, having replaced Marxism-Leninism around 1992.

MARXISM IS LIKE LAVA

Over the last hundred years or so, communist regimes have erupted around the world. They've spread virulently among the hearts and minds of both those who believed in their ability to save the world, as well as those who desired to *rule* the world. They have poured down the mountain in searing heat and through the sky with choking ash. They've killed the children of avarice that brought them, as well as the poor souls caught in their path with nowhere to turn—death from unstoppable, all-consuming pyroclastic flows.

But the reality with lava is that once it erupts, it will inevitably transform. When it's suddenly exposed to air and rapidly cools, it can harden into volcanic glass and, in so doing, becomes breakable. Communist regimes don't last forever, and the weight of their existence is eventually susceptible to a hammer-blow. They average a lifespan of just thirty-seven years, so most people who experience them will thankfully outlive them. There have been many regimes in the past, but there are currently only four countries officially following the historical Marxist-Leninist faith that defines communism as we know it.

CHAPTER TWO: LIES UNLIMITED

Table 2: Communist Regimes, Past and Present[2,3]

Country	Name under Communism	Start (Year)	End (Year)	Lifespan (Years)[4]
China	People's Republic of China	1949	N/A	74
Russia[5]	Soviet Union	1917	1991	74
Laos	Lao People's Democratic Republic	1953	N/A	70
Mongolia	Mongolian People's Republic	1924	1992	68
Cuba	Republic of Cuba	1959	N/A	64
Vietnam	Socialist Republic of Vietnam	1976	N/A	47
Yugoslavia	Socialist Federal Republic of Yugoslavia	1945	1992	47
Albania	People's Socialist Republic of Albania	1946	1991	45
Bulgaria	People's Republic of Bulgaria	1946	1990	44
North Korea[6]	Democratic Republic of Korea	1948	1992	44
Poland	Polish People's Republic	1945	1989	44
Romania	Socialist Republic of Romania	1947	1989	42
Czechoslovakia	Czechoslovak Socialist Republic	1948	1990	42
East Germany	German Democratic Republic	1949	1990	41
Hungary	Hungarian People's Republic	1949	1989	40
Congo	People's Republic of the Congo	1969	1992	23
Mongolia	Tuvan People's Republic	1921	1944	23
Republic of Yemen	People's Democratic Republic of Yemen	1967	1990	23
Somalia	Somali Democratic Republic	1969	1991	22
Angola	People's Republic of Angola	1975	1992	17
Ethiopia	People's Democratic Republic of Ethiopia	1974	1991	17
Madagascar	Democratic Republic of Madagascar	1975	1992	17
Cambodia	People's Republic of Kampuchea	1975	1991	16
Benin	People's Republic of Benin	1975	1990	15
Mozambique	People's Republic of Mozambique	1975	1990	15
Afghanistan	Democratic Republic of Afghanistan	1978	1992	14
Grenada	People's Revolutionary Government	1979	1983	4

---

[2] Wikipedia, s.v. "List of Socialist States," July 10, 2023, https://en.wikipedia.org/wiki/List_of_socialist_states.

[3] Wikipedia, s.v. "Juche," December 3, 2023, https://en.wikipedia.org/wiki/Juche#.

[4] The lifespan of communist regimes was estimated from the year 2023.

[5] Includes Belarus, Estonia, Lithuania, Latvia, Tuva, and Ukraine.

[6] North Korea officially changed from Marxism-Leninism to the Juche ideology in 1992.

PART I: INTRODUCTION

ORTHODOX MARXISM VS. MARXISM-LENINISM

Now, hold on for a moment. Didn't we just say these are all *Marxist-Leninist* regimes? What's the difference between that and Orthodox Marxism? It turns out that there's an important distinction. In truth, Marxist-Leninist regimes are dominantly guided in both social and economic policy by the ideology of Orthodox Marxism, but there's a key difference in that the first communists insisted that their followers "do not set up any sectarian principles of their own, by which to shape and mould the proletarian movement."[7]

The ideology of Leninism, on the other hand, requires something referred to as a "vanguard party" (a combined military and political party) to direct and manipulate the proletariat movement into communist revolution. That's why all the countries above are listed as Marxist-Leninist: they required a political/military party to effectively force the people into communism. All the regimes in Table 2 are a combination of the Marxian dream of workers rising up in revolution to attain communism combined with the stark reality that workers never actually did this. The only way communism occurred was by force and coercion, and this meant Leninism.

History has proven that workers needed dictators, soldiers, and secret police to force them into what was purportedly "best" for them. So perhaps it wasn't "best" after all.

When we look to communist China, now the longest lasting Marxist-Leninist machination, what can we see? Is the Chinese Communist Party a recent eruption? Does it have much longer before it too cools? How has it survived so long while Soviet Russia, East Germany, and the victims of the Iron Curtain, Afghanistan, Cambodia, and the Congo have all witnessed communism to have come and gone? Will communism erupt again?

The most critical example of a communist regime that was smashed following its mass exposure was the Soviet Union. It was eventually exposed to the rest of the world, but there were also many Russians living in the Soviet Union who were aware of the true nature of Marxist-Leninist ideology.

Aleksandr Solzhenitsyn, a dissident against communism, famously warned his Russian countrymen on the day he was exiled from the Soviet Union, February 13, 1974, that they should "live not by lies." Solzhenitsyn had concluded that the quintessential communist tactic of suppressing the truth, especially in the most fundamental form of speech, was a way to kill everything that humanity

---

[7] K. Marx and F. Engels, *Marx/Engels Selected Works, Vol. One: Manifesto of the Communist Party (1848)* (Moscow: Progress Publishers, 1969), 98–137.

really was. He knew that was how Marxist-Leninists maintained power. He knew suppression of truth was not sustainable, and that after tens of millions of murders and seemingly endless suffering, the Soviet empire of lies would be pulverized.

Solzhenitsyn was proven correct.

The Soviet Union ultimately dissolved in August 1991 under Mikhail Gorbachev, unable to sustain its own corruption. The decades of lies, persecution, and death under the Communist Party of the Soviet Union finally met with a leader who could not or would not propagate it any longer. The West has, ever since, viewed this as the definitive victory and end to the Cold War.

But was Marxism defeated? There is no killing an idea. The West has had its own struggles dealing with the threat of totalitarian ideologies. Although it may sometimes seem like North America has constantly been under a veiled assault from communist ideology, that awareness waxes and wanes. At our weakest points in history, communist ideology has subtly penetrated society deep enough to invade schools and churches. At other times, governments were prepared to deal with the looming threat of communism in a significant, generally peaceful manner. At still other times, there came to be an almost paranoid preoccupation with eliminating the *Red Menace*, particularly during the McCarthy era in the United States. The geopolitical climate has worked a long way to influencing what individual nations and their policies have enforced to deal with the threat of communism.

In 1993, for instance, following the collapse of the Soviet Union, the US government was focused enough to decide that the recurring threat of communism must be indelibly written into the American psyche. To that end, the Victims of Communism Memorial (VOC) Foundation was created in 1993 by a unanimous Act of Congress. The VOC's website today warns that there have been over 100 million deaths worldwide under communist regimes.[8] That estimate is over double the number of Allied troops and civilians killed in WWII.

CAPITALISM CAN BRING DISASTER TOO

The first officially recorded communist ideology, typically referred to as Marxism, is named after German economist Karl Friedrich Marx (1818–1883). Marxism is built on promoting falsehoods, but so are a lot of capitalist strategies. Just think of the global financial crisis of 2007–2008. That crisis occurred due to a system of lies to deceive investors in the US housing market. Hungry investors

---

[8] "Victims of Communism Memorial Foundation (n.d.)," Victims of Communism, Retrieved July 12, 2023, https://victimsofcommunism.org/.

gobbled up variable rate, sub-prime mortgages just after house prices peaked in 2006. When the value of those houses suddenly and drastically declined in the following years, investors were left holding the bag. They had been suckered into buying badly over-valued houses.

A huge portion of these investors simply defaulted on their loans. That might not sound terrible for the rest of us, but those sub-prime mortgages were tied to securities: tradeable, non-physical assets whose value are defined by contracts. Securities that were backed with these sub-prime mortgages correspondingly lost all their value, as investors defaulted on the loans that backed them. This led to a rapid collapse in the US housing market. Although this phenomenon of market collapse began in the US, global growth brutally slowed as faith in the US markets tanked. All this because of lies: the over-valuing of houses that eventually corrected. The housing bubble before the financial crisis of 2007–2008 led to a terrible crash, from which the world was slow to recover.

The world was bailed out because the banks were bailed out. What could have happened—perhaps what should have happened—was that the US banks be allowed to collapse completely in the domino-like after-effect of the sub-prime mortgage crisis. We might then suddenly and irrevocably understand the fate of lying about the value of our assets, or the fate associated with exploiting people under false pretenses.

To the amazement of all, however, the major banks were bailed out by the US government and continued to operate. All the capitalist strategists who willfully got on board with the corrupt scheme to defraud investors were never ultimately held accountable. It turns out that the ones who suffered were the victims of exploitation, exactly the type of situation that would have Karl Marx chuckling to himself. One system of lies laughing at another.

There are many differences between capitalism and Marxism, but—importantly—this book is in no way intended to be a defence of the capitalist system. Instead, requisite falsehoods involved in maintaining an ideology are warning signs that it is not sustainable. For Marxism, that broadly includes suppression of free speech as part of an overall impetus to maintain state control. For capitalism, that includes avenues that may be abused by the human propensity for sin. The difference seems to lie in the necessity of lies in Marxism versus the susceptibility to lies of capitalism. For one ideology deception is a requirement, while for the other it's a glaring weakness nearly impossible to avoid.

PART II
THE SEED IS DEVOURED

CHAPTER THREE
THE NEW LEFT

WE WILL BEGIN our discussion on dialectical leftism by first examining how it interacted with the largest generation in history, the Baby Boomers (born 1946–1964). This examination is critical to the state of Marxism-based ideology today because a correspondingly large effect was passed from Boomers onto subsequent generations. That effect has gone a long way to determining what appears to be a kinder, gentler Marxism in the twenty-first century in the woke ideology. Appearances, as we all know, are only skin-deep.

In this chapter, the most important takeaway is this: beginning in the 1960s, a dramatic shift toward the ideological left occurred, concomitant with a move away from church membership and activity. The move away from churches is evident in both Canadian and American data. During the 1960s, the radical left was most popularly represented in the New Left movement, a rejection of Orthodox Marxism that abandoned class antagonism and aimed for a cultural revolution. The New Left on the streets had a counterpart in academia in the Neo-Marxist Frankfurt School, which we will examine in Chapter Eight. The New Left also had the rare public support of a celebrity in pediatrician Dr. Benjamin Spock.

Child-rearing from the time of the Baby Boomers' first births was under the auspices of modern psychology and pediatrics, and this was well-represented in Dr. Spock. Spock's world famous *The Common Sense Book of Baby and Childcare*, first published in 1946, sold more than 50 million copies by the year 2000. From that book's earliest editions, the implication to not indoctrinate your children into Christianity was widely adopted. That suggestion seemed to cause societal problems that Dr. Spock felt he needed to address. Later editions would include

> explicit advice that participation in religious activity was of psychological benefit to children.
>
> The question arises: could Dr. Spock's book have so adversely affected the Baby Boomers that it contributed to their leaving church in unusually high numbers? Whatever part it played in that initiative, it's likely there was some effect from Spock's book because of its unrivaled influence on child-rearing.

According to statistics, the Baby Boomer generation conducted the greatest move away from religious activity in Canada and a significant move away from religious membership in the United States. In more recent times in the US, the largest drop in church membership occurred between Generation X and Millennials, which is quite curious. The origins of the move away from religious activity and membership seem to fall back on the later Silent Generation, suggesting the momentum of abandoning church began at the earliest part of the twentieth century. As we shall see in the next chapter, that partially overlaps with the time of the first wave of the Social Gospel (1880–1920) and the initial influence of dialectical leftism within the Christian Church itself.

The Baby Boomers are the most socio-economically dominant generation in recent history. They have an inordinate effect on the planet in many ways because they are literally a population explosion that dwarfs other generations.

After WWII ended, there was some freedom across the world, but there were still austerity measures in countries like the United Kingdom of Great Britain and Ireland, which suffered a continued lack of resources and foodstuffs. That meant one of the cheapest, most fun things to do immediately after the war was to come home, get married (in most cases), and have sex. And *boom*, pregnancies went through the roof, because this was before the widespread use of medical birth control.

Never has a society provided so much peace, wealth, and opportunity to a generation as it did to the Baby Boomers, the post-WWII generation. And with that great prosperity and opportunity came an entirely new concept: choice.

DR. BENJAMIN SPOCK

Parents were told to offer children choice on everything, from what to do, to where to live, and even what to believe. That much freedom had never been permitted in history. The Boomers were also the first children to be raised under the tutelage of modern psychology and pediatrics, which included pediatrician Dr. Benjamin Spock (1908–1998).

Although they were raised by parents using that book, the Boomers would also end up using it with their own children. It was that famous for that long, selling over 50 million copies and remaining as the number two best-seller of all time (up to the year 2000), according to the *New York Times*.[1] Only the Holy Bible sold more copies during that time frame.

Dr. Spock's approach to parenting centred on affirmation for mothers, insisting that their natural instincts were often correct and could thus be safely followed. It was the kind of self-help advice that literally instructed you to "help yourself," and it could have been written by Family Guy's atheist dog, Brian Griffin. In an episode of the *Family Guy* cartoon, Brian famously (and fictitiously) wrote a self-help book called *Wish it. Want it. Do it.*, which amounted to the same kind of self-help approach as Dr. Spock's advice.[2] The overall approach of relying heavily on the individual who bought the book was the hidden theme. Brian's book contained fifty blank pages for the buyer to fill in themselves.

Dr. Spock's advice on how children should be raised was anti-authoritarian in the permissiveness and borderline lackadaisical attitude it promoted in its very first edition. Here's a review of that edition (which, by the way, currently sells for around $1,000 CAD), printed in 1996 on the fiftieth anniversary of its publishing:

> The assumption is that parents generally are steady, decent people of good judgment who will raise healthy, happy children as a matter of course. "Trust yourself. You know more than you think you do," runs the fabled opening. Be the reasonable, attentive person you are, and your baby's own natural development will lead him to fit in with your family's way of doing things. "Each child wants, himself, to eat at sensible hours, and later to learn good table manners" counsels the kindly doctor. "The desire to get along with other people happily and considerately develops within him as part of the unfolding of his nature, provided he grows up with loving, self-respecting parents."[3]

---

[1] E. Pace, "Benjamin Spock, World's Pediatrician, Dies at 94," *New York Times*, March 17, 1998, https://www.nytimes.com/1998/03/17/us/benjamin-spock-world-s-pediatrician-dies-at-94.html.

[2] "Wish It, Want It, Do It [Video]," Family Guy Fanon Wiki, September 2, 2019, https://familyguyfanon.fandom.com/wiki/Wish_It,_Want_It,_Do_It.

[3] C. Winkler, "DR. BENJAMIN SPOCK … NEOCONSERVATIVE?" *Washington Examiner*, December 29, 1996, https://www.washingtonexaminer.com/weekly-standard/dr-benjamin-spock-neoconservative

It seems irresponsible to promote such attitudes—that is, until you look at previous authors of child-rearing books from the early- to mid-twentieth century, such as Dr. John B. Watson (1878–1958), who advised parents to "Never hug and kiss them," and to "Never let them sit in your lap … If you must, kiss them once on the forehead when they say goodnight. Shake hands with them in the morning." These words he published in 1928 in his book *Psychological Care of Infant and Child*.[4] It's quite possible such harsh advice, in the face of post-war anti-authoritarianism and later the sexual revolution, was over-corrected for by Dr. Spock's ever-evolving work. Spock admitted changes to counterbalance permissiveness were something he included following *The Common Sense Book of Baby and Childcare*'s first edition:

> Some people think I am the Pied Piper of Permissivism. The original edition in 1946 was part of a reaction against rigid rules which had laid down precisely when a baby should be fed and handled. This reaction was so successful that I became frightened by the swing to permissivism, and in the second edition I changed a lot.[5]

THE NEW LEFT

Dr. Spock revealed his true ideological colours when he declared he was a socialist in the 1960s, beginning with his membership in a rising movement, a descendant of Marxism called the New Left. Although the New Left no longer associated itself with the Orthodox Marxism that defined socialism and communism, it did propose a cultural revolution instead of a class-based one. The New Left saw Orthodox Marxism as a failure, and despite their continued belief in Karl Marx's goal of revolution to overturn society and redistribute wealth, they sought new methods to bring about such a crisis.

They pushed for women's rights, abortion rights, gay rights, drug-user rights, anarchism, and an end to the Vietnam War. These goals are sometimes referred to as Cultural Marxism, although this term erroneously carries the racist-based stigma of blaming its inception on German-born Jews who moved to the US (the Frankfurt School, which we will discuss in Chapter Eight). In the same

---

[4] John B. Watson, *Psychological Care of Infant and Child* (London, UK: George Allen and Unwin Ltd., 1928), https://archive.org/details/dli.ernet.7917/page/n5/mode/2up?view=theater.

[5] "'Pied Piper of Permissivism': Dr. Spock Talks about Baby and Child Care—Archive, 1962," *The Guardian*, June 23, 2017, https://www.theguardian.com/lifeandstyle/2017/jun/23/dr-benjamin-spock-baby-and-child-care-1962

manner today, Black Lives Matter (BLM), an organization built on a Marxist framework, can't simply be attributed to Black people. Both BLM and Cultural Marxism are examples of ideological choices of individuals who choose to join those movements—they are not implications of either skin colour or ethnicity. The New Left had an unofficial leader in the Neo-Marxist Herbert Marcuse, a German sociologist who escaped the Nazi regime to spread his ideas in the US.

The New Left rejected Orthodox Marxism but ultimately didn't survive as an independent sub-category of communism. There were just too many ideological similarities with Marxism that prevented them from permanently becoming a unique entity. The only appreciable, stand-alone element to the New Left was its pacifist stance, which slowly eroded into radical violence that alienated many. The anti-war sentiment at the beginning of the movement put the New Left at odds with communists over continued involvement in the Cold War (especially Vietnam), but this was ultimately an insufficient breaking point. History has revealed that the New Left and communism ended up existing in poorly separated ideologies that today operate in tandem. An example of this co-existence is contained within the violent extremist group Antifa, which houses ideological differences in socialism, communism, and anarchism, all under one roof.

But the most surprising reality of all is that the New Left, despite disappearing from the streets at the end of the 1970s, did not die. They instead found a new home in the halls of academe. This is explained in Dr. James Lindsay's *Race Marxism: The Truth about Critical Race Theory and Praxis* (2022):

> [T]he New Left became the Academic Left and did so continuously enough so that what is usually referred to as the "New Left" now should be understood to have been merely a turbulent early period of activism as various radical movements fused together and were infused with "Critical Marxism" (i.e. Critical Theory). The result was precisely the "Identity Marxist" identity-politics-based movement[.] [6]

TANKIES AND TROTS

The New Left was formed first in the United Kingdom, when a sudden rift caused Marxist sub-groups to splinter off from their communist parent but also amalgamate with other groups that were Marxist but didn't fall under the Soviet

---
[6] J. Lindsay, *Race Marxism: The Truth About Critical Race Theory and Praxis* (Independently Published, 2022), 157.

style. In fact, it was the violent suppression revealed in Soviet-occupied Europe that would frighten many people into abandoning communism—they had never really understood what Marxism entailed.

In response, the New Left broke off as an independent, originally peaceful movement. It was a cobbling together of various smaller movements such as feminism, Black liberationism, Neo-Marxism, Cultural Marxism, Critical Legal Theory, and several disenfranchised groups. (We will discuss these movements and some of their most important contributors in Chapter Eight.) This amalgamation of groups into the New Left was the biggest product of the rift in Marxism.

The New Left then labelled those who held to Marx's original ideas and favoured Stalinist authoritarianism and violence (Orthodox Marxists) as "tankies." This term referenced Soviet tanks rolling into Hungary in late 1956 to suppress dissidents, which horrified many around the world.

Conversely, the members of the New Left who didn't embrace the violent methodology of Stalin were referred to as "trots," short for Trotskyites. Leon Trotsky (1879–1940), whose real name was Lev Davidovich Bronstein, was a revolutionary Marxist. He aided Vladimir Lenin (1870–1924) as a Bolshevik leader in the October Revolution in overthrowing Russia's provisional government. He followed this stint as People's Commissar for Military and Naval Affairs of the Red Army during the Russian Civil War, which Lenin's Bolsheviks also won. After Lenin died, Trotsky was soon exiled under Josef Stalin (1878–1953) for his dissenting views on revolution. Trotsky wanted worldwide communist revolution, whereas Stalin was focused on Soviet Russia. Trotsky became a fierce critic of Stalin, for which he was ultimately assassinated in 1940.

Like their namesake, the trots of the New Left weren't as interested in affecting state-wide revolution either, but they accepted the existence of a democratic state within which they operated unfettered toward their Marxist goals. The trots worked toward a world-wide continuous revolution through existing political means.

The slang terms tankie and trot, despite their age, have experienced a recent revival over the internet, over fifty years since their inception. They only appear to be useful identifiers to those operating within the communist ideology itself, as tankies and trots often operate entirely within each others' parameters, and only their acts of violence may reveal which is which. The New Left made this distinction between tankies (Orthodox Marxists and Marxist-Leninists) and trots (the New Left and Neo-Marxists) explicit for a time, and it was the pacifist stance that allowed big names like Dr. Spock to publicly attach themselves to a new kind of communism.

Affluent and well-educated, Dr. Spock belonged to what turned out to be a neo-communist cult in the 1960s and 70s in the New Left. He was, at the same time, a man who wrote one of the best-selling books of all time, and that book was telling parents how to raise their children. In fact, one of the earliest and most poignant criticisms of Spock's work is that it told parents not to indoctrinate their own children but implied instead that those children should be left open to find their own way in life. What this advice really amounted to was an indoctrination by the world—a much more uncertain scenario. Chance would become a much greater determinant in who one's children met and who they chose to learn from.

Is it possible that after the Second World War, parents were being subtly manipulated by the type of anti-Christian pedagogy common in socialism and communism? Did Dr. Spock contribute to this in *The Common Sense Book of Baby and Child Care*? Radical left ideologies typically push toward atheism to ensure that the power of the state is absolute and can't be seriously challenged by any external forces civil society might contain. One way to push for atheism is to suggest people not participate in church. There are, however, more forceful ways to effect such change.

JOSEF STALIN'S WAR ON CHRISTIANITY

Take the Soviet Union under Stalin as a case in point. Beginning in 1928, Stalin targeted the Russian Orthodox Church to try and purge it from society. He purged Christianity from the Communist Party and from school curricula beginning in the first grade. Tens of thousands were murdered, including many priests, while others were sent to gulags. Thousands of churches were razed to the ground.

Under relentless pursuit of purification, a second purge of Orthodox Christians began with Stalin's League of the Militant Godless from 1932 to 1937. This time frame was what Stalin referred to as the Five-Year Plan of Atheism, a horrific communist initiative that involved terror and murder to be carried out over a standard time frame of five years. Of course, things rarely go according to plan. There was a third and final round of purges before WWII that extended into 1938, a year after the planned end of the Five-Year Plan of Atheism:

During the purges of 1937 and 1938, church documents record that 168,300 Russian Orthodox clergy were arrested. Of these, 106,300 were shot. Many thousands of victims of persecution became recognized in a special canon of saints known as the "new martyrs and confessors of Russia".[7]

While simple instructional books for parents would never have suggested such rank evil as Stalin conducted, it's possible that some books did subversively push to stop Christian indoctrination of children. This could be accomplished by suggesting the parent let the child decide their future and beliefs for themself. Yet even if this was the case with Dr. Spock's famous child-rearing book, it wasn't something he ignored—which suggests it might have been a lack of care on his part in earlier editions.

An agnostic, Dr. Spock became dissatisfied with the situation of the typical American family during the 1960s. He worried that his book, then around twenty years in print, hadn't been as empirically based as it should have. To that end, he revised *The Common Sense Book of Baby and Childcare* several times, included admissions of his own personal mistakes, and eventually added the suggestion that churchgoing served a positive psychological function for children. That he only included this claim in later editions and that he rejected the Christian God in his own life may have inadvertently stymied the revisions he added.

In the same vein, assuming a single book, however popular, was solely responsible for the moral failings of an entire generation is a fantastic stretch. It's much more likely that Dr. Spock's book both contributed to and reflected the countercultural zeitgeist of the post-war era. Nevertheless, the biggest historical move away from going to church appears to be—statistically speaking—conducted by the Boomers in North America. We'll look at some statistics on religious activity from two sources: one for Canada, and then one for the US for the sake of comparison.

---

[7] Wikipedia, "Persecution of Christians in the Soviet Union," July 6, 2023, https://en.wikipedia.org/wiki/Persecution_of_Christians_in_the_Soviet_Union.

CHAPTER THREE: THE NEW LEFT

Figure 1: Participation in a group religious activity at least once a month, by year of birth, Canadian-born individuals, 1985–2019[8]

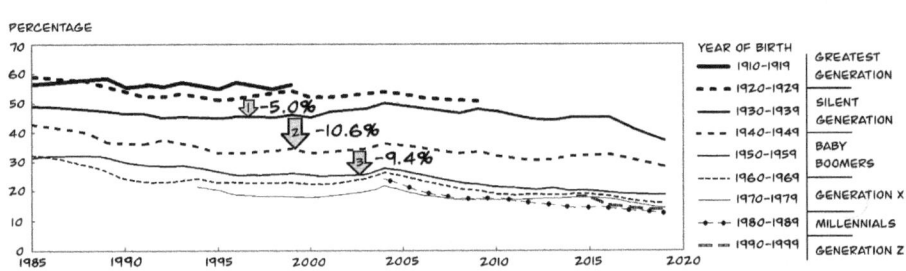

Are your eyes glazing over, like chocolate Timbits? Hang in there—this will be brief. The first and most certain thing to note is that as time goes on, and through the generations, group religious activity (church) is declining substantially in Canada. It's declining not only between the groups but within the groups as well, meaning each generation overall goes to church less and less as they get older, and each new generation goes to church less than its predecessor.

Several Statistics Canada surveys from different years were compiled to make the graph above. It shows a pronounced drop between the early-to-middle Silent Generation, jumping to the late Silent Generation/early Baby Boomers. That pronounced drop averages around 10.6 per cent (arrow #2 above). That drop is the greatest between any two contiguous groups on the graph.

The next biggest drop comes between the late Silent Generation/early Baby Boomers and the middle Baby Boomers. That drop averages around 9.4 per cent (arrow #3 above). Thus, the Baby Boomers were involved in an overall drop of group religious activity of approximately 20 per cent.

But before we blame the Baby Boomers for destroying Western society by not going to church (or any other such hyperbole), it appears that the move away from religious activity in Canada was already well underway with the Silent Generation.

The Silent Generation dropped noticeably below the Greatest Generation for religious activity, with an average drop of around 5 per cent (arrow #1 above). This suggests that the roots of moving away from group religious activity in

---

[8] L. Cornelisson, "Religiosity in Canada and Its Evolution from 1985 to 2019," Statistics Canada, October 8, 2021, https://www150.statcan.gc.ca/n1/pub/75-006-x/2021001/article/00010-eng.htm. An adaptation of this graph was made to include arrows with pct. drop and also generation names.

Canada may extend to pre-WWII times, and perhaps even the earliest part of the twentieth century. It certainly did accelerate under the Baby Boomer generation, however.

Data from the United States suggest a similar drop between the Baby Boomers and previous generations as significant but not as startling as the surprising drop between US Generation X (1965–1979) and the US Millennials (1980–2000), reported at 12 per cent.

Table 3: Changes in US church membership by generation over time

Generation	1998-2000 %	2016-2018 %	Change pct. pts.
Traditionalists (born 1945 or before)	77	68	-9
Baby boomers (born 1946-1964)	67	57	-10
Generation X (born 1965-1979)	62	54	-8
Millennials (born 1980-2000)	n/a	42	n/a

Source: Gallup

In this data compilation by Gallup, church membership as a percentage of generations is measured. Please note that this is not directly comparable to the previous graph from Statistics Canada, which instead looks at percentage of group religious activity. Being a member of a church doesn't automatically imply group religious activity, but there must certainly be a correlation of some sort. So we can say that the two datasets are somewhat related, but you can't directly compare them, just notice general trends in each.

As noted, the largest drop in church membership is between US Generation X and the US Millennials at 12 per cent. Importantly, there's no such equivalent drop of Canadian Millennials from Canadian Gen-Xers in the preceding Statistics Canada graph. In fact, the Canadian data suggest just a 0.9 per cent average drop in religious activity of Canadian Millennials from mid-to-late Canadian Generation-X. This raises the question of why such a difference might occur between the two nationalities (US vs. Canadian) of Millennials and Generation-X, as they don't seem to follow a pattern that extends across the border. However, that trend does show up markedly in a category reported by Statistics Canada called "religious affiliation," which could be closely linked to church membership in the Gallup poll. Let's look:

Figure 2: Percentage reporting religious affiliation, by year of birth, Canadian-born individuals, 1985–2019[9]

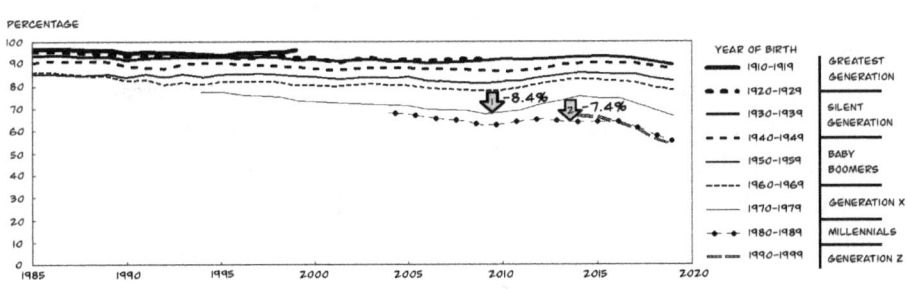

Although reported religious affiliation in the Statistics Canada survey isn't identical to church membership in the Gallup poll, the same pattern appears. There is a similar drop between Canadian Generation-X and Millennials at -7.4 per cent (arrow #2 above). That means the drop between these two generations is recorded in both Canada and the US in slightly different ways (religious affiliation vs. church membership). It should also be noted that there's an even more pronounced drop between Canada's late Baby Boomers/early Generation-X and later Generation-X at -8.4 per cent (arrow #1 above) in religious affiliation. The US didn't see such a marked drop between those two generations in church membership, however. All in all, the Boomers are at the heart of the greatest descent in group religious activity and church membership for the sizeable data compilations presented here.

Born in 1903, Dr. Spock belongs to the Greatest Generation (born from 1901–1927), which Gallup lumps together as part of the Traditionalists Generation (born before 1946). Spock wrote *The Common Sense Book of Baby and Childcare* while in the medical corps of the US Navy Reserves, during WWII. He had been a practising pediatrician since the 1930s, and at the time his individualistic approach to child-rearing was considered revolutionary. It was certainly a great deal more open and loving than Dr. Watson's had been.

But Dr. Spock made basic, sometimes dangerous, mistakes, pioneering the treatment of children as individuals. Some of these errors were concrete physical ones, like wrongly promoting that babies sleep on their stomach—later discovered to significantly increase sudden infant death syndrome (SIDS)

---

[9] L. Cornelisson, "Religiosity in Canada and Its Evolution from 1985 to 2019," Statistics Canada, October 8, 2021, https://www150.statcan.gc.ca/n1/pub/75-006-x/2021001/article/00010-eng.htm. An adaptation of this graph was made to include arrows with pct. drop and also generation names.

risk.[10,11] Others were ideological: parents naturally had the answers, and kids were naturally angels, were two faulty ideas from the first edition.

When he was accused of promoting avoidance of church-going behaviour by Pastor Norman Peale, and of permissiveness by US Vice President Spiro Agnew, the charges stuck. Both detractors claimed Dr. Spock's book had created a weak generation that suffered from his corrupt teaching. But whether Dr. Spock's libertarian socialist views did that much damage is still a debatable topic. The fact that the Baby Boomer Generation reveals the greatest decline of church membership and group religious activity in North America is instead a statistical reality.

---

[10] "Ways to Reduce Baby's Risk," Safe to Sleep, retrieved July 12, 2023, https://safetosleep.nichd.nih.gov/reduce-risk/reduce.

[11] J. Summer and Dr. N. Vyas, "When Can Babies Start Sleeping on Their Stomachs?" Sleep Foundation, July 17, 2023, retrieved August 1, 2023, https://www.sleepfoundation.org/baby-sleep/baby-sleeping-on-stomach#.

CHAPTER FOUR
THE SOCIAL GOSPEL

IN ADDITION TO cultural influences suggesting parents avoid indoctrinating their children into Christianity, an earlier movement saw the co-optation of the institution of the Church itself by social justice initiatives, beginning in the 1880s in Canada. These initiatives were referred to as the Social Gospel movement. Over time, they would be most clearly identified with the United Church of Canada (UCC), which began as a coming together of Methodist, Presbyterian, and Congregational denominations in the summer of 1925. The Methodists in particular were devoted to addressing social wrongs associated with industrialization—especially through the implementation of labour laws. Their earnestness extended into foreign countries and even missionary work in China.[1] The first iteration of what came to be known as the Social Gospel movement lasted from approximately 1880 to 1920 in Canada.

In this chapter, the key takeaway is that Canada's societal ills from 1880–1920, caused largely by industrialization, contributed to left-leaning Christian churches reassessing the core of their belief system. The sight of too much human suffering demanded change. There were also pressures on the Church initiated from positivism, Charles Darwin's *On the Origin of Species*, and higher criticism of the Holy Bible, questioning authorship of the Synoptic Gospels.[2] The answer of the left-leaning church to all these worldly concerns was the Social Gospel movement.

---

[1] See Chapter Three of J. Manthorpe, *Claws of the Panda* (Toronto, ON: Cormorant Books Inc., 2019).

[2] The Synoptic Gospels are the Bible's books of Matthew, Mark, and Luke, which contain substantial overlapping material.

The Social Gospel movement undermined the importance of an individual's salvation by teaching that God's work on earth was not completed because so many were suffering. Therefore, a collectivist approach to addressing the ills of society, or a *societal regeneration*, would become the primary goal of the church. This would replace the goal of *individual regeneration* (salvation). To overwrite the focus on individual salvation has, over time, arguably led to increasingly radical ideologies within the left-leaning church in Canada. It has allowed dialectical leftism to flourish within Canada's left-leaning churches.

While the left-leaning church reveals no historical lineage of Marxist indoctrination (unlike universities, as we shall see), there are examples of gradual Marxist subversion. Methodist minister Albert Edward Smith and his gradual subversion from social gospeler into Marxist-Leninist is a demonstration of the radical change that could and did occur. The striking worldview similarities between the Social Gospel and communism allowed for such change with relative ease.

Another socialist-centred ideological change was witnessed on a large scale by the creation of the Labour Church, founded in 1918 by Methodist minister William Ivens of Winnipeg, Manitoba. The Labour Church was ostensibly created to reconcile alienation between Church and working class. A.E. Smith likewise founded the People's Church in 1919 in Brandon, Manitoba, a separate but ideologically similar institution to the Labour Church. These churches imitated the Labour Church formed in England thirty years earlier.

From 1880 to 1920, Canadians experienced mass immigration, rapid urbanization, and growing industrialization. This combination of factors created widespread social problems in newly-minted Canada's post-Confederation society. Poverty was the biggest issue, with slums expanding in major cities where many could barely afford to live. Wage increases failed to meet the soaring cost of living. There was a clear economic inequality demonstrated by a middle and upper class that controlled significant wealth and was able to afford the increasing costs of goods and services. Poor health was another serious issue for a significant portion of the population. Poorer areas of town were dirtier, and most cities lacked a reliable sewage system. Drinking water supplies were often subject to contamination.[3]

---

[3] See Section 7.6: "Social Gospel" in J. D. Belshaw, "Canadian History: Post-Confederation," BCcampus, 2016, https://opentextbc.ca/postconfederation/.

All these societal problems nagged at the conscience of those well-off enough to weather the storm, many of whom were left-leaning Protestants. At the same time, those Protestants were also dealing with newly discovered scientific challenges to their faith, as explained by University of Waterloo professor and historian of sociology Rick Helmes-Hayes:

> Especially noteworthy are the Protestant churches respective theological and practical responses to three sets of events: 1) the rise of science, especially Charles Darwin's writings; 2) the development of scholarly literary and historical criticism of the Bible; and 3) the growth of widespread social problems that bedeviled Canadian society during the period.[4]

The Methodists, Presbyterians, and Congregationalists looked to the conservative establishment churches (the Catholics and Anglicans) in Canada and didn't see the sort of response they believed essential to Christianity. The three proto-UCC denominations also unfortunately began to adopt Darwinism, which made them question their focus on salvation of the individual, or what is sometimes called *individual regeneration*. Science ate away at their faith in God and in His ability to save the suffering humans around them. Although the effects of the Age of Enlightenment had been dogging the Old World for hundreds of years already, the effect of science to delegitimize Christianity was a relatively new phenomenon in Canada. That scientific focus, coupled with the new higher criticism of the Bible, saw a marked effect on left-leaning churches that tried to marry such concerns with Christian theology and practice.

At that time they began to question their whole raison d'être. While the purpose of the Church had always been the conversion and salvation of the individual, it now seemed to be an irresponsible goal to focus on such a minute portion of the population. With all the poor and suffering flooding big cities like Toronto and Montreal, how was a large portion of society supposed to come to know God when they couldn't so much as feed themselves? This rationalization would strike into the hearts of many.

---

[4] R. Helmes-Hayes, "'Building the New Jerusalem in Canada's Green and Pleasant Land': The Social Gospel and the Roots of English-Language Academic Sociology in Canada, 1889–1921," *The Canadian Journal of Sociology/Cahiers Canadiens de Sociologie*, 41(1), 1–52. 9, 2016, https://www.jstor.org/stable/canajsocicahican.41.1.1.

> [S]ocial gospelers argued that the church should worry less about saving souls for the hereafter and more about creating the Kingdom of Heaven on Earth in the here and now. [...] Indeed, they argued that social regeneration was "at least as important as" and would have to "precede rather than follow individual regeneration". They acknowledged that individuals had faults and that led to sinful behaviour, but reminded traditional members of the pious middle and upper classes that in many respects, people were products of their environment.[5]

It's important to point out here how dialectical leftism overlaps with the Social Gospel. A clear similarity exists in the determinist perspective, turning people into a product of their environment and limiting or even eliminating the possibility to affect their own lives and salvation through faith. That premise begs for a statist solution. Another connection between the Social Gospel and dialectical leftism is the idea of making heaven on earth a priority, and not necessarily putting faith in the salvation through Christ that is referenced in the Bible, which comes only after death. Like the worried social gospelers, Marxist materialism also contained a significant focus on aiming toward an earthly utopia to solve all of society's ills. Again, this begs for a statist solution. The closest any major church came to espousing support for communist policies during the first wave of the Social Gospel was seen in 1918 at the Methodist Church of Canada's (MCC) General Conference:

> At that remarkable event, the Methodists endorsed a slate of motions that: i) condemned special privileges, autocratic business organizations, profiteering, and all unearned wealth; ii) called for "the development of democratic forms of industrial organization"; iii) advocated the nationalization of natural resource industries, means of communication and transportation and public utilities"; iv) spoke in favour of the establishment of an old age pension scheme.[6]

This reads very much like a list of communist initiatives, or even a communist critique of a capitalist society that's meant to improve it. A communist critique

---

[5] Ibid., 10

[6] Ibid., 12.

of capitalist practice could certainly include an objection to "autocratic business organizations," which would give too much power to a non-government individual. Calling for "democratic forms of industrial organization" requires state influence directly applied to the means of production, a staple of communist regimes. Moreover, calling for "nationalization" of any kind of industry leaves the state responsible for controlling that business once it's usurped. The closer the churches came to suggesting the state should control the means of production, the closer they were coming toward espousing communist ideology.

There was evidence that some social gospelers were at least careful about the possibility of adopting Marxist ideology. One of Canada's most prominent and radical social gospelers, James Shaver Woodsworth (1874–1942), rejected the Communist Party of Canada and their push for violent revolution. Woodsworth was a Methodist minister and activist, but also a pacifist. His contribution as a protest organizer led to him being arrested during the Winnipeg General Strike of 1919 and charged with sedition. Ultimately, he spent just five days in jail before the charges against him were dropped and he was released. If he had demonstrably incited the workers, as some other organizers did, he wouldn't have been so lucky. As we shall expound upon in Chapter Nine, the promotion of violence is one of the hallmarks of Marxist ideology, and thus greatly helps to identify its adherents.

For all its drive and support, the Social Gospel movement eventually ran out of steam, as explained by historian and former Ontario MPP Richard Allen:

> The reasons for decline in the 1920s were manifold: the accomplishment of many reforms; a delayed disillusionment with the war, a weariness with doing good and a general abandonment of moral earnestness for a new hedonism; and the decline of idealism as a reigning philosophy. The Social Gospel, ideologically bound to the primacy of reason in a being vitally attuned to a benevolent God, could hardly survive in a world apparently animated by power and unreason on the one hand and frivolity on the other.
>
> However, under the impact of the Great Depression, a new younger generation combined the insights of Alfred North Whitehead, Reinhold Niebuhr and Karl Marx to fashion what some termed a new Social Gospel, others a form of "radical Christianity," which recognized the need for personal as well

as social renewal, accepted the importance of class struggle and sought a society of "mutuality." [7]

At the end of WWI, when the MCC lost its fervour for the Social Gospel, a minority of its members still held radical perspectives. Those radicals often felt there was too much inequality in society and that something should be done about it.

Although the nickname "Roaring Twenties" is generally applied to the American economy of that time, Canada's economy was eventually moving in the right direction in the 1920s too. However, as urbanization surpassed rural living in Canada for the first time, there were still sectors that perceived unjust economic inequality and were determined to use unions, church leaders, and politicians to push for their due. In Western Canada, this meant that rural Methodist churches, which included workers from railways and farms, had members open to radical ideology while still aligned with the dying Social Gospel movement.

ALBERT EDWARD SMITH: COMMUNIST MINISTER

Albert Edward Smith (1871–1947), an MCC minister and social gospeler, came to minister to the people in Brandon, Manitoba in 1913. After Smith preached the Social Gospel for the first several years of his ministry there, he began to read Marx in 1917, when the October Revolution captured his interest. Smith admired Lenin, but his early communist leanings didn't make him a communist, as he continued to publicly endorse social democratic policy. Behind closed doors, however, something different was happening. Smith saw a connection between the Social Gospel he was preaching and the communist faith he was studying.

It wasn't a paradigm shift that Smith would have to experience to make the adjustment from Social Gospel to communism. The Social Gospel provided fertile ground for such an extremist ideology, as explained by historian and archivist emeritus for the University of Brandon, Tom Mitchell:

> Smith's turn to Communism required no profound epistemological change. Moreover, little adaptation of Smith's Social Gospel critique of capitalism was required for him to come to general agreement with members of the Communist movement on economic, social, and political questions.[8]

---

[7] R. Allen, Social Gospel. The Canadian Encyclopedia. Last modified March 4, 2015, https://www.thecanadianencyclopedia.ca/en/article/social-gospel.

[8] T. Mitchell, "From the Social Gospel to 'The Plain Bread of Leninism': A.E. Smith's Journey to

Many who continued to espouse the Social Gospel after it lost the widespread support of the MCC appeared to be radicalized. Another Methodist minister, William Ivens (1878–1957), was opposed by his congregation in Winnipeg and forced to step down for his anti-war sentiment in 1918. This was odd because Ivens was a pacifist, so he didn't endorse violent revolution as a Marxist would, but his anti-war stance was considered un-patriotic. After he was removed from the MCC pulpit, he formed the Labour Church in 1918, which was quickly patronized by many disgruntled workers and veterans returning from the war. The question became: Why did Ivens need to make a new church focused on class differences? A potential answer came a year later when Ivens was charged with seditious libel for his contribution to the organization of the Winnipeg General Strike in 1919 and spent a year in prison.

Like Ivens, A.E. Smith wanted to be a contributor to the socialist cause in Canada, though Smith originally claimed that he didn't want anyone to break the law. However, during a strike in Brandon in 1919, Smith decided to join in the strike action, after which his congregation decided they'd had enough of his activism. They forced him to step down from his MCC pulpit after preaching the Social Gospel for six years in Brandon.

Smith responded by doing the same thing as Ivens—he founded his own church. Smith named it the People's Church, taking several hundred members out of the MCC in the process. The problem with these new churches, which were both considered to be Labour churches, was that they prioritized the class struggle occurring in Western Canada, and they weren't focused on Christianity. They began to attract the attention of the Royal North West Mounted Police (RNWMP), which decided that the "work" Smith was conducting could lead to serious trouble.

> RNWMP surveillance of Smith's activities beginning in the spring of 1919 was part of a larger state reaction against perceived protagonists of crisis. An early report characterized Smith as "an agitator of the Soviet system ... more dangerous than any other Bolshevist agitator for he has intelligence and influence." In October 1919, this surveillance continued; the RCMP Officer Commanding at Brandon was instructed to

---

the Left in the Epoch of Reaction after World War I," *Labour/Le Travail*, 1994, 33, 144. https://doi.org/10.2307/25143791.

detail a constable in plain clothes to report on meetings of the People's Church.[9]

Smith's activism and his participation in the strikes of 1919 demonstrated to the MCC that he was no longer conducting himself in an acceptable fashion for a minister, but this wasn't proof he endorsed communist ideology. The RNWMP and RCMP were on the right track, however, for although Smith continued to preach the Social Gospel until at least the year 1923, his viewpoint on social democrat policies is less certain. That viewpoint seems to have been affected dramatically by the defeat of the social democrats in Italy in 1922, after which the fascists rose to power under Mussolini. Eventually, Smith would set the record straight and never look back: "Any doubt about A.E. Smith's future was resolved 12 February 1925, when Smith and his wife joined the English branch of the Communist Party of Canada in Toronto."[10]

While the first wave of the Social Gospel movement between 1880–1920 provided the groundwork for radicalization, it wouldn't be until the second wave of the Social Gospel, the period following 1920, that radicals such as A.E. Smith came to prominence. In that type of radical Christianity, A.E. Smith referred to Jesus as a revolutionary and Mary as a mother who pushed her son to be a radical. At the same time, Jesus was stripped of his divinity.

It's important that the newest forms of Marxism today could be equated with a newest Social Gospel movement enveloping left-leaning churches, a third wave entirely separate and with different focus than either the original Social Gospel (1880–1920) or the second, post-1920 Social Gospel wave that gave rise to a radical Christianity. Since its earliest beginnings, the influence of Marxism has substantially grown within the left-leaning Christian church.

Marxist influence in the Church typically connected to concerns over social inequality, although exactly which social inequalities have changed over time. In its second wave, the Social Gospel demonstrated an Orthodox Marxist focus on labour and class relations. In the third or newest wave, that has changed to a Neo- and Cultural Marxist focus on sexual orientation, race, and then gender.[11] Even so, there are still arguments being made for an approach of Orthodox Marxism

---

[9] Ibid., 131.

[10] Ibid., 145.

[11] "Gender, Sexuality, and Orientation," The United Church of Canada Website, retrieved August 1, 2023, https://united-church.ca/community-and-faith/being-community/gender-sexuality-and-orientation.

within Western Christianity today.[12] In similar fashion to the institution of the Church, in Chapters Five and Six, we'll focus on the institutions of education. Therein we will discuss the dialectical thought process that first replaced Christianity in education using Orthodox Marxism, and then led from class-based Orthodox Marxism into the newer forms.

UNITED CHURCH OF CANADA AND MODERN SOCIAL JUSTICE

The most recent wave of the Social Gospel, the third wave that we infer, may be the most egregious regarding sheer dissonance with scripture. The author will briefly discuss his own experiences with the changes in this most recent wave of the Social Gospel, beginning in the early 1980s:

> During my childhood in the late 1970s and early 80s, church was something I attended weekly growing up, due in large part to my Christian parents' insistence. I remember it being quite an enjoyable experience, both in Sunday school and when the minister would talk to the children during service. He was a kind, charismatic man. We (the kids) would attend the church service as well as Sunday school. Can you picture kids sitting through two hours of church today? We would all end up being called to the front of the church during the service, where we entered a discussion led by the minister about whatever the sermon was for that day, but in a form we could understand. I can only remember positive experiences from those early church days, and that was as a member of the UCC back in the 1980s, a time when society had not been hit with many of the alarming consequences of modernity, and we were blissfully moving along as a prosperous nation.
>
> Even as recently as the 1980s, the United Church was undergoing a radical change from societal pressures, especially small groups of activists. These were entities that had been financially supported by the Liberal Party of Canada directly through government initiatives created under Pierre Elliot Trudeau.

---

[12] T. F. Kauffman, (2014). "Workers of the Church, Unite!: The Radical Marxist Foundation of Tim Keller's Social Gospel," *The Trinity Review*, 2014, 317–318, https://doi.org/https://www.trinityfoundation.org/journal.php?id=301.

> Things changed at my church before I knew it. The church was undergoing internal arguments, which were far beyond my understanding at that time, about the possibility of permitting homosexual ministers.
>
> Later in life, I would always find this something of a contradictory concept—one that still makes no sense. The Bible is clear that homosexuality is a sin, so why would a confirmed, unrepentant, and open sinner be teaching the congregation? It would be the same if we had a heterosexual minister leading the church who was married but also in an open relationship. If he wasn't shy about what he was doing, he was openly declaring himself an adulterer and was pushing for acceptance of his non-scriptural sexuality both in society and at church. That would make no sense either. You cannot have someone who normalizes what the Bible calls sin as the leader of Christian people, who are supposed to be fighting against temptation, who even pray not to be led into temptation.

As we saw with the first wave of the Social Gospel movement, a focus on social justice is not the same as a focus on individual salvation. Social justice is based on many perceived worldly inequalities the Bible does not prioritize or even mention. The Bible prioritizes the salvation of the individual through faith in Christ, and it neither asks humanity to become its own saviour in the interim nor to right social inequalities it doesn't even consider.

As time went on, the UCC became so distant from Christianity that if you now look up its website, you'll see that it is first and foremost an organization dedicated to social justice, and only afterward acknowledges the Word of God as a secondary focus.[13] This is a reflection of the earliest wave of the Social Gospel, which proposed societal regeneration must precede individual regeneration. It must be disheartening to see that the list of inequalities only seems to be increasing with time, and that the concept of societal regeneration is as far away—or farther—than it has ever been, at least in the eyes of radical ideologues who see nothing but injustice in the world.

In the newest (or third) wave of the Social Gospel, the UCC picks and chooses the parts of the Bible it believes best suited to promoting its agenda,

---

[13] "Welcome to the United Church Canada," The United Church of Canada, retrieved July 12, 2023, https://united-church.ca/.

CHAPTER FOUR: THE SOCIAL GOSPEL

which focuses largely on the victimhood of people of colour and the LGBTQ community.

The UCC set a precedent by being the first church in Canada to ordain a female minister (Lydia Emelie Gruchy in 1936) and also to ordain the first homosexual minister (Tim Stevenson in 1992). It prided itself on supplanting scripture and being the most progressive church possible. But even the UCC ran into serious problems when a minister "came out" as not believing in God but wanted to continue her job.

GRETTA VOSPER: ATHEIST MINISTER

In 2016, CBC journalist Wendy Mesley interviewed UCC Minister Gretta Vosper at West Hill church in Toronto.[14] Gretta, formerly known as Margaret Ann Vosper, had decided to make a public statement endorsing atheism in the wake of the Charlie Hebdo Massacre in January 2015. In that incident, two French Muslims murdered twelve people and injured another eleven at newspaper outlet *Charlie Hebdo* in Paris, France, all for making cartoons about the prophet Muhammad.[15]

How Vosper managed to conflate the Charlie Hebdo massacre with Christianity is a testament to the hodgepodge of confusion produced from modern schools of divinity. It's possible Vosper was using this as an opportune time to promote atheism among her congregation and others she could reach through various media. Perhaps she thought that massacre might create a crisis of faith in others, asking "How could God allow this?" As if it was the only horrible incident in history. As if it was God's fault.

What's truly telling is how during her 2016 CBC interview with Mesley, while answering what would happen if she were removed from the ministry, Vosper implicated the United Church of Canada in her answer. She suggested *the* United Church had created who she was, which must include her atheism:

> And as I've said elsewhere, [if removed from the UCC,] I will feel betrayed by the church because it has created who I am. It has been a major force in my life. It has taught me what I know.

---

[14] "Gretta Vosper | The Atheist Minister" [Video]., CBC News, retrieved March 31, 2024, https://www.cbc.ca/player/play/652504643698.

[15] Wikipedia, s.v. "Charlie Hebdo shooting," July 27, 2023, https://en.wikipedia.org/wiki/Charlie_Hebdo_shooting.

It has given me the tools to explore. It has demanded that I do that and so, I've done that and here we are.[16]

It's hard to imagine a better example of the *slippery slope* argument in today's churches that have decided to abandon scripture. Vosper's own words point to a permissive church that decided it should allow all sorts of worldly ideologies to break down its doors. The result is the story we just read: Gretta Vosper teaching a congregation that God doesn't exist, and hoping her message is normalized. In the end, Vosper, who was dealing with substantial legal bills fighting the UCC, settled out of court with them. She continues to preach at West Hill to this day.

There is currently a third wave of the Social Gospel that has submitted to the theory of *intersectionality*, addressing inequalities surrounding sexual orientation, race, and gender. How does this compare to the second wave of the Social Gospel that focused on class relations, in accordance with Orthodox Marxism? Let's look to historian Tom Mitchell to see if his assessment of the first and second waves of the Social Gospel could apply to the third wave today.

> Yet the Social Gospel had a number of limitations as a guide to social analysis or as a basis for political action. First and foremost, the Social Gospel reduced the purposes of God to merely human purposes and conceived of God's purposes as purely temporal. As well, it was excessively optimistic and utopian and, among adherents, the doctrine promoted a naïve notion of the character of conflict and social change. Lastly, the Social Gospel posited an "untenable conception of linear universal human progress."[17]

Although this critique was intended to address the first and second waves of the Social Gospel, it appears as if it could be an equally valid critique of the Social Gospel's third wave.

---

[16] "Gretta Vosper, "The Atheist Minister" [Video]., CBC News, retrieved March 31, 2024, https://www.cbc.ca/player/play/652504643698.

[17] T. Mitchell, "From the Social Gospel to 'The Plain Bread of Leninism': A.E. Smith's Journey to the Left in the Epoch of Reaction after World War I," *Labour/Le Travail*, 1994, 33, 144. https://doi.org/10.2307/25143791.

CHAPTER FIVE
EDUCATION, THE STATE ... *AND RELIGION?*

HOW EXACTLY DID we get to a point where Christian theology is shunned in schools while the education system, now clearly consumed with woke ideology, tries to instill a belief system built on unscientific claims and outright falsehoods? Why was it impossible for Christian theology and science to co-exist in the same institution?

In this chapter, a brief tour through the initial formation of a tangible Western education system will begin to explain how we ended up here. This brief tour will argue three key points:

First, in the Western world, Christianity was originally the primary focus of institutions of *both* religion *and* education, which is completely at odds with the modern concept that religion and science are mutually exclusive. Compare this to the woke ideology of today, which rejects reason and the scientific method. Christian theology remains much more compatible with those tools than do the ideologies of postmodernism and Marxism.

Second, modern universities evolved out of early Christian monastic and cathedral schools. Although they greatly expanded their curriculum in the transition, Northern European universities remained strongly focused on Christian theology, especially within German-speaking lands.

The third and final point is that the institution of the university provided the theological grounding to make repeated challenges to the late-medieval papacy through John Wycliffe, Jan Hus, and Martin Luther. In this manner, education interacted with Christianity to reflect Renaissance humanism and pull Christianity back to the scripture on which it is founded. This further suggests that Christian theology and education are not mutually exclusive.

PART II: THE SEED IS DEVOURED

IN THE BEGINNING ... OF EDUCATION

Universities and colleges have been, for a long time, the bastions of reason and learning in the Western world. Some might argue that they still are, but herein we argue that they have become peddlers of radical indoctrination, which has greatly hindered their ability to provide instruction or conduct research.

When they first started popping up across Europe, universities were little like the modern institutions we have today. And their history reveals a much more dramatic gap in both function and purpose. Today's universities began as tiny schools in single rooms, with just a handful of students, completely devoted to the studying and teaching of the Holy Bible. That antithesis of the current situation may be hard to fathom, because the clash between education and religion is so firmly ensconced in the Western mind.

The clash even permeates pop culture. This is much like a memorable *Simpsons* cartoon moment, in which Superintendent Chalmers pops into Springfield Elementary to check on how the school is going under Principal Skinner's replacement, Ned Flanders. He hears Flanders' voice crackle over the P.A. system: "Well cockaly-doodly-do, little buddies! Let's thank the Lord for another beautiful school day!" Chalmers instantly loses it: "Thank the Lord ... thank the Lord? That sounded like a prayer. A prayer! A prayer in a public school! God has no place within these walls! Just like facts have no place within organized religion."[1]

Of course, Ned Flanders is a clever caricature of a Christian, one so focused on love and acceptance that he's willing to be continually abused by his neighbour, Homer Simpson. Though Flanders is nominally Christian, he is a stereotype that can subversively dissuade people who might have a legitimate interest in Christianity. His kindness is so foolishly overblown it extends into a lack of respect for himself. Matthew 22:39 reads: *"And a second is like it: You shall love your neighbor as yourself"* (emphasis added). Ned doesn't love himself at all if he's willing to take abuse like he does.

Superintendent Chalmers accurately portrays the modern-day hatred of associating Church and state, especially in the critical sub-form of Church and education. It's especially interesting that he says, "facts have no place within organized religion," because historical evidence proves the exact opposite to be true.

For centuries, the only Western institutions that kept and reproduced books were monasteries. Monks are credited with keeping the works of classical

---

[1] ThingsICantFindOtherwise, "God Has No Place within These Walls! (The Simpsons)," YouTube Video, 0:20, October 7, 2015, https://www.youtube.com/watch?v=AG26IoRBuWQ

philosophers such as Plato and Aristotle alive during the early medieval period through their practice of transcribing worldly books in their free time. Yes, you read that right. They copied out entire books (by hand—no typesetting) in their free time.

That Christian monks kept, studied, and reproduced books appears to be widely accepted today, but any time Christianity is considered in historical context, it's important to be aware that people struggled to reconcile it with the emergence of science, especially in the field of philosophy. Throughout history, there were those who thought the two irreconcilable, those who thought they were separate but reconcilable, and those that thought science and religion were all part of the same greater whole.

In 1905, a famous US General, William Birney (1819–1907), also a lawyer and publisher, argued that not only did Christian monks not preserve, reproduce, or study the classics, but the only reason archaeologists found any non-religious books in monasteries was because they had been donated. This he elaborated upon within a turn of the century polemic he wrote for *The Monist*:

> It is by these gifts, made by the learned civilians and semi-secular dignitaries of the Church, and the fact that, as a general thing, the monasteries were respected in time of war, that in my opinion, the finding of classics in the monasteries can be accounted for. To infer that the monks copied them because they had them would be as loose as to infer that the Venetian Senate had copied the many valuable manuscripts found in their library, all of which were either presented or bought.[2]

At the time of his writing, Birney addressed what he considered errors in the historical Christian practice of monasticism. He believed Christian monks attempted to obliterate science and the possibility of a classical education by destroying ancient books and killing educators. Birney was a student of monism, the idea that the separation between spiritual and material realms (dualism) was an illusion and they were instead one (monism). Thus, the destruction of science to him was a destruction of a critical contribution to existence. As we shall discuss in Chapter Seven, the monist school of thought featured prominently at the beginning of Marxism under Marx's mentor, G.W.F. Hegel, when Hegel

---

[2] W. Birney, "Did the Monks Preserve the Latin Classics?" *The Monist*, 15(1), 87–108, 1905, retrieved April 2, 2023, http://www.jstor.org/stable/27899562.

attempted to marry religion and philosophy. However, Hegel's monism was abandoned by Marx because it attempted to hold on to Christian faith.[3]

While Birney believed Christian monks actively attacked pagan works like the Greek classics and tried to eliminate them, he had very little evidence to explain why such books were found intact in Christian monasteries. Moreover, evidence of the keeping and reproducing of books in monasteries would grow with the expansion of Christendom and a rudimentary school system.

MONASTIC SCHOOLS AND CATHEDRAL SCHOOLS

In AD 380, *The Edict of Thessalonica* from Emperor Theodosius I made Christianity the state religion of Rome.[4] This was during the very last days of the empire as it gradually disintegrated. After the Edict was declared, it became a punishable heresy to deny Christ, including punishment for those who believed in Christ's existence but denied his divinity.

So much for shaking the dust off your feet!

In fact, the earliest disciples were asked to simply walk away from those who did not choose to convert:

> And [Jesus] called the twelve together and gave them power and authority over all demons and to cure diseases, and he sent them out to proclaim the kingdom of God and to heal. And he said to them, "Take nothing for your journey, no staff, nor bag, nor bread, nor money; and do not have two tunics. And whatever house you enter, stay there, and from there depart. And wherever they do not receive you, when you leave that town shake off the dust from your feet as a testimony against them." And they departed and went through the villages, preaching the gospel and healing everywhere. (Luke 9:1–6)

While shaking the dust off your feet was symbolic among the Jews of what we understand to be "I wash my hands of what happens to you," it was also a completely non-violent and earthly declaration to leave others alone. It was understood then that judgement was God's alone, as is written many, many times

---

[3] E. Digby, "Hegel's Monism and Christianity," *The Monist*, 7(1), 114–119, 1896, retrieved April 2, 2023, http://www.jstor.org/stable/27897390.

[4] Christianity in this sentence should be equated specifically with the Catholicism of the Nicene Christians.

in the Bible, and that it wasn't the place of the disciples to exact punishment.[5] How unbelief began to be interpreted as punishable by human means doesn't seem clear, as there is no instruction for it in the New Testament. This may suggest that insistence on punishment was more a product of the condition of the world and an associated lack of basic human rights at that time. Recent history reveals that blaming Christianity is frequently a fashionable choice.

However, when people identified as Christians conduct acts of violence, those individuals risk being accused of religious instruction having predicated such acts, often by those who haven't read the text they are blaming (the Bible). In this way, an individual who reads that Christians were violent at some point in history can claim that humanity (without Christianity) is basically good but that Christian belief caused violence and death. Such simplifications might indicate a lack of study on the part of the claimant as opposed to some deep philosophical truth.

Insistence on earthly punishment (which, as we noted, isn't in the New Testament) could also be seen in Christian institutions that pre-existed the Edict. One Christian institution that had already been around for a century before Rome's conversion to Christianity was the monastery. The prototype for our modern-day Western universities began all the way back here, under the auspices of early Christian monasticism. A concrete but very weakly connected education system was created within these monasteries beginning around the fifth century AD, within monastic schools.

Monastic schools were typically small, with just a handful of pupils, taught by a single monk (called an abbot or "father"), and housed within Christian monasteries. The original focus of these teachings was asceticism, a brutal practice of self-deprivation for one's faith. It was taken from Middle East tradition. Anthony the Great (251–356), sometimes recognized as the *Father of all Monks*, is remembered for devotion to such an isolated and painful life, which today is referred to as eremitic:

> In regions around the eastern Mediterranean in the late third and early fourth centuries, men and women like Anthony—whose biography provided a model for future monks—withdrew into the Egyptian desert, depriving themselves of food and water as part of their effort to withstand the devil's temptations. The

---

[5] See for instance James 4:12, Luke 6:37, Matthew 7:1–2, 1 Corinthians 4:3–4, Acts 17:31, Hebrews 9:27, and Romans 2:1–3.

ideal of the saint alone in the wilderness retained its appeal, but Pachomius (died 312/13) and others living along the Nile River pioneered an irresistible alternative in cenobitic monasticism, that is, retreat into a community of like-minded ascetics committed to daily regimens of work and prayer. In western Europe, some monks and nuns settled far from cities and towns, seeking lives of devotion and self-denial in inhospitable or fortified locations, but other communities flourished in populous places, where they might withdraw from the world in spirit and yet remain nearby to offer instruction and guidance.[6]

Anthony the Great's focus on asceticism was gradually replaced by cenobitic monasticism with biblical teaching, recitation, reading, and writing, all in small groups. Children as young as six were accepted to monastic schools, both boys and girls, sometimes offered as gifts from their parents, so they might serve God. More rarely, a child would claim to have the devotion necessary to want to serve under their own volition.

Monks weren't always wonderful students, either. They were only loosely tied to their teacher, and troublesome students could move from monastery to monastery, as recorded by Benedict of Nursia (480–548), considered the founder of Western Christian monasticism. This realistic observation of bad students by St. Benedict was recounted by Abbot Herbert Byrne of Ampleforth Abbey (1884–1978):

> [T]he monk either persevered in his solitude or passed from teacher to teacher, receiving from each some special lesson, some further benefit. But it obviously left the unstable soul without support and opened a fairly comfortable career to the work-shy. Indignant descriptions of some unsatisfactory types enliven the first chapter of St. Benedict's Rule.[7]

Monastic schools included teaching for both monks (boys) and sometimes nuns (girls). Through certain periods of time, it was considered acceptable to

---

[6] J. Sorabella, "Monasticism in Western Medieval Europe," The Met, retrieved July 25, 2023, https://www.metmuseum.org/toah/hd/mona/hd_mona.htm.

[7] H. K. Byrne and Abbot of Ampleforth, "Benedictine Monasticism. Life of the Spirit," (1946–1964), 2(21), 382–385, 382, 1948, http://www.jstor.org/stable/43702988.

have double monasteries, where both nuns and monks were housed separately but served at the same church and facilities. There were also convents solely dedicated to the practice and teaching of nuns, concomitant with male-exclusive monasteries. Even after its change from asceticism, monasticism was designed to be a lifelong devotion and involved both strict rules and corporal punishment (physical beatings).

Along with existing monastic schools, cathedral schools effectively arrived with the formation of the Western Roman Catholic Church and its initial dioceses in 590 under Pope Gregory I, often considered the first medieval pope. The first cathedral schools in England, for example, include Canterbury Cathedral (597) and Rochester Cathedral (604). Both buildings were rebuilt in the eleventh century in a beautiful gothic style that has largely survived to this day. These schools were originally dedicated to teaching choir to boys.

By the early eleventh century, monastic schools began to be superseded by cathedral schools, where church leaders would educate future clergy in a manner vaguely like what we have in modern times. In cathedral schools, students would attend classes during weekdays for several hours each day before departing to their proper homes, to return the next weekday. This was much different than monasteries, where the students would permanently reside.

Despite being open to the public under Emperor Charlemagne (747–814) as early as the ninth century, cathedral and monastic schools during the medieval period bore little other resemblance to public education today.

The later arrival of cathedral schools saw greater restriction regarding who was eligible to be educated. Although children were included in cathedral schools, it was only children of noble birth, and of those nobles, only boys, so they might be trained to join the clergy. Women were prohibited from joining the clergy and thus also prohibited from joining the cathedral schools.

The weakly connected system of monastic and then later cathedral schools was, in effect, the first institutionalized and widespread education system in Western society.

MEDIEVAL UNIVERSITIES

The first universities materialized in the late eleventh century, roughly halfway through the medieval period. Universities were frequently associated with—or even directly created from—monastic and cathedral schools. The University of Paris, for example, among those universities first founded (1150), arose directly from Notre Dame cathedral school, and was first dedicated to teaching theology and philosophy. Universities would have additional opportunities for higher learning in the trivium and the quadrivium. The subjects for an undergraduate arts degree, for example, consisted of grammar, logic, and rhetoric (the trivium); and arithmetic, geometry, music, and astronomy (the quadrivium). The trivium would be taught first.

Universities were dominantly Christian inventions that included the Word of God when they first began. Superintendent Chalmers, who thought facts had no place within organized religion, was obviously not a medieval history buff. Nor perhaps were the writers for *The Simpsons*. Most people today believe the education system should be devoid of spiritual content, and atheism continues to grow rapidly in Canada.[8] Unlike today, however, atheism was relatively obscure during the medieval period, the term having yet to be coined. Still, writings as early as those of Anselm of Canterbury (1033–1109) acknowledged the existence of unbelievers.[9]

Near the end of the medieval period, universities remained thoroughly involved with the Church, but they also experienced a growing influence from the state. Of course, Church and state had not yet been separated as in modern society. Universities received their charters—official recognition as institutions—from such high dignitaries as popes, emperors, and kings. Such charters were necessary so that the degrees attained would enable students to practise throughout Christendom. Medieval universities were also subject to the petty politics of men. A vicious fight for separation of Church and state, one which affected the development of universities, erupted in the latter half of the twelfth century.

Assassination of Thomas Becket. When then King of England, Henry II, a monarch renowned for his fiery temper, banned Englishmen from attending the University of Paris in 1167, it expedited the development of English universities. This was good for education in England, but not so good for England's relations with France, or the king's relations with the Church of England. Henry was having a spat with the Archbishop of Canterbury, his former chancellor, Thomas Becket (1119–1170). He had nominated Becket for Archbishop and wrongly hoped that nomination and subsequent election would help him maintain power over the Church of England through his former subordinate.

---

[8] "The Canadian Census: A Rich Portrait of the Country's Religious and Ethnocultural Diversity," Statistics Canada, October 26, 2022, retrieved July 12, 2023, https://www150.statcan.gc.ca/n1/daily-quotidien/221026/dq221026b-eng.htm.

[9] Wikipedia, s.v. "History of Atheism," July 11, 2023, https://en.wikipedia.org/wiki/History_of_atheism.

CHAPTER FIVE: EDUCATION, THE STATE...*AND RELIGION?*

Following his election, however, Becket began fighting to put the government in its place, eventually excommunicating three of Henry's key supporters. The spat also fuelled Henry's rivalry with King Louis VII of France, who was greatly concerned over Henry's growing power and expanding kingdom. Louis provided Becket refuge for a time to vex the English king, before supporters of Henry II assassinated Beckett in 1170 at Canterbury Cathedral, hacking him to bits—*inside* the church. That event was recorded by a monk from Cambridge, Edward Grim, who attempted to save Beckett but had his arm nearly severed off in the process. Grim recorded a firsthand account of the murder:

> … the impious knight … suddenly set upon him and [shaved] off the summit of his crown which the sacred chrism [had] consecrated to God … Then, with another blow received on the head, he remained firm. But with the third the stricken martyr bent his knees and elbows, offering himself as a living sacrifice, saying in a low voice, "For the name of Jesus and the protection of the church I am ready to embrace death." But the third knight inflicted a grave wound on the fallen one; with this blow … his crown, which was large, separated from his head so that the blood turned white from the brain yet no less did the brain turn red from the blood; it purpled the appearance of the church … The fifth—not a knight but a cleric who had entered with the knights … placed his foot on the neck of the holy priest and precious martyr and (it is horrible to say) scattered the brains with the blood across the floor, exclaiming to the rest, "We can leave this place, knights, he will not get up again."[10]

New universities were going to pop up, chop chop!

Due in part to Henry II's banning of the University of Paris, two of the most famous English universities established themselves with greater enrollment near the end of the twelfth century: the University of Oxford (1167), and the University of Cambridge (1209). These are two of the most prestigious and storied learning institutions to this day. Beckett didn't spill his brains all over Canterbury Cathedral for nothing!

---

[10] D. M. Hayes, "The Murder of Thomas Becket," Internet Medieval Sourcebook, retrieved July 12, 2023, http://fs2.american.edu/dfagel/www/MurderOFbecket.htm.

As for the University of Paris, unlike its early Northern European contemporaries, it now exists in a much different form. It was officially closed and sold off during the French Revolution in 1793. After it reopened as the University of France in 1806, it continued to operate as a single entity until 1970, when it was divided into thirteen independent universities.

For many centuries in the medieval period, Western universities remained subject to Roman Catholicism and associated religious traditions. That changed upon the arrival of the Protestant Reformation, a culmination of several independent initiatives.

Jan Hus burned at the stake. One of the first, often overlooked, proto-protestants to have a high position in a university was the Bohemian Jan Hus (1370–1415). Hus was born into a poor family in Husinec, Bohemia (modern day Czechia) and educated in a monastic school beginning at the age of ten. He later moved to Prague and was admitted to Charles University (founded 1348), where he proved to be a dedicated student, earning a master's degree before turning thirty. He would go on to teach at Charles University and rapidly rose in administration to the level of dean and then proctor. He began preaching at Bethlehem Chapel at the age of thirty-two. Everything seemed to be going very smoothly for Hus, and he was a model of success for his fellow Bohemians. Problems arose when he gained a reputation as a preacher with very different views.

Some big liturgical differences Hus incorporated while preaching at Bethlehem Chapel from 1402–1412 included comparing the veneration of art with idolatry, introducing scripture readings in the vernacular (instead of Latin, which only the clergy understood), and hymns in the vernacular for the congregation to sing along with, instead of just to be sung or read by clergy.[11] Rome was not a fan of this approach.

Hus's outspoken nature against the practices of the Catholic Church as he preached in Bohemia didn't go unnoticed in Rome. He was vehemently opposed to papal indulgences (which were exchanges of money to free the trapped souls of your dead relatives) and other issues, such as the righteousness of the crusades. Many of Hus's views were directly inspired from an English Catholic priest who was also a university professor, Oxford's John Wycliffe (1328–1384). Wycliffe, whose views often questioned the legitimacy of Catholic practices, would escape persecution, and was only declared a heretic posthumously in 1415.

---

[11] Enrico C. S. Molnar, "The Liturgical Reforms of John Hus," *Speculum*, 41(2), 297–303, 1966, https://doi.org/10.2307/2851264.

Hus detested that the Catholic Church engaged in non-scriptural practices—stuff that wasn't instructed in the Holy Bible but which the papacy had added through its practice of tradition. He presented his issues to the theology faculty of Charles University, but, in cowardly fashion, his peers refused to support him. This lack of university faculty support was no minor detail, as we shall see when we come next to the Protestant Reformation. It left Hus isolated and a much easier dissident to handle.

For his differing views and practices, Hus was excommunicated by the Church and spent two years under enforced exile. All his protestations had occurred during the Catholic Church's protracted Western Schism from 1378–1417, during which two and then three separate papal candidates had been elected by various Church bodies. All three candidates laid claim to the papacy, one from Avignon, one from Rome, and one from Pisa. The Catholic Church was torn apart, and this gave Hus indirect security for a short time.

Beginning in 1414, the Council of Constance was called by King Sigismund of Hungary (1368–1437), future emperor of the Holy Roman Empire, to reunite the Catholic Church and bring together all three popes to sort out things. It ended up taking three years. Over that time, two claimants were denounced as antipopes and removed from office, while a third was excommunicated. A fourth pope, Martin V (1369–1431), was then elected as the genuine article in 1417, ending the Council of Constance. Martin V now held office over the re-unified Catholic Church and Papal States.

Jan Hus was summoned to that same Council of Constance by Sigismund to present his dissenting views against the practices of the Catholic Church, but with the promise of safe passage. He trusted the promise of the king and made his way. However, as soon as he arrived in Constance in 1415, Hus was arrested and thrown in prison. Sigismund had been convinced of Hus's guilt by Church officials and reneged safe passage.

Hus was instructed to immediately recant his views or suffer the consequences. When he refused, he was burned alive at the stake. His lack of support, especially from his peers at Charles University, was a key reason he didn't get far with his dissident preaching of both his own and Wycliffe's views.

The reaction to Hus's execution was swift. The Bohemians (and Moravians) moved away from papal authority and declared that anyone who believed in the persecution of a good and just man like Jan Hus was a traitor of the worst kind. They let Sigismund know what they thought of him, and this incensed the king. Sigismund sent angry letters warning Bohemians that anyone who followed the teachings of either Hus or Wycliffe would be executed. In response to the withdrawal from papal authority, Martin V endorsed five separate crusades against Hussites and Wycliffites in Bohemia, beginning in 1420.

The result was the Hussite Wars (1419–1434), in which ingenious Bohemian generals would defeat the papacy's dominantly German Catholic crusaders. A peace settlement acquiesced to by a beleaguered King Sigismund would see the Hussite religion practised freely in Bohemia for the next two hundred years. The Catholic Church, however, was unchanged by Hus's dissenting views.

The Protestant Reformation. The Protestant Reformation began in 1517, and the separation of the Lutheran, Calvinist, and Zwinglian Churches from Roman Catholicism followed, driven chiefly by friar and professor at the University of Wittenberg, Martin Luther (1483–1546). The Church of England also took control of the institutions of the Catholic Church within its borders, beginning in 1534, by making the king their supreme leader. This was accomplished under Henry VIII (1491–1547), the fat-faced monarch who kept chopping off his wives' heads when they couldn't bear him an heir.

And so the Catholic Church became chopped into many pieces, where certainly geography and distance from Rome had a part to play. Chop chop!

Yet one of the biggest supporting roles to play in the Protestant Reformation would be that of the northern European universities of Germany (as opposed to those universities in France or England, or those in southern Europe, which were predominantly Italian). The universities to the south differed greatly from their northern cousins.

In southern European universities, law and medicine doctorates were the goal of most students. The faculty were typically aged professionals loosely tied through the university but generally having their classes and material decided by student-body voting. This was the practice in place at the University of Bologna, for example, the oldest university in the West, founded 1088.

In contrast, and as well-explained by professor emeritus of the University of Toronto, Paul Grendler, in his 2004 paper *The Universities of the Renaissance and Reformation*, northern European universities had a completely different focus and organization from their southern counterparts. The place of theology was much more significant in German universities, and those German universities were much more organized. They possessed a senate with power to make academic changes. They employed deans to lead their various faculty, including theology. They had numerous young masters, who had just completed their education but would remain on to teach undergraduate courses. Some German universities even maintained strong relations with religious orders, an important product of the days of monastic schools. At the University of Wittenberg, for instance, there was a close tie with the Augustinian Hermits, who provided students, professors, and residence.

These physical or institutional advantages prefaced a critical and well-supported challenge to the medieval papacy. At the time, and despite Jan Hus and John Wycliffe's earlier protestations, the papacy continued selling indulgences. Professor Grendler explains the institutional pre-conditions that allowed Luther the opportunity to proceed with a dispute against such venality as the indulgences spread:

> The Protestant Reformation began as a common academic exercise, a proposed disputation. Martin Luther had been concerned about the indulgence trafficking in and around Wittenberg since 1514. This led him to examine and find wanting the biblical and theological support for indulgences. In late October 1517, Luther drafted Ninety-five Theses, or propositions of debate, concerning indulgences, in preparation for a public disputation about them. This was normal procedure for a university disputation by a professor who wished to attract attention to himself and his views. Luther had engaged in previous disputations in September 1516 and April 1517, in which he attacked [medieval] Scholasticism. The ideas in the Ninety-five Theses (or On the Power of Indulgences) were revolutionary. But the theses were written in academic disputation prose, which was just as dreary as it sounds. The number of theses that Luther proposed to debate was about average for a disputation led by a professor.[12]

This was a curious circumstance. What some argue to be the *Renaissance humanist* approach (not to be confused with contemporary humanism) was being used to critique the Catholic Church and its practice. Renaissance humanism refers to the attempt to go back and re-study works of antiquity from their original texts, all to aid the individual with critical thinking and perspective. Martin Luther was demanding a return to the instruction in the Bible. Education

---

[12] P.F. Grendler, "The Universities of the Renaissance and Reformation," *Renaissance Quarterly*, 57(1), 1–42, 14, 2004, http://www.jstor.org/stable/1262373.

was helping provide opportunity to question the unbiblical practices of the Roman Catholic Church, and in some regard was therefore working with the Church—the body of believers—to try and produce the truth. Perhaps Luther's strongest argument (put together many years ago by both Jan Hus and, before him, John Wycliffe) was that there was no biblical impetus for the selling of salvation for souls in a purgatory, and that the traditions of the Catholic Church had gone too far afield in the name of making money.

It would have been extremely difficult for a reformation to have occurred within the Catholic Church itself because of the inordinate power the papacy held. This power transfer to an individual, considered to directly have begun from Christ, was not recorded within scripture, either. There was no clear handing of the leadership of the Church to St. Peter (considered to be the first pope in Roman Catholicism) written within scripture. This transfer was instead assumed to have been established through tradition in the earliest Church. The closest passage that could be interpreted as giving Peter charge of the Church is probably the following:

> Now when Jesus came into the district of Caesarea Philippi, he asked his disciples, "Who do people say that the Son of Man is?" And they said, "Some say John the Baptist, others say Elijah, and others Jeremiah or one of the prophets." He said to them, "But who do you say that I am?" Simon Peter replied, "You are the Christ, the Son of the living God." And Jesus answered him, "Blessed are you, Simon Bar-Jonah! For flesh and blood has not revealed this to you, but my Father who is in heaven. And I tell you, you are Peter, and on this rock I will build my church, and the gates of hell shall not prevail against it. I will give you the keys of the kingdom of heaven, and whatever you bind on earth shall be bound in heaven, and whatever you loose on earth shall be loosed in heaven." Then he strictly charged the disciples to tell no one that he was the Christ. (Matthew 16:13–20)

It's an interesting answer that Jesus first receives, one that reminds me of what it's like to run an online site where you ask everyone's opinion. You get all sorts of answers, and most of them are easily proven wrong. People thought Jesus was John the Baptist, Elijah, Jerimiah, or other prophets, but they were all incorrect. That must have been frustrating for the disciples to hear, but God had not yet allowed Jesus' divinity to be revealed. The key statement here is, of course, *"And I tell you, you are Peter, and on this rock I will build my church, and the gates of hell shall not prevail against it."* From this line, some derive an understanding that Peter is the rock upon which Christ built the Church, and this is used to explain that Peter was the first pope. Protestants contest the interpretation of this statement, suggesting instead that Christ was the rock upon which the Church was built.

The instructions following the declaration of building upon the rock are less open to interpretational challenges and are commonly understood to be the *Office of the Keys*: the power to forgive sins or to withhold forgiveness if someone doesn't repent. According to Roman Catholic tradition, this power was reserved strictly for the pope—and anyone the pope approved.

The institution of the university provided the societal and, surprisingly, the *theological* grounding Luther needed to be able to question the Roman Catholic Church, with support of his peers and the German princes shortly thereafter. Contrast this to the tribulations of Jan Hus, whose views were rejected at Charles University in Prague and whom the German Princes came together against at the behest of Sigismund of Hungary and Pope Martin V.

Luther's ability to translate, assess, and bring the message of the Holy Bible directly to the common people, who were generally illiterate in Latin, was critical. Most people only received reading of scripture at church, and that was always in Latin. Both Wycliffe and Hus would have greatly approved of this initiative, which they both attempted in their own ways. It's also important to note that Luther was inspired by the work and sacrifice of Hus.

Martin Luther helped disseminate the message of Christ by promoting that *everyone* should read the Bible and thus understand directly what they must know. He even translated the entirety of the Holy Bible from Latin into German by 1534, using language that was clear and concise. His translation proved greatly influential to the spread of the Word in the vast expanse of German-speaking territory in Europe. It would be another four centuries before the Gideons came along with their tradition of putting those little red English Bibles in hotel rooms (beginning in 1908), which is a similar initiative to bring the Bible to everyone and is still done today.

CHAPTER SIX

SIGNS OF A TRAJECTORY

We're now going to leap ahead from the time of the Reformation by about three centuries, to the next big ideological developments that concern us. In skipping from roughly 1500 to 1800, we dodge big events like the Thirty Years' War, the formation of the Anglican Church, the implementation of the Gregorian calendar, the Spanish Inquisition, various plagues across Europe, and the War of Spanish Succession. Not much, really, compared to the number of iPhone updates that could have been created over that time frame. From this point forward, there will be no more gaps in history, since dialectical leftism can be traced directly to this era and has existed ever since. The preceding chapters on history were an absolute necessity to explain how dramatic a shift has occurred from theology to ideology and why.

The mid-1800s were a time of great activity for the Western world. Industrialization was roaring in late bloomers France and Germany, who could now be considered industrial powers along with England. The Napoleonic Wars had caused the fall of the Holy Roman Empire, and following that, the influence of the Catholic Church in Europe was greatly diminished under the new liberalism. The French monarchy was at last abolished. Nation-states Germany and Italy began to unify, and there was general instability as the established powers continued to diminish in the face of growing secular power.

In this chapter, we'll focus on how the mid- to late-1800s saw institutions of education remove their affiliation with Christianity, which mimicked the larger secularization across Europe. This spiritual but palpable change was witnessed by philosopher Friedrich Nietzsche, who recorded it by decrying that "God is dead!

> God remains dead! And we have killed him!"[1] This secularization was likewise seen in Germany's Kulturkampf, where a newly unified Germany sought to exorcise the influence of Rome from its borders. From there, we'll look to when secularization of education spread to the New World, in North America.
>
> The point here is to demonstrate that this fall away from Christianity—a kind of miniature second fall from grace—left a large vacuum that secularists assumed scientific objectivity would be able to maintain. They may not have realized that in removing the Catholic Church's influence, they also removed a good deal of Christian influence and threw the Holy Infant out with the bathwater. The Enlightenment thinkers couldn't have imagined what was going to come further down the road to fill the empty tub. The answer to that is the inception of *dialectical leftism*, which will be covered in detail in the next chapter.

Before we start talking about this second, miniature fall, we'll look back to the first, big fall to recall why that didn't destroy us.

For humanity, that big fall from Paradise was bitter and all-consuming. The Bible says that after being expelled from Paradise, man then had to eat by the sweat of his brow and toil all the days of his life.[2] No more were the sun, the plants, or the animals a beautiful backdrop of joyful experience at the beck and call of humanity's interest. Now everything, from the roaring waters of the ocean to the whirling sky of the tempest, was a threat—a cause to fear mortality. The old Adam in each of us was bound through original sin, and therein condemned under the law of God. And breaking so much as one iota of that law was the same as violating all of it: insurance that none escaped death.[3]

The coming of Jesus culminated in reconciliation of man to God. An answer to the fall for humanity, but not for the cursed earth beneath their feet. A reconciliation so great and holy it could only be achieved by God Himself. In the manifesto of the accuser, Satan, who was happy to drag down man with the temptation to be like God, there was no salvation. A lawyer of inhuman cunning, Satan argued man would never be able to resist his weak flesh with the existence

---

[1] F. Nietzsche, *Nietzsche: The Gay Science: With a Prelude in German Rhymes and an Appendix of Songs*, B. Williams, Ed.; J. Nauckhoff and A. Del Caro, Trans. (Cambridge: Cambridge University Press, 2001).

[2] See Genesis 3:19.

[3] See Romans 6:23.

God granted him, which required unswerving obedience. Yet God didn't leave His creation to its own devices. Under the auspices of the Creator, through the witness of Christ, man would become perfected, no longer vulnerable to the temptations of the old evil foe. This was the way back from the fall.

But man still has to die first, believing in Christ and (hopefully) baptized to receive the free gift of salvation. He must join in Jesus' death and resurrection in Word and Sacrament during his time on earth, which bears witness not to his merit, but his faith. Following his death, man will be represented to God through His Son, Jesus, who will testify that man is known.

When universities first began to attack faith in God, they initiated a kind of miniature fall from grace.

For a time, universities enjoyed growth and prosperity. Certainly that time was far from perfection or anything like Eden, and with a great deal of bloody mishaps like what happened to Becket or Hus, but they focused on teaching and learning about the world around them. This practice, even though some disparage as positivist, was at least based in truth of witnessing that which could be seen, whatever the limit of such an approach. The stunning eventuality was that when mankind decided he was dissatisfied with studying and reporting on what could be seen, he attempted to make reality into his own vision and fell right back down into what could not be seen. This time, without God.

One of the most famous atheist minds of the nineteenth century, one whom many people admire and wish to emulate to this day, is the German philosopher and philologist Friedrich Nietzsche (1844–1900). Nietzsche is known especially for his hackneyed quotation "God is dead," which came from his work *The Gay Science*, published 1882. We will examine some of Nietzsche's contribution to the fall of the university away from Christianity, an ironic turn of events, as Nietzsche himself was denied a position at the University of Leipzig in 1883 "owing to the fact that the Faculty would never dare to recommend [him] to the Board of Education in view of [his] attitude towards Christianity and the concept of God."[4]

Nietzsche has received a boost in his present popularity thanks to Canadian clinical psychologist Dr. Jordan Peterson and his books *12 Rules for Life: An Antidote to Chaos* (2018) and *Beyond Order: 12 More Rules for Life* (2021). Those books, of which *12 Rules for Life* has sold over ten million copies, heavily reference the works of Nietzsche.

---

[4] Friedrich Nietzsche, "Letter to Peter Gast," August 26, 1883, retrieved from https://en.wikisource.org/wiki/Selected_Letters_of_Friedrich_Nietzsche#To_Peter_Gast_-_July,_1883.

NIETZSCHE'S *THE GAY SCIENCE*

Here is an apt time in our lightning-paced history lesson to pause for thought. Where we left off in the last chapter, the Protestant Reformation had a renewed focus on what Dr. Jordan Peterson refers to as "… the strange Christian insistence that salvation could not be obtained through effort or worth—through 'works'."[5] Peterson included this quotation in his self-help book, *12 Rules for Life*, because the Protestant Reformation watered down *the imitation of Christ* in the eyes of his influencer, Friedrich Nietzsche.

Yet Martin Luther wasn't asking Christians to conduct fewer good works. He was asking the office of the papacy to repent. Luther saw papal indulgences as a completely corrupt practice and used them as his chief evidence in his 95 Theses. The highly organized German universities provided him the institutional legs to stand on and present such a criticism.

In this instance, it's possible the pattern of criticism initiated under Renaissance humanism did in fact benefit Christian believers, but only because the papacy had gone so far astray from scripture. The skills to educate one another, especially to educate and protect the laity, don't appear to be used to challenge God—or try to become like God—in this unusual instance. Remember, the fall from Eden was caused by the temptation to be like God.[6] Luther's criticism of the papacy didn't fit the well-established and very human pattern of the eating of forbidden fruit. There's little evidence at all that Luther was trying to remove the imitation of Christ either, as Christ never busied Himself selling indulgences.

Nietzsche's understanding of Christianity was one of someone who practised little but read a lot: largely theoretical and lacking experience. Someone detached from the real-world traditions he was evaluating. That doesn't mix well at all. It's like a colleague that never shows up for work but does it all from home. How much respect or trust do you have for that colleague? How about for his work? It's not so simple to evaluate.

To explain Nietzsche's approach, we need to understand that he was a rationalist in the classical sense of the word. He believed empirical evidence wasn't necessarily needed to discover the truth, and that truth could instead be reasoned out by the power of the human mind. Therefore, reading Nietzsche's *The Gay Science* (1882) gets to the heart of his popular "God is dead" conjecture. His writings suggest that he was overwhelmed by the secularization and related

---

[5] Dr. J. B. Peterson, *12 Rules for Life: An Antidote to Chaos* (Toronto, ON: Random House Canada, 2018), 186.

[6] See Genesis 3:5.

wars occurring throughout Europe at the time. He was clearly terrified of what he believed to be the struggle to address existential angst and meaninglessness, otherwise he would hardly have produced so many works on the subject.

Nietzsche's conclusion was that God was a construct of human weakness that had been disproven by truth and destroyed. That destruction was creating the suffering he witnessed during the wars associated with the secularization of Europe. Now another social construct based on lies, be it liberalism, socialism, or utilitarianism (none of which he believed in) would have to take God's place. And that too would fail and lead to still more suffering.

Nietzsche saw nothing but failure in the constructs of man that didn't uphold what he believed to be the truth. How could man escape this horrific trajectory? Nietzsche saw the falling away from Christian dogma as creating a void that would have to be filled, and he argued that what came next would be much worse. While we would argue that the general thrust of his assertion was correct, the scope of that assertion was not. Nietzsche believed Christianity would collapse in its entirety across the world. The historical evidence, which we can boldly proclaim but Nietzsche couldn't have guessed, shows that Christianity collapsed only within certain institutions of society, education being chief among them.

Ultimately, Nietzsche's solution for the coming absence of Christian dogma was that individuals had to become capable of defining their own values to be able to accept the truth and not avoid it with social constructs that would cause suffering for society. This new man, capable of such self-definition, would be a kind of moral Superman—or *Übermensch* in German. We will leave it to Dr. Peterson, who is not beyond questioning his influencers, to deconstruct the idea of the *Übermensch*:

> ... the psychoanalysts Jung and Freud put paid to [the concept of an Übermensch], demonstrating that we are not sufficiently in possession of ourselves to create values by conscious choice. Furthermore, there is little evidence that any of us have the genius to create ourselves "ex nihilo"—from nothing— particularly given the extreme limitations of our experience, the biases of our perceptions, and the short span of our lives.[7]

---

[7] Dr. J. B. Peterson, *Beyond Order: 12 More Rules for Life* (Toronto, ON: Random House Canada, 2021), 164.

One can hardly blame Nietzsche for being preoccupied with suffering and the "death of God," as all of Europe was in upheaval at that time, and the papacy had lost a great deal of its territory, power, and influence. The works Nietzsche believed "that Jesus demanded," however, were nothing like what the medieval Catholic Church conducted in their penitence cycle.[8] How could he not see this?

In fact, the editor of *the Gay Science* for the translated edition examined for our research, Oxford University professor Sir Bernard Williams (1929–2003), went so far as to accuse Nietzsche of reproducing argumentation Roman writers used. This would make some sense, as it would be easy for a philologist like Nietzsche to (either knowingly or unknowingly) incorporate such rhetoric he had not only studied but was a professor of.

> The idea of nihilism which is so important in his later works is undeniably relevant to modern conditions, but his discussions of such subjects as "corruption" [...] borrow a lot from the rhetoric of the Roman Empire and the disposition of its writers to praise the largely imaginary virtues of the vanished Republic.[9]

In the same way as he did regarding "corruption," as Sir Williams delineates, it's possible Nietzsche also over-valued the practices of the Roman Catholic Church, the so-called practice of the "imitation of Christ." Was Nietzsche just indulging in Romanesque rhetoric again? Did Nietzsche not realize that the "death of God" was tied to specific institutions of society and not to individual believers the world over?

It almost doesn't matter what Nietzsche thought, because in the end, the Christian Church has expanded greatly since his time. The empirical evidence—two billion Christians in the West today—destroys the rationalist's conjecture.[10] Nietzsche's colourful story of a terrified man bearing a lantern, looking to alert others to the "death of God" amidst ridicule, was only right in one regard: he was too soon. He will always, in fact, be too soon.

---

[8] F. Nietzsche, *The Will to Power*, 1968, retrieved from https://ia803205.us.archive.org/27/items/FriedrichNietzscheTheWillToPower/Friedrich%20Nietzsche%20-%20The%20Will%20to%20Power.pdf.

[9] F. Nietzsche, *Nietzsche: The Gay Science: With a Prelude in German Rhymes and an Appendix of Songs*, B. Williams, Ed.; J. Nauckhoff and A. Del Caro, Trans. (Cambridge: Cambridge University Press, 2001).

[10] Wikipedia, s.v. "Western Christianity," June 21, 2023, https://en.wikipedia.org/wiki/Western_Christianity.

THE KULTURKAMPF

By the time of Nietzsche's writings (1872–1888), secularization and annexation had redrawn the face of Europe. In Nietzsche's native Prussia, German unification was occurring under Minister-President and Lutheran Otto von Bismarck (1815–1898). Bismarck was engaged in the most definitive attempt to secularize Germany in history, called the *Kulturkampf* (1872–1878), an attempt to remove the papacy's power from within German borders.

The contemporaneous nature of Bismarck's *Kulturkampf* and Nietzsche's writings should not be understated. The forcible removal of Roman Catholic dogma from German borders greatly distressed Nietzsche's wandering mind. Similarly, the motivations of Bismarck's *Kulturkampf* shouldn't be relegated to only theological concerns, as that would be too narrow. Pure and simple politically motivated greed can explain a good deal of what happened. Bismarck didn't care what religion was dominant within Germany, as long as it had no power to challenge the state. This is well-explained by American historian Francis Arlinghaus (1905–1993):

> Bismarck denied that he was himself an enemy of religion or that he had any quarrel with the Pope as a religious leader; instead, he insisted he was merely opposed to the political influence of the Church. As a matter of fact he would not have objected even to the political influence of the Pope or the Church if he had been able to manipulate that influence for his own purposes.[11]

Where were Bismarck's staunch Lutheran convictions against the papacy?

For Bismarck, the ends justified the means. He didn't much care what one's convictions were. This is in stark contrast to Nietzsche, who blamed Lutheranism and the Protestant Reformation as the primary driver for all the human suffering he was witnessing in Germany. He believed a change in the convictions of Germans had watered down the imitation of Christ, and that was going to allow in the monster of nihilism.

Nietzsche was likely bitter against Lutheranism because it gave the average peasant the ability to challenge the Roman Catholic Church's hold over Christendom, albeit through education. It thus had contributed to the collapse of the dogma of the papacy—part of the glue of the Holy Roman Empire. That

---

[11] F. A. Arlinghaus, "The Kulturkampf and European Diplomacy, 1871–1875," *The Catholic Historical Review*, 28(3), 340–375. 340-341, 1942, http://www.jstor.org/stable/25014177.

dogma, however, had clearly gone astray. Papal indulgences were concrete proof. A papal bull claiming infallibility of ex cathedra doctrines in 1870 was also not a product of scripture.[12]

The *Kulturkampf*, which translates to "culture struggle," was symptomatic of the much larger power struggle throughout Europe. It was a result of secularization displacing the Catholic Church in the wake of the Reformation, the effects of the Age of Enlightenment, the collapse of the Holy Roman Empire, and continuous warring between royal houses and secular powers.

The myth is that the *Kulturkampf* was solely based on religion and a completion of the Reformation. The reality was that this was dominantly a greed-driven struggle like any other. It was simply convenient to have the religious angle to abuse to further the cause of controlling German citizens under the power of the state. If Bismarck could have enforced the power of the state through the papacy, he would have kept Catholicism full force in Germany.

In the Franco-Prussian War of 1870, Bismarck and Prussia led the Northern German confederation to victory against the Empire of France under Napoleon III. The war served to unify northern and southern German states and to expand the power of the House of Hohenzollern (the German monarchy) so that Wilhelm I became Emperor of Germany in 1871. Wilhelm I was crowned at the Palace of Versailles after the defeat of the French. This was a coup for Bismarck, as he wanted to put into place a system of elites that would reinforce the power of the state above all.

The *Kulturkampf* was no completion to the Reformation, just as the Thirty Years' War wasn't something Luther would have ever desired. Luther didn't want a war or even a new church when he drafted the 95 Theses in 1517. He would have despised all this conflict. He wanted a *reformation* of the Catholic Church within itself.

But that didn't happen.

What happened was intermittent fighting punctuated by a bloody war, killing approximately six million Europeans between 1618 and 1648, all supposedly for religion. Then came even more war all throughout Europe, the conquests of Napoleon, and, later, secularization. The papacy was collapsing in part because of the Reformation but also because of the rapid rise in nationalism, rationalism, atheism, and materialism, driven by the Age of Enlightenment. Rome was losing to increasingly secular nation-states that amalgamated and vied for their piece of

---

[12] Wikipedia, s.v. "Papal Infallibility," July 18, 2023, https://en.wikipedia.org/wiki/Papal_infallibility.

Europe, all amidst the smoldering embers of the Holy Roman Empire and the Church.

In this European battle between Church and state, it was Prussia's turn in the hot seat. Bismarck would try to force the power of Rome out of his borders—but through legislation. His plan for a power shift began immediately following the unification of Germany. It was also an opportune time to make such a move because the papacy's military force had been crushed in 1870 by newly crowned King Victor Emmanuel II and his Italian army. Unified Italy conquered all the Papal States following a withdrawal of French military support.

Germany likewise began unification of German-speaking lands in 1866 and completed the process in just five years. The German states all unified to fight France in the Franco-Prussian war under the leadership of King Wilhelm I, Bismarck, and Prussia. Bismarck's subsequent *Kulturkampf appeared* to chiefly revolve around removing the Catholic Church from schools in Germany, which fit in well with most Prussians, who were Lutheran.

In response, Rome doubled down on its papal bulls, proclaiming new dogma such as papal infallibility in 1870, which stated that the papal office could only make perfect doctrine—as if it were Christ. In terms of all that was going on, all the territory it had lost, all the power it now lacked, this might be seen as an act of desperation.

To Nietzsche, it must have seemed like the world was literally ending. When he implied that Christian dogma was dead, he was most likely reflecting the near total defeat of the papacy and the dogma it enforced throughout Europe. What he may have failed to fully realize amid the turmoil was that this was just a fundamental power shift within the realms of man—specifically the state—and didn't actually involve the destruction of Christianity as a belief system.

Universities have religion removed. By the mid-1800s, even before the Kulturkampf arrived for Germany, Christianity was effectively removed from universities in France and England. It had occurred much earlier in France. The University of Paris, which as we mentioned had been closed and sold off during the French Revolution, was reopened under the name Université de France. The facilities were new, and it was then a completely secularized institution under Napoleon.

In England, the University of Oxford and the University of Cambridge underwent reforms in 1854 and 1856, respectively, which removed the requirement for students to register religious affiliation. There was a related and continual decrease in chapel attendance in the years following those reforms.

The results of the *Kulturkampf* in Germany, and of the twenty-two laws to cement the power of state over Church, were crushing for the papacy. Although the pope's office had already lost a substantial number of ecclesiastical estates in the mediatization of Germany, about one-third of the German population remained Catholic.

The German state had gone right after the papacy and local Catholic clergy with, for example, *the Pulpit Law (1871)*. Clergy were expressly forbidden from discussing state matters from their pulpits, where they might have an opportunity to promote dissent among the masses.

If you want to know how much trouble can be caused from a pulpit, think of all those North American churches that had anti-mandate narratives between 2020–2022. Those pastors helped incite mass dissent against the government initiative for vaccine mandates here in Canada as well as in the US.[13,14] This explains the persecution by the Canadian government of the Christian pastoral office during the pandemic, across Canada.[15,16,17] The battle between Church and state suddenly sprang to life again in the twenty-first century. Whether you believe such action by the modern Church was justified or not, it was certainly interesting to see both how much influence even a single church could spread, and how worried the Canadian government was about such influence.

German schools have religion removed. The most strenuously contested aspect of the *Kulturkampf* was addressed in the School Supervision Act (1872), which gave the state complete authority over schools and removed the entirety of the Church (both Protestant and Catholic) from any supervisory or teaching roles.

---

[13] A. Ghobrial and M. Bond, "Hamilton Pastor under Fire for Providing Hundreds of Religious COVID-19 Vaccine Exemptions," City News, November 22, 2021, https://toronto.citynews.ca/2021/11/22/hamilton-pastor-religious-exemptions-covid/.

[14] E. Dias and R. Graham, "White Evangelical Resistance Is Obstacle in Vaccination Effort," *New York Times*, April 5, 2021, https://www.nytimes.com/2021/04/05/us/covid-vaccine-evangelicals.html.

[15] A. Donnini, "Church of God Pastor Convicted after Attending Anti-Lockdown Rally, Fined $5k," CBC News London, December 1, 2022, https://www.cbc.ca/news/canada/london/church-of-god-pastor-convicted-after-attending-anti-lockdown-rally-fined-5k-1.6670811.

[16] D. Naylor, "WATCH: Calgary Police Arrest Pastor Pawlowski for Breaching COVID Lockdown," *Western Standard*, May 8, 2021, https://www.westernstandard.news/news/watch-calgary-police-arrest-pastor-pawlowski-for-breaching-covid-lockdown/article_9dee54fc-1134-5f17-9d16-120a6f04f690.html.

[17] J. Wakefield, "Edmonton Trial Begins for GraceLife Church Pastor Charged with Ignoring COVID-19 Health Rules," *Edmonton Journal*, May 3, 2021, https://edmontonjournal.Com/news/local-news/edmonton-trial-begins-for-gracelife-church-pastor-charged-with-ignoring-covid-19-health-rules.

Bismarck did this because he believed the Church was using indoctrination of the young as a tool to attack the state. Teachers didn't have pulpits, but they certainly had students who were forced to listen.

Throughout it all, bishoprics in Germany were emptied until they reached about a one-quarter vacancy rate. *Kulturkampf* laws put laymen in charge of vacancies if there was no clergy present. About 1,800 Catholic clergy were either imprisoned or exiled, and half of the population of monks and nuns left.

The Catholic Church throughout Germany was now a shadow of its former self. The state had taken all the Church's power to make decisions that impacted individuals, including Church-imposed punishments and penalties. If in any doubt about his autonomy, all a German citizen had to do was renounce their church membership before a Justice of the Peace and the process was complete.

Bismarck's government eventually came to reconcile with the papal office in 1887, whereafter the Catholic Church gained back the power to at least govern their own clergy. But the deed was done; there would be no more religion in schools, as the state of Germany had assumed complete control of education.

We've taken time to discuss the deeper history of Western education in some detail, recounting how the medieval university was an outgrowth of the collapsing Roman Empire. We traced the course of education over a millennia-and-a-half from there to the end of the 1800s and Bismarck's politically motivated *Kulturkampf.* Along the way, the educational institution became much more than just itself. The university was as critical to the Protestant Reformation in its theological contribution as it was for the Renaissance in its humanist contribution. It seemed to be, up to this point in time, an incredible edifice, defying the backdrop of war-weary Europe. It offered a chance for thought instead of battle, a new venue from which people could challenge each other. Despite this, academics often descended into ego-driven squabbling, just as they do today, and the Reformation saw numerous dismissals of professors when universities swapped theological affiliations. Scientific achievements and the Industrial Revolution, which we will not expound upon here for the sake of brevity, were greatly aided by the presence of universities. The rudimentary Western education system was clearly beneficial to civil society as we know it. It was an institution largely free from state control, and it allowed the citizenry to challenge the state when it had become corrupted by its own dogma.

We need not discuss what happened next in terms of the early 1900s, or how WWI and WWII followed, as they're historic events that everyone understands on at least a cursory level. But what happened concurrently with those worldwide conflicts, as far as ideological development, was extremely important to the situation we find ourselves in today—and may be less well understood.

When we left off with the education system, religion was tossed (sometime around the early- to mid-1800s) from higher education in Europe. Religion had also been removed in the late nineteenth century from primary school systems where the Catholic Church had lost its influence to a nation-state, such as in newly unified Germany. France was another such example following "the Ferry (1882) and Goblet (1886) laws which respectively removed religious teaching and personnel from public schools in France."[18]

CHRISTIANITY AND EDUCATION IN THE ENGLISH-SPEAKING WORLD

In stark contrast, England would continue to hold on to its link between religion and schools in its primary education system: "The Elementary Education Act of 1870 in Great Britain recognized the role of religious schools, which were crucial in the British educational landscape."[19]

This adherence to tradition can be correlated to a degree with the British monarchy's persistence, although the Magna Carta's signing in 1215 by King John of England (1166–1216) has proven at least equally critical. Secularism, which deposed many rulers across Europe, failed to breach Britain's rocky coastline. Approximately 25 per cent of all English primary schools today are owned by the Church of England, and collective prayer remains a part of the relatively recent *School Standards and Framework Act 1998* for England and Wales.

Canadian schools remove religion. Unlike its forebearer, Canada would lose prayer permanently in schools in 1988 thanks to a challenge of the Charter of Rights and Freedoms brought before the Supreme Court of Canada in Zylberberg v. Sudbury Board of Education, 1988.[20] What was done for the sake of minority rights removed the last remnants of Christian practice from an institution of learning. This pattern would only increase as the 1982-founded Charter aged, and the protection of more and more discrete groups were put over the needs of civil society at large.

---

[18] Ismail Ferhat, "Religions and Education in Europe (Nineteenth to Twenty-First Century)," *Encyclopédie d'histoire numérique de l'Europe* [online], ISSN 2677-6588, published on 22/06/20, consulted on 24/03/2023. Permalink: https://ehne.fr/en/node/12463.

[19] Ibid.

[20] "Zylberberg v. Sudbury Board of Education," The Charter Rules, 1988 CanLII 189 (ON CA), retrieved July 13, 2023, from http://www.thecharterrules.ca/resources/zylberberg_v_sudbury_board_of_education_1988_canlii_189_on_ca.pdf.

Likewise, to the south, two key Supreme Court cases in the United States resulted in the prohibition of state-sponsored prayer and religious activity in US public schools. *Engel v. Vitale* (1962) led to the prohibition of state-sponsored prayer, while *Abington School District v. Schempp* (1963) led to the prohibition of religious activity—the reading of the Holy Bible—in schools.[21,22] It's noteworthy that the very practice that effectively created Western education in the first place, the reading and recitation of the Holy Bible in monastic schools, beginning in the fifth century AD, was now effectively abolished in the northern New World, about five hundred years since Columbus sailed the ocean blue in 1492.

Should Christianity return to public schools? Canadian society is too diverse and too unfocused to support or accomplish any such initiative. Despite remaining a predominantly Christian nation, Canada now has a population of over 1.8 million Muslims, as well as approximately 335,000 Jews (ethnic and religious). The growing atheist trend in Canada has now reached a staggering 12.6 million people, and any initiative to reintroduce Christianity into schools would leave civil society completely at odds with these Canadians. The time for Christianity and schools to be linked seems to have passed, because our society is now only nominally Christian. There also remain options for parents to send their children to private Christian schools.

The point of all this handwringing then is twofold. The first is to dispel the myth that Christianity is an anti-science religion or that it should somehow preclude rational thought. That is a comical stereotype worthy of *The Simpsons* or even the marginally cleverer, satire-driven *South Park*. The second is to reiterate that *there is no such thing as a school devoid of ideological indoctrination.*

Ideology, just like nature, abhors a vacuum.

The law, in our case the Charter of Rights and Freedoms, might promise us otherwise and *claim* to prohibit indoctrination from occurring in schools, but we have substantial proof that, in the absence of Christian indoctrination, the Western education system took on a much more insidious pedagogy. In fact, there are critical observations in Canada today that social justice, and preceding it, the school of critical legal studies in the US, were invasions into universities that taught law itself.[23]

---

[21] Wikipedia, s.v. "Abington School District v. Schempp," July 11, 2023, https://en.wikipedia.org/wiki/Abington_School_District_v._Schempp.

[22] Wikipedia, s.v. "Engel v. Vitale," April 19, 2023, https://en.wikipedia.org/wiki/Engel_v._Vitale.

[23] C. Blatchford, "The Wrong Kind of Justice Warriors at Canada's Law Schools," *National Post*, March 13, 2018, https://nationalpost.com/opinion/christie-blatchford-the-wrong-kind-of-justice-warriors-at-canadas-law-schools.

PART II: THE SEED IS DEVOURED

DIALECTICAL LEFTISM: THE NEW RELIGION IN SCHOOL

From a rational standpoint, it's not difficult to assert that pervasive radical indoctrination has overtaken the value system in most North American schools. Meritocracy (value derived through talent, work, or success) is now replaced with what Dr. Gad Saad, professor of marketing at Concordia University, lovingly calls "the victimhood Olympics," whereby the intersection of an individual's oppressed characteristics is equated with that person's value. Meritocracy is correspondingly dispensed with under claims of "White privilege" or even "White supremacy," either of which imply an oppressive stance that automatically devalues the accused and isn't subject to argument. These are tenets of critical race theory, which will be discussed in Chapters Ten and Twelve.

And race is not the endpoint of oppression, which has further expanded from the addition of postmodern ideology into the category of gender. This newest addition has invaded institutions of education throughout Canada. Recall for instance the male high school teacher, Kayla Lemieux, in Oakville, Ontario, who wore giant prosthetic breasts—complete with huge erect nipples—to teach shop class.[24] Or the fact that ultra-progressive Western University of London, Ontario, now includes both pad- and tampon-dispensing machines in men's washrooms.[25] Or the fact that radical activists from Saskatchewan were trying to eliminate separate gender washrooms, even when these washrooms were used by children.[26] How about the decision of the Ontario Human Rights Tribunal in *N.B. v. Ottawa-Carleton District School Board*, which ruled gender identity lessons taught to grade one students are not discriminatory?[27] Gender ideology's harmful-to-children, pervasive, completely unscientific influence is a clear sign things have gone off the deep end.

But in this book, we won't venture far into issues surrounding gender and transgenderism, because that would be somewhat outside the scope of Marxist

---

[24] M. Ashton, "Canadian Biologically Male Teacher Wears Massive Prosthetic Breasts to School," *The Postmillennial*, September 16, 2022, https://thepostmillennial.com/canadian-biologically-male-teacher-wears-massive-prosthetic-breasts-to-school.

[25] E. Cantin-Nantel, "CAMPUS WATCH: Tampon, Pad Dispensers Installed in Western University Men's Room," *True North News*, February 7, 2023, https://tnc.news/2023/02/07/tampons-mens-western/.

[26] M. Kotzer, "Moms of Trans Kids Use Men's Washrooms to Push Legislation," CBC Saskatoon, March 28, 2015, https://www.cbc.ca/news/canada/saskatoon/moms-of-trans-kids-use-men-s-washrooms-to-push-legislation-1.3013702.

[27] R. Antoniuk, "Canada: Tribunal Rejects Parent's Attempt to Challenge School Lesson on Gender Ideology," Mondaq, November 2, 2022, https://www.mondaq.com/canada/human-rights/1246350/tribunal-rejects-parent39s-attempt-to-challenge-school-lesson-on-gender-ideology.

ideologies and much more toward postmodernism. What we will discuss in the coming chapters is how dialectical leftism began its takeover of universities with something called critical theory, the precursor to critical legal studies and the more widely known critical race theory.

We saw a brief introduction to a cohort of critical theory in Chapter Three when we examined the inception of what was called the New Left. This Neo-Marxist movement was an admission of the failure of Orthodox Marxism, but it also tried to synthesize Orthodox Marxism with new schools of thought, such as Freudian ideas on repression, to devise a more practical and successful methodology. The chief architect behind that revival of Marxism was sociologist Herbert Marcuse and the Frankfurt School to which he belonged. We will come to Marcuse and the Frankfurt School in short order, but there are several earlier steps in how a new faith—*dialectical leftism*—took hold of the education system in the absence of Christianity. The interested reader is advised to purchase a copy of Dr. James Lindsay's *Race Marxism* (2022) to explain the lengthy and complicated history of corruption in the United States. It's of critical importance that dialectical leftism began where Christianity left off—that being the decision to remove Christian affiliation from universities during the early-to-mid-1800s.

PART III
THE VINE SUFFOCATES

CHAPTER SEVEN
ORTHODOX AND CULTURAL MARXISM

WHAT REALLY STARTS to happen following the departure of Christian affiliation in universities is an influx of those professors who are liberated and railing against God. We will examine a specific group of these people called the "Left Hegelians." This group includes Karl Marx, the father of communism, who wasn't a simple or even authentic atheist, although he famously called religion "the opium of the people."[1] In reality, Marx utterly despised Christianity and possessed a faith of his own.

In this chapter, we'll look at the founders of Orthodox Marxism and discuss what that ideology first entailed. While Orthodox Marxism is rightly attributed to Karl Marx and Friedrich Engels, it also includes earlier contributions on the chain of dialectical leftism from philosophers Ludwig Feuerbach and especially G.W.F. Hegel. All these characters will be examined in some detail, to give the reader a sense of what kind of person would contribute the ideas they did to dialectical leftism. For those looking for deeper study outside the scope of this work, the Utopian socialists Charles Fourier, Henri de Saint-Simon, and Robert Owen, whose ideas greatly influenced Marx and Engels, are a good place to start.[2]

To present an introduction to the ideology of Cultural Marxism, a methodological side-step in dialectical leftism, we will look to the Albanian-Italian Antonio Gramsci and his contribution to Marxist methods. Though Gramsci didn't construct an ideological

---

[1] K. Marx, *Critique of Hegel's Philosophy of Right* (Oxford, UK: Oxford University Press, 1970), 2, https://www.marxists.org/archive/marx/works/download/Marx_Critique_of_Hegels_Philosophy_of_Right.pdf.

[2] See my Woken Promises video covering the Utopian socialists: Marx, Engels, and the Abolition of the Family: Woken Promises: Episode 21, https://vimeo.com/756626469.

step forward in the historical evolution of Marxism, his concepts of civil society and cultural hegemony were powerful tools for future students to discover. They were successfully adapted by the later Neo-Marxists and other nefarious forces for the purpose of destabilization of a nation and proved more effective than clamouring for violent revolution.

G.W.F. HEGEL

Marx's most famous predecessor and, through works, his mentor, was the German philosopher Georg Wilhelm Friedrich Hegel (1770–1831) from the city of Stuttgart in the Holy Roman Empire. Hegel's importance to dialectical leftism can't be understated. He's the founder of the well-known *Hegelian dialectic*, an adaptation from the ancient Greeks' dialectical method, and that method underlies all additions of ideas to the radicalism that has taken hold today. Because of his great significance to the ideological revolutions that came after him, it's important to defrock this oft-revered character. Many students of philosophy today still create a kind of mystique around Hegel, when he exhibited normal, sometimes entirely mundane, characteristics.

As his portraits reveal, Hegel appeared older than he really was, perhaps a reflection of his sickly childhood. His skin was pitted from a smallpox infection he narrowly survived at the age of six. That infection was so bad it blinded him for over a week. At the age of eleven, his entire family was struck with bilious fever, and his mother died. Later in life as a student, Hegel contracted malaria, and it left him unable to function for several months.[3]

As his body struggled to meet the challenges of a harsh world, Hegel's mind was in a similar condition of episodic peril. Throughout his life, he suffered severe bouts of depression, evinced by his wretched poetry. His attempts at writing are considered by classical standards poor and prosaic, lacking the sort of imagination and beauty of a genuine artist.

Having followed with interest the French Revolution in his youth, and admiring Napoleon, Hegel was one of many intellectuals that longed for German-speaking lands to have a revolution of their own. Hegel was an idealist, however. He was only interested in theoretical or ideological revolution and had no appetite for bloodshed. His revolutionary fervour cooled abruptly when he learned of the mass executions during Maximillian Robespierre's Reign of Terror

---

[3] Georg Hegel, "George Wilhelm Friedrich Hegel in 90 Minutes," YouTube Video, 1:16:32, September 1, 2016, https://www.youtube.com/watch?v=-Tn-7rHyEak&t=2698s.

from 1793–1794. Kangaroo courts dispensing over 16,000 death sentences were a sign the revolution in France had gone too far.[4]

At the age of eighteen, Hegel entered theological seminary at the University of Tübingen in Southwest Germany. There he met two of his lifelong friends as roommates: the poet Friedrich Hölderlin (1770–1843) and the philosopher Friedrich Schelling (1775–1854). Schelling would achieve some fame during his lifetime, while Hölderlin's poetry would disappear until the early 1900s, when he was rediscovered. Hegel was called "old man" by his friends for his wizened visage and drab personality, even during his youth.[5]

Although we have claimed here to begin investigating the flooding of universities with those who railed against God, Hegel's descension from Christianity wasn't so clear. He was certainly a product of the zeitgeist, as his lifespan narrowly preceded the time frame when universities abandoned religion wholesale. His greatest problem with the Church was that it enforced what he viewed as Christian authoritarianism. This view was reinforced by his roommates in a kind of adolescent resistance to the seminary rules they were subjected to.

Instead of submitting to religious orthodoxy, Hegel tried to do what other famous philosophers and theologians have done when he tried to appropriate God into his own ideological framework. He probably figured that such appropriation was necessary because Christian orthodoxy was being challenged throughout Europe, and he still wanted to adhere to the parts of Christianity he found himself in agreement with. Hegel claimed he was a committed Lutheran and was especially fond of Martin Luther. This was because, like many Germans, Hegel viewed the friar as a hero who brought freedom to the German citizenry. Hegel wanted to be a kind of philosophical Martin Luther, a man of letters who would bring the difficult ideas of philosophy to the common man, like Luther translated the Bible for all Germans. In that way, perhaps he could free German-speaking lands from total secularization.

Hegel was a nerd of the highest order. As he worked his way through university, he wrote huge tomes recording his daily activities, journals that included footnotes of the most mundane observations one could imagine. His studies, supposed to be focused on theology while at Tübingen, secretly switched to philosophy, for which he developed a keen interest. He became engrossed in the works of the German idealist Immanuel Kant (1724–1804), especially Kant's

---

[4] Wikipedia, s.v. "Reign of Terror," July 25, 2023, https://en.wikipedia.org/wiki/Reign_of_Terror.

[5] Georg Hegel, "George Wilhelm Friedrich Hegel in 90 Minutes," YouTube Video, 1:16:32, September 1, 2016, https://www.youtube.com/watch?v=-Tn-7rHyEak&t=2698s.

Critique of Pure Reason, which expressed belief in the limitation of the human mind. Hegel was greatly influenced by Age of Enlightenment thinkers in general, and he shared another special interest in the works of Jean-Jacques Rousseau (1712–1778) with both his roommates.

Later in his life, Hegel tried to synthesize Kant's rational ideas with Christ Jesus in a work he titled *The Life of Jesus*. After shelving it for many years, he eventually opened it again to re-read and decided it was terrible. He hated it so much he attempted to destroy every existing copy. Theology always seemed to provide a stumbling block for Hegel, at least when he tried to marry it with philosophy. When Hegel completed his degree at Tübingen, his theological certificate included the vindictive description: "not much good at philosophy."[6] A callous reminder that he should not stray too far from orthodox theology.

Hegel was a charlatan. A flim-flam man. His journals of learning are today known to be waylaid with numerous errors, which he never bothered to correct. He made a habit of learning everything by memory but wouldn't design to look-up, verify, or check any claims he made against existing literature.[7] He was a master of misinformation long before the term was coined. This is an incredible point of fact considering his career choice to be a professor.

He began his career by tutoring an aristocratic family in the city of Berne, Switzerland from 1793–1796, while he quietly pressed friends to find a more prestigious appointment. This was a very difficult time in Hegel's life, one in which he felt deeply alone and often very depressed. Despite the stunning scenery all around him, with the Jura Mountains to the north and the Swiss Alps to the south, Hegel's poetry reveals that while living in Berne, he felt nothing but a sense of death about him.[8]

His relationship with the aristocratic family turned sour after several years, reflecting his own drained disposition. To make a rescue attempt, his old friend and roommate Hölderlin, who was then tutoring a banker's family in Frankfurt, suggested that he should go there. Hegel found the family of a rich wine merchant to tutor in Frankfurt, and in 1797 moved there. He ended up just as lonely, however, as Hölderlin was entangled in an affair with the wife of the banker whose family he tutored.

That foolishness blew up in Hölderlin's face and ultimately cost him his sanity.

---

[6] Ibid.

[7] Ibid.

[8] Ibid.

Meanwhile, Hegel struggled to find his feet.

Hegel's mystical vision. It was during this difficult time that Hegel studied the works of the Jewish-Dutch philosopher, Benedictus de Spinoza (1632–1677). Spinoza was another favourite figure of the Age of Enlightenment and a pantheist. During his life, Spinoza was censured among the Jewish community for his views challenging the Hebrew Bible and questioning the nature of God. That boldness to question God seemed to pass on to Hegel through his study of Spinoza.

It was during his time with the works of Spinoza that the most powerful recorded event in Hegel's life occurred. At this time of depression, loneliness, and endless study, Hegel experienced a profound and mystical vision. In this vision, he felt he had received insight into the nature of the very universe. One of the points he would remember and reiterate from that time forward was that everything in the universe was connected, and that division was only an illusion.[9] This would become a prominent feature in Hegel's philosophy, a focus on monism that challenged the conception of the material and spiritual realms as separate. Hegel was so affected by this vision that it caused him to discontinue all his journals, cease his poetry, and refuse to commit blasphemy. After this event, he decided that his life would be dedicated solely to his philosophy, where he would define a rational and intellectual basis for his monistic vision of the cosmos.

While Hölderlin had been caught in an affair and was suffering the consequences, Hegel's other former roommate from Tübingen, Friedrich Schelling, had found success and was now a professor at the University of Jena. Schelling invited Hegel to come to Jena and work there alongside him. After submitting a dissertation, Hegel was given the position of docent at the university in 1801.

Immediately upon beginning his university career, however, it became readily apparent that Hegel was an absolutely miserable lecturer. Instead of preparing a lesson beforehand or delivering it with any enthusiasm, Hegel would use his teaching time as an opportunity to test ideas and hypotheses. These impromptu scenarios he often created mid-lecture, testing them on his students. Even his greatest admirers among the student body were very aware of what tedium Hegel's lectures were. It's amazing that he survived as a docent—as such teachers were paid based on the number of students that registered for their courses. Hegel was lucky when enrollment for his class reached into the double digits, topping off at eleven in his second year of teaching.

---

[9] Ibid.

In a twist of fate, Hegel's revolutionary idol, the unstoppable Napoleon Bonaparte, attacked the Prussian Army just outside the village of Jena (home to the university) in October 1806. The result was a rout of the defending Prussians, and the city of Jena was torn asunder. In the aftermath, Prussia surrendered to France and lost about half of its European territory. The battle at Jena, resulting in a bloodbath of over 25,000 casualties near the entrance to the village of just 5,000 inhabitants, ruined potential enrollment at the University of Jena and effectively cost Hegel his job.

Hegel had witnessed Napoleon scouting through the streets of Jena the day before the battle occurred and romanticized his sighting of the emperor, but he may have never stopped to consider the implications. This seemingly wonderful event in his life prefaced yet more financial woes. Hegel is rumoured to have completed his most famous work, the *Phenomenology of the Spirit*, at the time of Napoleon's victory at Jena.[10]

As the years moved on, Hegel left Jena and worked at different universities in Heidelberg (1816–1818) and then Berlin (1818–1831). His students eventually became numerous and devoted enough that they began a following. These early followers of Hegel were later referred to as the "Right Hegelians." The Right Hegelians espoused a conservative interpretation of Hegel's work, which would soon prove more open to interpretation than anyone guessed.

THE HEGELIAN DIALECTIC

It was from the tedious lectures and books of Hegel, steeped in the dialectic used by Plato and Aristotle, that his new philosophy, centred around historicism, had to be painfully extracted by interested students. The key idea was that history was driven by the dialectical process, where an existing or current ideology, manifested in the state, must struggle to exist. That state would then come to face its contradictions and opposing ideologies in a struggle contesting its survival. The resultant synthesis of the state against its contradiction—two ideologies—a combination of some of their ideas and exclusion of others, would be the concrete result of the dialectic. A new form of government. This process of creating a new ideology is visualized in Figure 3 below:

---

[10] Ibid.

Figure 3: Visualization of the Synthesis of a New Ideology (Aufgehoben)

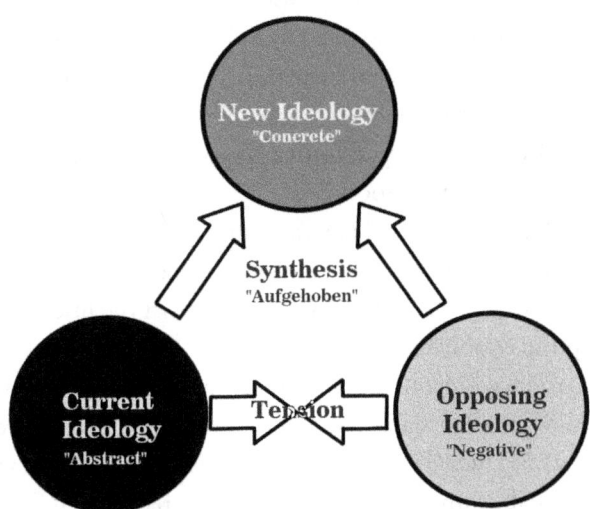

That new government, a synthesis, included aspects of both states/ideologies before it, while also containing aspects of neither. It would be a superior, more veridical ideology because it had eliminated aspects that were false or incorrect from its predecessors and, in so doing, transcended them. Hegel labelled this process as abstract, negative, and concrete. The "abstract" was the original or existing ideology, the "negative" was its contradiction(s), and the "concrete" was the result of the synthesis of the abstract with its negative. (Abstract, negative, and concrete are all marked in quotations in Figure 3 above.)

He therefore argued that throughout history, the dialectical method was driving ideology as materialized in the state, and that each step, which he called in German *aufgehoben*, got closer, nearer to perfection. The ultimate idea, the "absolute idea" in his terminology, would occur once all contradictions had been faced. The state would then reach perfection and see a materialization of the divine on earth. This was how Hegel had, perhaps inadvertently, appropriated God, by fitting Him into his own understanding of things.

An example Hegel witnessed of his dialectic in action was the invasion of Prussia by Napoleon, stemming from the French Revolution. This was a challenge to the existing state (and ideology) from a new state (and ideology). For Prussia, which largely held on to the old way of doing things after the Holy Roman Empire dissolved in 1806, that meant the Prussian royalty, coupled with feudal aristocracy and bureaucracy, remained as the existing state and conservative ideology. Napoleon represented the new, secular world order—a liberal ideology first manifested in France, which was now sweeping across Europe, deposing monarchies and the Church, the landowners, and those who held power. Napoleon had no regard for the divine right of kings. Although the French emperor would eventually be defeated, only a handful of monarchies survived the liberal wave that began under Napoleon, so in this sense, the appeal of Hegel's system can be understood.[11]

The Right Hegelians took Hegel's statist approach to philosophy as a suggestion that the existing Prussian bureaucracy was a higher, more tested form of government. They believed it therefore should resist the liberal wave in Europe and seek to keep the established order.

If Hegel experienced revolutionary fervour in his youth, he came to fear it as he grew in years. When Prussia became destabilized and there were riots seeking change in Berlin 1831, Hegel's views had tacitly switched from "revolutionary" to "supporter of the establishment." Now that he was a recognized figure throughout Prussia, including receiving the Order of the Red Eagle for his service to the state, his views had changed. Unfortunately, Hegel's habitual poor health didn't permit longevity, and despite trying to avoid exposing himself to a cholera outbreak in Berlin 1831, Hegel died from an intestinal infection that year.

Hegel's ideas, however, would not die with him. His historicism, driven by a dialectical process of abstract and negative, resulting in a concrete synthesis, would be taken up by a new generation of thinkers—the Left Hegelians.

KARL DAUB

In 1816, middle-aged G.W.F. Hegel was invited to teach at the University of Heidelberg by one of his most accomplished admirers. Heidelberg's head professor, who also happened to be a Right Hegelian, was a theologian and philosopher named Karl Daub (1765–1836). Daub had originally been very much interested in Kantian philosophy but took a sharp turn when he discovered the works of the two former roommates from Tübingen, Friedrich Schelling and Hegel. Daub published several pieces that clearly show how his development as a philosopher closely mimicked the paths of Kant, Schelling, and then Hegel. He would have been elated when Hegel accepted his invitation to teach at Heidelberg.

---

[11] Monarchies that were abolished in Europe include: Portugal (1910), France (1870), Italy (1946), Austria-Hungary (1918), Yugoslavia (1941), Germany (1918), Romania (1947), Bulgaria (1946), Greece (1973), Albania (1939), and Iceland (1944). The surviving monarchies to this day include: The United Kingdom, Denmark, Norway, Sweden, Belgium, the Netherlands, and Spain.

Just as Hegel had attempted in his work, Daub was concerned with constructing a reconciliation between philosophy and religion, to create a new Christian dogma—a dogma suitable for modern Germans with Enlightenment values. However, Daub's speculative theology met with widespread criticism and found few adherents. Thus, the works of Hegel represented a reconciliation between philosophy and religion that Daub couldn't discover on his own. Although Daub came to accept that he couldn't directly contribute to Hegel's philosophy, he eventually found someone with the necessary skills to do so instead. Someone who could find the solutions he wasn't able to.

LUDWIG FEUERBACH

Daub's best of intentions soon found a vehicle with which to reach its destination. In 1823, fifty-five-year-old Karl Daub met then nineteen-year-old Ludwig Feuerbach (1804–1872), a theology student from an academically successful family, who matriculated at Heidelberg. Hegel had already left Heidelberg University five years before Feuerbach arrived, back in 1818, to take up the chair of philosophy at the University of Berlin, where he would teach for the remainder of his years.

Just as Hegel had, Feuerbach arrived at university with the intention to serve the Church, but just as Hegel did, he quickly fell away from that focus. Noting Feuerbach's promising philosophical skills, Daub decided to introduce him to the works of Hegel. In short order, Feuerbach became convinced that it was in his best interest to move to Berlin and learn directly from Hegel at the university there.

It took some convincing for Ludwig's father, Paul Feuerbach, to go along with the scheme, but he eventually capitulated. The Feuerbach family was largely successful, and it's likely that Paul didn't want to jeopardize his reputation with this new Hegelian path in philosophy, which greatly contradicted the existing Prussian state. More importantly, he had already lost one son, who had been accused of being a dissident and committed suicide.

At the time, all of Europe had been reeling in the face of the French Revolution and the liberal wave sweeping through Europe. In 1815, a student association at the University of Jena conducted demonstrations to make clear they wanted a national, pan-German state and a liberal constitution. This was exactly the type of thinking the young Hegel admired, and it was now widespread throughout German-speaking states.

To fight this sentiment for unifying Germany and removing the feudal system, the German princes came together in 1815 and formed the German Confederation in the wake of the defunct Holy Roman Empire. This led to an increasingly authoritarian attempt to control matters by the conservative establishment, later called the *Vormärz* period. Both Prussia and Austria established police states, and they pushed the other thirty-seven German-speaking states to follow suit. Liberal dissidents often had to flee German-speaking territory to avoid persecution.

Whatever happened between student and administrator at the school isn't recorded, but the path Ludwig took once arriving at the University of Berlin was in complete opposition to Daub's conservative interpretation of Hegel. Feuerbach's understanding of Hegel instead fell in line with the newer, younger, and much more radical Left Hegelians. These were the new breed of Hegel's followers, who interpreted their mentor's work as proving violent revolution was the mechanism by which history moved forward. They had no intention of enduring the *Vormärz* period any longer than they had to.

Feuerbach became obsessed with Hegel's understanding of the dialectic, and even defended it in his early years. In line with the other Left Hegelians, the dialectic promised Feuerbach that revolution was the driving mechanism throughout the history of the state, and that meant, sooner or later, the Prussian authorities would be forcibly overcome.

Feuerbach's first publication, which he made anonymously in 1830 due to its highly controversial content, was called *Thoughts on Death and Immorality*. It contained a clear attack on the neo-Pietist (Confessional Lutheran) movement then occurring in Germany, a direct challenge to the intertwined religious authorities and the German royalty sustaining the authoritarian *Vormärz* period.

Martin Luther must have been rolling over in his grave witnessing the return of a state colluding with organized religion to impose strict protocol and taxation on the people, none of it being instructed in scripture. Once again, it was all about power. This terrible return fostered intense hatred in academic and peasant alike, and it pushed people away from the Church.

Anthropological materialism. Feuerbach, one of those academics harbouring resentment against the police state in which he lived, had been keeping a secret from the public eye, even as he was busy defending his mentor. It was a secret he wouldn't reveal until well after Hegel died. He began by first showing that he was prepared to detach from the ideology of Hegelianism—the reconciliation between philosophy and religion—when he wrote an essay titled "Toward a Critique of the Hegelian Philosophy" in 1839. Two years later, in 1841, Feuerbach published his most infamous work, The Essence of Christianity, which finally revealed how he was going to cut ties with his mentor. Feuerbach had discovered the fatal flaw in Hegel's vision for the cosmos: God wasn't real. In fact, no gods, ever, were real. Feuerbach became convinced of his own brilliance in a philosophy of what can today be called anthropological materialism.

From his narrowly focused and highly rational approach, Feuerbach created a philosophy that explained the existence of religion. It was clear to him that the Christian religion, although valuable for the reflection and amplification of contemporary values, was devoid of any supernatural aspect. Instead, Feuerbach postulated that Christianity and other religions around the world were social constructs, made from the fantasies that reflected temporal cultures and societies where the religion was first constructed. These various fantasies and desires were projected onto a god, with the intention of showing the most enviable traits of the human race. There was a dire need for religion, Feuerbach believed, because the human condition left the individual in a state of dissonance between humanity, a vision of perfection to Feuerbach, and themselves.

All religion was simply anthropology to Feuerbach then, as each belief system was insight into the psychology and societies of humanity through its history. Any predicates ascribed to God were just the more important or desired values of the time from which they were derived.

If Hegel, and before him Spinoza, had opened the door to questioning God, Feuerbach kicked it in. His radical approach didn't come without serious cost, either. Because he had dared to publish such atheistic claptrap during the heavily enforced *Vormärz* period, Feuerbach effectively destroyed any chance he had at becoming a university professor. Atheism remained a serious charge at a university and would later also be levelled against other famous names, like Friedrich Nietzsche, to keep them from potential appointments. This was a serious blow, as Feuerbach's skills in philosophy were of limited use outside the ivory tower. Feuerbach would live out his days in relative obscurity with his wife, and together they lived comfortably for a time off her inheritance.

KARL MARX

As Feuerbach faded from prominence, a new figure emerged among the Left Hegelians as his successor. It was a young and brash student named Karl Marx (1818–1883), who initially struggled with the Hegelian dialectic and its entanglement with divinity. Despite being a disciple of Hegel's reconciliation of religion and philosophy, Marx despised Christianity, though the seeds of his disenchantment had been sown much earlier.

Karl, like his father, Heinrich Marx (originally Herschel Marx, 1777–1838), was an Enlightenment thinker.[12] Heinrich had constantly read to Karl when he was a young boy—not from the Holy Bible and probably not from the Brothers Grimm's *Kinder- und Hausmärchen*, but from Enlightenment thinkers.[13] Apparently, Voltaire was a favourite of Heinrich's to read aloud to his boy. Heinrich home-schooled Karl until he was twelve.

Above all things, Karl was influenced by a love of those Enlightenment thinkers, coupled with a growing dissonance with all things Christian. Political scientist Dr. Paul Kengor reveals how Marx's childhood indoctrination was responsible for his Enlightenment values, but also for his need to challenge religious orthodoxy.

> [Heinrich Marx] was much more liberal [than his orthodox Jewish relatives], a product of the Enlightenment, who, tellingly, if not fatefully, had read Voltaire aloud to young Karl. He knew Voltaire and Rousseau by heart. With the sort of candor and disdainful language his son would use, Heinrich denounced what he called "the Gospels polluted by ignorant priests," in favour of what [Marx biographer Jonathan Sperber] described as a "liberal and enlightened Protestantism, not entirely separate from deism, that would be Heinrich Marx's Christianity of choice."[14]

Karl was baptized as a Lutheran at the age of six, and just as Hegel did, he admired Martin Luther for his ability to "free" the German citizenry from the oppression of the Church. But even an adult Karl Marx couldn't possibly understand what Luther had really hoped to achieve through reform of the Catholic Church. The most violent portions of the Protestant Reformation, which Luther wasn't alive for and would have greatly lamented, gave sanguinary

---

[12] Hershel Marx changed his name to Heinrich to facilitate acceptance in German society and avoid antisemitism, the same reason he adopted the Lutheran faith.

[13] *Grimms' Fairy Tales*, originally known as the *Children's and Household Tales* (German: *Kinder- und Hausmärchen*) had subtly antisemitic stories such as "The Jew Among the Thorns," which Hershel Marx would likely have disapproved of, considering his ethnicity.

[14] P. Kengor, *The Devil and Karl Marx: Communism's Long March of Death, Deception, and Infiltration* (Charlotte, NC: TAN Books, 2020), 58.

Karl a twinkle in his eye. Yet such crucial details weren't so important to the Marx family. Heinrich had the whole family adopt the Lutheran faith. This might have seemed odd, since most of the Marx's relatives were in fact orthodox Jews, including several rabbis in their extended family. However, Germany's virulent antisemitism was on the rise in the nineteenth century, furthering its development as a long-standing issue in the Holy Roman Empire. Heinrich wanted his family to fit more easily into society and be able to climb the social ladder without any bigotry getting in the way.

When he finally allowed his child to attend school, Heinrich Marx carefully selected an educational option that supported his Enlightenment views. This was during the aforementioned *Vormärz* period, however, and Heinrich's inclinations were not an acceptable education choice according to Prussian bureaucracy. The high school to which Karl Marx went, Friedrich Wilhelm Gymnasium, was situated in his hometown of Trier and run by one of Heinrich's friends. The school espoused liberal humanism as a core ideology.

The secret got out eventually. The Gymnasium was raided by Prussian authorities and several teachers were removed because they actively promoted liberal views to their students. The young Marx witnessed these authoritarian measures firsthand. They no doubt increased his ire toward the establishment and helped form his revolutionary vision for the future.

Karl Marx enrolled in the University of Bonn at age sixteen as a student of law. Despite his father's hope for his success, Karl quickly ran into trouble with his grades. He switched from law to philosophy, as he had always intended to. Heinrich responded by forcing his son to transfer, after just one year at Bonn, to the University of Berlin, in a kind of all-or-nothing gamble. Either Marx was going to get it right or he was going to be cast out from the hallowed halls of academia altogether.

At the age of nineteen, Karl was introduced to the Left Hegelians, including then thirty-three-year-old Ludwig Feuerbach. The Left Hegelians were an irreverent and aloof bunch who demonstrated their dissatisfaction with the establishment by defying secular authority and conducting acts to ridicule Christianity. They saw religion and authority as part-and-parcel of the whole bourgeois package. Marx joined in the fun one day with the Left Hegelian Bruno Bauer (1809–1882).

Bauer's claim to fame was his rationalist approach to critiquing the New Testament. He went so far as to deny the historicity of Christ and, following that, concluded that the Synoptic Gospels were pure fiction. If Bauer had criticized the Holy Bible in any kind of relevant or meaningful way—and that's unlikely, since he denied historical fact—his importance was buried under ridiculous events like the stunt he and Marx pulled one holiday:

> For that Easter season in 1842, Bruno and Marx went to the nearby village of Godesberg, which was a favourite excursion site from Bonn, rented donkeys, and road them through the village in what was a direct and deliberate parodying of the entrance of Jesus into Jerusalem.[15]

That same day, they would drink themselves into a stupor and then attend church, laughing and snickering all the way through.

Marx's contempt for Christianity was palpable. The Left Hegelians included many atheists, with Bauer, Feuerbach, and Marx key among them. Yet Marx, like his Left Hegelian brethren, had been bitten by the Hegelian bug. Hegel's historicism and the Hegelian dialectic seemed entirely correct to Marx, if he could only get that "divinity" rubbish out of the way. After all, for Hegel the state was the manifestation of the dialectic process. Eventually, the state would reveal the divine on earth.

What if it didn't have to be a divine revelation at the end of history? What if, instead, it could be a secular one?

To find the answer he needed, Marx had to wait for the 1841 publication of Ludwig Feuerbach's *Essence of Christianity*. Even then, it might not have come to him right away. In the meantime, Marx had achieved his doctorate in philosophy that same year, arguing in his dissertation that philosophy must take precedence over Christianity. It was a more honest version of what Hegel attempted but also much more antagonistic. Marx's dissertation was also far too liberal for the dominantly conservative University of Berlin, so he submitted it to the University of Jena instead, which awarded him his Ph.D. The Prussian authorities, who Marx believed were in bed with the neo-Pietist awakening in the aristocracy, would have torn up his dissertation. Marx didn't dislike religion—he hated it. He hated Christianity. Evidence from much more personal sources testify that his emotions on the subject were not calm or logical.

Marx was something of a passionate poet throughout his years, although the works he produced revealed influences that were clearly violent and arguably demonic. In 1841, his poem "The Player" was published in the Berlin literary

---

[15] Ibid., 14.

magazine *Athenaum*. It referenced the tortured existence of a protagonist who played the violin and included the following lines:

> Look now, my blood-dark sword shall stab
> Unerringly within thy soul.
> God neither knows nor honors art.
> The hellish vapors rise and fill the brain,
> Till I go mad and my heart is utterly changed.
> See the sword—the Prince of Darkness sold it to me
> For he beats the time and gives the signs.
> Ever more boldly I play the dance of death.
> I must play darkly, I must play lightly,
> Until my heart and my violin burst.
> The player strikes up the violin,
> His blond hair falling down.
> He wears a sword at his side,
> And a wide, wrinkled gown.[16]

What's entirely surprising about this dark poetry by Marx is that it doesn't deny the existence of the supernatural in the slightest. In fact, it references both God and the devil and suggests that the focus of the poem, the violin player, has been given his sword and an impetus to play the violin from Satan. These don't seem like the musings of a detached atheist. They seem like the thoughts of someone who drew inspiration from forces that challenged God. "The Player" even includes a quaint little criticism (an infinitesimal fraction of Marx's ruthlessness) when Marx writes "God neither knows nor honors art." Perhaps Marx could never serve God because he felt his art, that is, his ideology inspired by the Enlightenment thinkers, would never be appreciated by the Most Holy.

For a time, Marx's life might have had the appearance of normalcy, despite all his dark poetry or his occasionally ridiculous behaviour. He had many friends and an active social life, and eventually a marriage to the love of his life, Jenny von Westphalen (1814–1881) in 1843. He went on to have seven children with Jenny, of which only four survived to reach adulthood. He would also make the most important friendship of his life in 1844, when he met for the first time Friedrich Engels (1820–1895).

---

[16] Robert Payne, *The Unknown Karl Marx* (New York, NY: New York University Press, 1971), 59–60.

PART III: THE VINE SUFFOCATES

FRIEDRICH ENGELS

Engels must not be considered some simple henchman to Marx, or even a friend who didn't have his own understanding of communism. Engels was very much a communist ideologue who agreed fully with Marx's radical views, though through his own study, and believed in the need to overturn bourgeois oppression through violent revolution. However, we won't spend the pages here that it would take to distinguish between what came from Marx and what came from Engels, as it's enough that their major ideas are understood. The key to remember is that Engels was more than just a friend to Marx, and they collaborated on many works, beginning immediately after they met at the Café de la Régence in Paris, 1844.

Engels commitment to communist ideas was equalled by his commitment to Marx. He financially supported Marx when his good buddy ran out of resources. He even went so far as to help Marx find a home for an illegitimate child Marx had with a housemaid, a woman named Helena Demuth (1820–1890), whom Marx's children lovingly referred to as Lenchen. Engels and Demuth collaborated after Marx's death in 1883 to put together his unpublished and unfinished work.

Marx eventually renounced his Prussian citizenship. His radical left views promised him nothing but trouble anywhere that answered to the Prussian authorities. They had already been silently following him around because of his frequently published diatribes, and they would have been much happier if he were in prison or dead. Marx didn't just attack the establishment in Germany, either. In one instance, during the year 1843, Marx's denouncing of the Russian monarchy in a newspaper article was so off-putting, Tsar Nicholas I called a few official meetings and had that newspaper banned from all of Russia. This was a very smart move, because Russia's monarchy ultimately fell to the Bolshevik revolution some seventy-five years later.

Marx moved to Paris in 1843 and began work challenging all the ideas he had taken for granted at university. This was a recurring theme throughout his life. A brutal, rational approach of inexhaustible criticism. It would cost him the majority of his friendships and often leave him intellectually isolated.

Isolated but free from the watchful eyes of the Prussian police, Marx began work as a co-editor for the *Deutsch-Französische Jahrbücher* (*German-French Annals*), a far-left newspaper designed to bring together German and French radicals seeking revolution. His days were full of endless mulling and writing and a new focus on the economy that he deemed necessary for his critique of society.

Engels was crucial to this new focus on economic analysis, because he provided firsthand observations in his book *The Condition of the Working Class in England in 1844*. Engels provided a missing puzzle piece with this contribution, and now the Hegelian dialectic was finally beginning to make sense to Marx and his class-based focus. The revolutionaries that Karl sought to enact his overturning of society, the step forward in the dialectic, were going to be the victims of capitalist oppression—the workers themselves. This byproduct of the Industrial Revolution was more easily witnessed in the factories in England, as Germany's industrialization lagged.

Marx was getting closer to solving his problem with the Hegelian dialectic, that nagging metaphysical component and also that reference to "divinity" he so despised. Now he had a partner with whom to challenge Hegel's ideology. Together, Engels and Marx studied Feuerbach's *Essence of Christianity*, and together they were inspired by its liberating qualities, as Engels later revealed:

> Then came Feuerbach's Essence of Christianity. With one blow it pulverized the contradiction, in that without circumlocutions it placed materialism on the throne again.... The spell was broken; the 'system' was exploded and cast aside, and the contradiction, shown to exist only in our imagination, was dissolved. One must oneself have experienced the liberating effect of this book to get an idea of it. Enthusiasm was general; we all became at once Feuerbachians.[17]

They had the key to the next step in the dialectic: to drop all this metaphysical and especially religious nonsense and put Feuerbach's materialism inside of the Hegelian dialectic. The result was a godless, soulless system they fittingly called "dialectical materialism."

Dialectical materialism. The march through history was still contained in the state as it had been for Hegel, but now, since the Left Hegelians could philosophically claim that God wasn't real, using Feuerbach's analysis, Marx and Engels envisioned the end of history as a communist utopia. That was the secular equivalent to the divine manifesting itself on earth. Perfection. Equality for all. Equality of opportunity, of course. But also, equality of outcome! This is one aspect that has not changed since Marx and can still be found among the most recent iterations of dialectical leftism.

---

[17] F. Engels, "Ludwig Feuerbach and the End of Classical German Philosophy," *Die Neue Zeit (The New Era)*, 1886.

Everyone, from the lowest radical left-wing initiate to the highest anti-capitalist professor, speaks of the communal revolution to come. They call each other comrades. They speak about oppression as if they know it better than any other generation.

No more were Germans going to chase ideas or simply witness as innocent bystanders of history as it went step-by-step through ideas battling one another for supremacy. That was the old Hegelian dialectic. Using Feuerbach's materialist approach, the focus became not to study the changes that were occurring but to actually implement them oneself. This is why communist thinkers refer to each other and to their heroes as revolutionaries. They are the instrument of change that forces the dialectic forward.

One of the most vicious of these "heroes" who well understood the dialectic, and therefore pressed it forward, was Vladimir Lenin (1870–1924). According to his understanding of dialectical materialism, and exactly as Marx had indicated, the faster the dialectical process (revolutions) were moved through, the faster the end of history would arrive, and the faster the communist utopia would come to materializing in the state. This explains Lenin's desire to push through violent revolution that killed many for the "greater good" of speeding through the dialectic and achieving utopia.

If Hegel's historicism had been a pipe dream, Marx's dialectical materialism attempted to make it attainable. It was Feuerbach's materialism that allowed everything Hegel created to have rational grounding. The new impetus of the revolutionaries to get involved and foment societal upheaval, to actively make the dialectic move through history, was also a call for revolution that would ultimately result in the death of an estimated 100 million human lives. That's the current death toll for communism worldwide. No one can say if that is where it will end.

Marx claimed that he had no belief in a god, but his writings and his poetry and even his vision for utopia on earth point to the existence of belief in the supernatural. Marx wasn't a staunch atheist but rather a man in love with his own stupidity. The rationalists who followed Feuerbach, including Marx, lost the humility of the philosophy of Kant that warned that human reason had its limits. Kant implied that it would simply be a waste of your time, since it was, quite literally, beyond you to find the solutions to some problems. Yet there was a second, much worse implication of Kant's limitation of the mind: Trying to construct philosophical or ideological solutions to problems that were beyond us could also end up doing horrific damage to everyone around us.

The power of an idea must not be underestimated. Even a bad idea.

Marx destroyed most of the key friendships he made with the Left Hegelians. He stole what he thought best of the works of Feuerbach but also made his own very clear attempt to show that he had surpassed Feuerbach when he wrote *The German Ideology* in 1845. With the help of Engels, Marx also did the same thing with the works of Bruno Bauer, contesting the Left Hegelian in Marx and Engel's work *The Holy Family* in 1844. Marx had a habit of treating his friends as if they were literally subjects of the dialectic, who could be casually discarded once their most important bits had been extracted. Marx and Engels were selfish and opportunistic in this attempt to find glory for their own ideas.

The Manifesto of the Communist Party. The most memorable work produced from the prolific writing careers of Marx and Engels remains The Manifesto of the Communist Party, published in 1848. The Manifesto is a call to arms for all communist ideologues, and specifically commands: "Working men of all countries, unite!"[18] It's a short book that aims to be easy to read and instructional to all comrades of the communist faith.

In the first section of four, Marx and Engels begin by explaining their concept of historical materialism, the entirety of history driven by dialectical materialism. Every revolution throughout history, every step in the dialectic, is simply a class struggle where the majority, comprised of the oppressed, overthrows the minority, an oppressive ruling class. Marx argues that although the ruling class had once been the Church and the intertwined royalty throughout Europe, the replacement of feudalism by industrial capitalist society rendered (or was in the process of rendering) a new ruling class. Now the ruling class was composed of (or was going to be) the bourgeoisie, the filthy rich capitalists who owned the means of production and exploited the workers with insufficient pay, insurance, or care for their efforts.

In the second section of the *Manifesto*, we see the distinction between Orthodox Marxism and the Marxism-Leninism that defines communist regimes we listed at the beginning of the book: "[Communists] do not set up any sectarian principles of their own, by which to shape and mould the proletarian movement."[19] Leninism requires a vanguard party to direct and manipulate the

---

[18] K. Marx and F. Engels, *Marx/Engels Selected Works, Vol. One: Manifesto of the Communist Party (1848)* (Moscow: Progress Publishers, 1969), 98–137, https://www.marxists.org/archive/marx/works/download/pdf/Manifesto.pdf.

[19] Ibid.

proletariat, while even the Neo-Marxism we cover in the next chapter requires academicians to push for a critical consciousness. This section also contains some of the more serious implications of communism, including that they "overthrow the bourgeoisie" and push for the "abolition of private property."[20] Those goals have historically proven to require coercion and violence.

In the third section, defining various forms of socialism, we see the violence required in Marxism made explicit:

> [Utopian socialists] reject all political, and especially all revolutionary action; they wish to attain their ends by peaceful means, necessarily doomed to failure, and by the force of example, to pave the way for the new social Gospel.[21]

Marx and Engels believed history taught that the only real revolutions were violent ones. Thus, the communist revolution in various areas of Europe was going to cost lives if it was going to be successful. The Utopian socialists, who idealistically wanted to push for their desires through example and peaceful means, were never going to succeed in the eyes of Marx and Engels.

The final section of four is just a single page and reminds us of something that remains important in our day and age: that communists are to ally themselves with social democrats to achieve their goals. Social democrats started to come back into fashion when Bernie Sanders pushed that ideological moniker during his campaign for the 2016 US presidential election.[22] Of course, that was before the mainstream Democrats sabotaged his campaign because he was getting too much popular support compared to Hillary Clinton.[23]

After the works of Marx and Engels were published, their inflammatory rhetoric spread the world over, inspiring communist thinkers everywhere. But something happened that neither of them predicted. The premise of their revolutionary communist ideology was that the capitalist system continued a ruling class (after feudalism died), and it too must ultimately be overthrown—but by the oppressed workers (instead of Napolean and secularization). It would

---

[20] Ibid.

[21] Ibid.

[22] S. Frizell, "Here's How Bernie Sanders Explained Democratic Socialism," *Time*, November 19, 2015, https://time.com/4121126/bernie-sanders-democratic-socialism/.

[23] D. Glanton, "DNC Betrayed Bernie Sanders and the Rest of America," *Chicago Tribune*, July 25, 2016, Retrieved July 27, 2023, from https://www.chicagotribune.com/columns/ct-dnc-sanders-glanton-talk-20160725-column.html.

be from a complex combination of the dangerous working conditions, the exploitation of hard labour, and even from the societal abuses the proletariat suffered that they would ignite into violent revolution. At least, that was the prediction in the *Manifesto of the Communist Party*. After history moved past the Industrial Revolution, however, and past what we could call industrial capitalist societies, there was a stunning goose egg when it came to the scorecard for Marx and Engel's prediction. Among industrial capitalist societies around the world, absolutely none had seen a revolution or an overturning of society conducted by the working class.

It all turned out to be fantasy.

From the time the *Manifesto* was published in 1848, it took sixty-nine years before the October Revolution in Russia, and that wasn't an uprising of the workers in an industrial capitalist society. The Russians had been abused for decades under the brutal Romanov dynasty, an effective autocracy that gave Russian peasants little in the way of anything, including human rights. The Romanovs were so exceedingly opulent and oppressive that they were violently dethroned and brutally murdered by the Bolsheviks who captured them.[24] But that had nothing to do with industrial capitalism at all.

In fact, over a prolonged period, Marxist ideologues were starting to realize that the stability and wealth created within industrial capitalist societies was so prevalent that it left the average working man with little desire to rise up, unless it was to go to the pub and get a beer. Where was all the anger and resentment that Marx and Engels were trying to harness?

Just like Hegel saw before creating his ideology centred around historicism, Marx witnessed revolutionary fervour firsthand in Germany and France. He assumed that he could recreate it en masse through propaganda, based on his own analysis. But the sheer reduction in abject poverty thanks to industrial capitalism was so drastic and widespread that it left workers dumbfounded with their autonomy. Poverty and risk of starvation were now relegated to a much smaller portion of the planet's population.[25]

---

[24] Tsar Nicholas II, his wife, and their five children (ages thirteen, seventeen, nineteen, twenty-one, and twenty-two) were murdered in July 1918 by Lenin's Bolsheviks. They were shot and stabbed to death in the basement of the Ipatiev house in Yekaterinburg, Russia. Vladimir Lenin was never proven to be directly responsible, although he endorsed the murders. See: Wikipedia, s.v. "Murder of the Romanov Family," July 24, 2023, https://en.wikipedia.org/wiki/Murder_of_the_Romanov_family.

[25] L. Ladan, "Capitalism Remains the Best Way to Combat Extreme Poverty Both in America and Abroad," Catalyst, June 14, 2019, https://catalyst.independent.org/2019/06/14/capitalism-remains-the-best-way-to-combat-extreme-poverty/.

PART III: THE VINE SUFFOCATES

It was a frustrating time to be a Marxist between 1848–1917. As much revolution and tumult as was witnessed across Europe, none of it was revolutionary Marxism. One of the key ideologues who lived during some of this time frame was the Albanian-Italian Antonio Gramsci (1891–1937), from a small town called Ales on the Island of Sardinia off the west coast of Italy.

ANTONIO GRAMSCI

Gramsci grew up as the son of parents who, despite possessing a rare, middle-income stability in Sardinia, ran into trouble with the law. When his father was arrested and imprisoned for embezzlement, Antonio, then just seven-years-old, was forced to leave behind his schooling to support his family. He would continue to do so until the age of thirteen. By the age of eight, Gramsci had already begun to think about what career he might need to have to support his family in the long term. He decided that being a carter, the driver of a horse-drawn cart, was an honorable profession. In the meantime, he did whatever odd jobs he could find to support his family. This would have been an especially difficult task, since Antonio was not a particularly fine physical specimen. Even once he reached adulthood, he was incredibly short for a man—under five feet—and had a hunched back from what some suggest was tuberculosis of the spine. This would have meant physical labour and even simple ambulating were much more demanding for Antonio. He coped with all these hardships beginning at a very young age.

As an islander, Antonio witnessed the suppression of his fellow Sardinians by mainland Italians, and he resented especially how they were being economically exploited. This was most keenly felt in the rudimentary mining industry, where the rapidly growing number of Sardinian workers saw their profits and their best ore shipped directly to the mainland, with no return of investment in the mining operations themselves.

The Sardinians had only recently been added to the Kingdom of Italy, Sardinia having first been ceded to the Italian royalty from the Spanish in 1720. They lacked a substantial education system, as their population generally were families that either worked in agriculture or mining. Even after the unification of Italy in 1861, the Savoy dynasty retained its authority over Sardinia and didn't allow the kind of liberal constitutions the mainland developed. This reality would have caused a tangible resonance when Antonio studied Marx's historical materialism, or at least would have given Gramsci hope that there was a chance for revolution to end such inequality.

Gramsci was gifted intellectually. He was clearly creative and saw things from a perspective similar but not identical to Marx, and this allowed him to revise some of Marx's ideas. When he was finally able to resume schooling, he applied for and received a scholarship to the University of Turin at the age of twenty. The city of Turin was among the northernmost in Italy, moving through industrialization when Gramsci arrived. He was able to see firsthand the conditions of workers not just from his exploited home of Sardinia, but also those workers in the north and the conditions they were subjected to.

Things moved quickly for Gramsci when he joined the Italian Socialist Party at the age of twenty-two. He would become absorbed with the cause for socialism, and he lost appetite for his studies. He also ran into financial trouble around this time and was unable to complete his degree. Instead, he began work as a propagandist for socialist newspapers, including *Il Grido del Popolo (The Cry of the People), Avanti! (Forward!)*, and *L'Ordine Nuovo (New Order)*. Antonio's focus on literature during his time in school allowed him to write well and make a name for himself in print. His work demands only grew, and occasionally included public speaking for socialist causes in Turin. He watched with vested interest in 1917 as the October Revolution turned the largest country on its head, from autocracy to communist. He must have been chomping at the bit. Gramsci joined the Third International, an international communist movement, in 1919 and was noted by Vladimir Lenin as being one of the Italian supporters most suitable to form a vanguard party like the Bolsheviks.

In 1920, The Italian Socialist Party performed miserably, and it was clear that the opposing fascist party would come to power. As revealed in his propagandist publications, Gramsci lamented what he saw as a conspiracy between the Vatican and the fascists. In his mind, the papacy was nothing more than a state that owned private property and exploited the people. Gramsci became angry with the Italian Socialist Party's policy of compromise and began to espouse the need for violent communist revolution, which at the time meant Leninism. He joined the newly founded Italian Communist Party (1921) and began to outspokenly pronounce the need for desperate measures. The key difference between Leninism and Marxism was the inclusion of a vanguard party—a group of representatives of the workers (instead of the workers themselves) that could execute ideas and imperatives that forced more people to awaken to the communist cause. This would necessarily involve violence.

As the representative of the newly formed Italian Communist Party, Gramsci travelled to Moscow for meetings in 1922. As if by magic, the incredibly short

PART III: THE VINE SUFFOCATES

but smart Antonio found his future wife in Moscow within less than a year and married her. He returned from Soviet Russia with his wife, Julia Apollonovna Schucht (1896–1980), a violinist. Julia had a sister, Tatiana, who lived in Italy and would later become crucial to supporting Gramsci. Antonio and Julia had two sons in rapid succession, but Antonio wouldn't be involved in any physical capacity with the raising of his children.

Under leader Benito Mussolini (1883–1945), the Italian fascists had rocketed to power during Gramsci's absence. After a supposed attempt to assassinate Mussolini, the fascists instated emergency powers in 1926. They used those powers immediately and arrested many of their political opponents, including Gramsci. This strategy would later be copied by Adolf Hitler after the Reichstag burned down in 1933. The fascists were very aware of Gramsci's hardcore communist stance and his travel to Moscow. Like Leninists/communists, the fascists were also extremists with murderous intent, so they captured Gramsci to make him disappear.

A decision was made. To avoid martyrdom, they would let Antonio rot in a jail cell, ideally far from the mainland. Gramsci was forced through a kangaroo court and expedited trial and sentenced to twenty years in prison for trumped up charges. He was eventually imprisoned in Turi, Apulia, in Southern Italy.

Gramsci's most influential work came from the time he spent studying and philosophizing in prison, especially when he was allowed medical leave for several years. Though he wasn't allowed to have writing material, he was secretly given books to read, as well as notebooks and pens with which to record his thoughts. Perhaps the most important concept Gramsci came up with, catalyzed by his failure to achieve violent, Leninist revolution, was the idea to subvert civil society.

CIVIL SOCIETY AND CULTURAL HEGEMONY CONCEPTS

In Gramsci's understanding of the whole of society, at the bottom was the working class, and above it was the state, separated into civil society and political society. This is different than the current way we think of the state as exclusive to government. Gramsci argued that civil society, comprised of groups outside control of government that were associations of citizens in marriages, churches, corporations, unions, and other institutions, was occupied by a bourgeois cultural hegemony. He believed it was necessary to attack that bourgeois hegemony by culturally subverting it with values of the proletariat. It was critical to implant communist thinkers into the various institutions, like churches and corporations, and have them advocate communist, counter-cultural thinking to challenge the bourgeoisie's way of doing things. This subversive method was an entirely new concept that challenged Marx and even Lenin's idea of violent revolution as the sole method to implement communism. It was fiendishly clever, and it remains a slower but much more successful technique used to this day by communist agitators.

Gramsci didn't do well in prison. The isolation, coupled with his frail health, exacerbated stressors he couldn't possibly handle. His sister-in-law, Tatiana Schucht, kept correspondence with him to keep his spirits up, but it wasn't enough. His condition became so bad, with frequent coughing and vomiting of blood, that he was allowed medical release to a hospital beginning in 1933 (age forty-two). It was during this time that he feverishly recorded what are now called *The Prison Notebooks*. These amounted to thirty notebooks filled with thoughts on history and relevant analysis, including on Marxism, totalling about three thousand pages. A great deal of Gramsci's ideas have been retrieved from these notebooks. The material for writing was secretly given to him by his friend Piero Sraffa (1898–1983), an Italian economist and professor at the University of Cambridge. Sraffa went so far as to sneak books in for Gramsci to study, including works of Marx. It would be thanks to Sraffa that *The Prison Notebooks* would be preserved and published after Gramsci's death.

Gramsci's tortured life fuelled within his soul a deep spite for the bourgeois hegemony he believed responsible for the ills of society. This was the only way a man suffering as greatly as he did would have continued to write so much despite what eventually became a paralyzing illness. He died of heart disease and tuberculosis in 1937 at the age of just forty-six. What Gramsci did, unlike the other contributors we've looked at so far, was not to affect the dialectic by revision of Marxist ideas directly but to add a new methodology to achieve the desired goal of revolution. Gramsci's concept of a cultural hegemony and the attempt to subvert that hegemony with a cultural revolution would inspire a whole new generation of Marxist thinkers.

CHAPTER EIGHT
NEO-MARXISM

AS GRAMSCI ROTTED to death in prison, many other Marxist thinkers were actively searching for a way to advance their ideology. The rise of fascism in Spain, Italy, and Germany as an extreme answer to the social problems at the beginning of the twentieth century saw a mirrored response in the rise of the radical left.

In this chapter, we'll examine how the rise of the radical left occurred right under America's nose at Columbia University. Perhaps because they were so pre-occupied with the Great Depression and concerns over the rise of fascism in Europe, the US government made a highly questionable decision. They allowed a neo-communist think-tank called the Institute of Social Research to transfer from Frankfurt, Germany to New York in 1934. The think-tank, colloquially referred to as "The Frankfurt School," housed professors who espoused a kind of uber-Marxism meant to perfect a new social philosophy based on empirical research. They began to call that philosophy critical theory. Of these new critical theorists, the most prominent was the German philosopher Herbert Marcuse, who, despite moving to America, slowly began developing and publishing ideas aimed at subversion of the US government.

The key takeaway from this chapter is that critical theory, which can be equated with Neo-Marxism and the Frankfurt School, was the next step in dialectical leftism after Orthodox and Cultural Marxism. It inspired the rise of the New Left, despite Marcuse's denial of any such connection. It opened the door to new Marxist methods and approaches, including using modern psychology to manipulate the populace into revolution. Marcuse's works, some of which are examined here, show a clear progression using analysis of world events (a kind of empirical data) to aim to foment revolution and improve Marxist methodology. The chapter ends with Marcuse's most dramatic connection to a new proletariat, the idea that he could use "the ghetto population" of the US as the "most natural force of rebellion."[1]

THE FRANKFURT SCHOOL

In Germany of the early twentieth century, Marxism was a very popular subject in university, included in classes on sociology, economics, and philosophy. The dream of a communist utopia infected students to such a degree that it would last a lifetime.

One such student from the University of Frankfurt was Felix Weil (1898–1975), a native Argentinian who had moved to Germany at the age of nine. Felix's wealthy father was a Jewish grain merchant who could afford the best education available. At the time, many in academic circles were convinced of the viability of revised Marxism. Felix earned his doctorate at Frankfurt, where he became good friends with Friedrich Pollock (1894–1970), another dedicated Marxist. Pollock had studied economics and sociology before achieving his philosophy doctorate at the University of Frankfurt. The two became convinced that the work of Marx had to be continued, and new solutions devised to address the historical failures of Orthodox Marxism. To that end, Felix gathered his inheritance and approached the University of Frankfurt with the idea of starting what would be called the Institute of Social Research in 1923. Widespread support from the German academic left made this initiative become a reality. The Frankfurt School was born the next year, in 1924.

The first director of the Frankfurt School was the economist Carl Grünberg (1861–1940), who was then sixty-three. Grünberg was of Jewish descent, born in Romania before moving to Austria. He was the editor of several socialist journals and had spent a good deal of his career as a professor at the University of Vienna. He was a key figure in the socialist movement in Austria, later dubbed Austro-Marxism.

Just four years after his appointment to the directorship of the Frankfurt School, Grünberg fell ill and was forced to resign. To immediately fill the position, co-founder Pollock stepped in and took over as director in 1928, but this was only a temporary solution, as Pollock already had his own professorial duties.

---

[1] H. Marcuse, *An Essay on Liberation*, first edition (Boston, MA: Beacon Press, 1971), 57–58.

There was an abundance of candidates among German academe to replace him. A friend of both founders, Weil and Pollock, was soon chosen. The replacement was agreed to be the philosopher Max Horkheimer (1895–1973), who had been teaching at the University of Frankfurt for several years.

MAX HORKHEIMER

Horkheimer was also of Jewish descent and came from a wealthy family of textile factory owners in Stuttgart, Germany. Like many philosophers before him, Horkheimer believed that philosophy held the key to all the other sciences. After he became the director of the Institute of Social Research in 1930 at the age of just thirty-five, he delivered his inaugural lecture in January 1931. His first presentation clarified that it was necessary to move away from specialization in science and toward a more holistic, interdisciplinary approach. This made perfect sense to him, as then it would be the philosopher who was required to amalgamate all the data from the various sciences and interpret them in terms of the current social climate. From that contemporary analysis of empirical research, he could discover which conclusions were verifiable and which were only enforced by the current social conditions.

CRITICAL THEORY

Horkheimer is also of importance for having been the first philosopher to officially label his approach to sociological problems as "critical theory," which he initially referred to as a materialist approach. That materialist approach clearly reflected the earlier tension between Ludwig Feuerbach and G.W.F. Hegel, which as we saw was synthesized by Karl Marx.

Horkheimer defined critical theory in his 1937 essay, *Traditional and Critical Theory*, which compared the traditional approach of philosophers like René Descartes to the modern, Marxist critical/activist approach. The idea for critical theory was a kind of uber-Marxism, where ideas would be ruthlessly attacked using all methods at the theorist's disposal, including empirical evidence. Empirical evidence was crucial, Horkheimer believed, because the outcome of various experiments was always, in his mind, dependent on the current sociological settings and would therefore change as society changed. Thus, science was beholden to both philosophy and sociology, ironically the two disciplines for which Horkheimer was accredited.

The key goal of all the work, the critical theory, to be done under his directorship was invariably focused on the alleviation of human suffering.

While Horkheimer also argued that the pursuit of happiness was an important contributor to the study of social philosophy, he did not believe that the pursuit was sufficient motivation to explain the actions of classes in society. To him, the proletariat was motivated chiefly by the hope of alleviating human suffering, an emancipatory goal that was directly in line with Karl Marx's original collectivist ideas.

Horkheimer believed that suffering existed in the world because of the lack of rational organization in society. The capitalist mode of production, to him, was irrational and created abundant suffering, a false sense of achievement, and a preoccupation with products. If the Institute of Social Research was to be successful, it would have to empirically discover a new, more rational organization to society that would answer a lot of the capitalist-caused problems that led to suffering. Like Marx, Horkheimer presupposed that some variant of communism would contain such answers, if properly investigated. This was an interesting point of contention at the Frankfurt School, whose theorists frequently argued that they were not in favour of Orthodox Marxism or communism but were nonetheless dialectically tied to it.

Although he wasn't originally a Marxist, Horkheimer was influenced by other Institute members in that ideological direction, especially the German psychologist Erich Fromm (1900–1980), who would push the ideas of both Marx and psychoanalyst Sigmund Freud (1856–1939) into the scope of Horkheimer's radar. Horkheimer's shift to Marxism over his years as director is gradual but discernable. Horkheimer brought Fromm into the Institute, largely because Fromm was a Neo-Freudian psychologist. The critical theorists would use Fromm's psychoanalysis to help explain why the proletariat didn't head toward revolution in capitalist societies.

Another approach to sociological problems that Horkheimer eschewed in favour of critical theory was G.W.F. Hegel's metaphysics, because it couldn't be empirically tested. That was probably a very sound decision, as relying on Hegel's monism and understanding of the universe, which as we saw came to him in a vision, was unscientific. Yet could re-instating Marx's ruthless pattern of criticism promise anything more? Horkheimer believed it could, as did many of the Frankfurt School, so this new "critical theory" is equated directly to the term "Neo-Marxism," although it clearly included ideas from both Orthodox Marxism and Gramsci's Cultural Marxism.

Just short of the Frankfurt School's tenth anniversary in 1933, the dominantly Jewish faculty there witnessed the appointment of Adolf Hitler to Chancellor of Germany. With this ascension of racist extremism came sweeping powers to the Nazis, which saw fascism literally flood the streets. The Frankfurt School was seized by the Gestapo and boarded up. All the professors officially lost their jobs because the Institute for Social Research was a communist think-tank, and communism was, according to Hitler, the ultimate enemy of fascism.

Horkheimer was officially fired from his professorship and, with many other professors at the school, fled to Geneva, Switzerland to open a branch of the Institute and continue work. During their time in Geneva, Friedrich Pollock's secretary opened negotiations with Columbia University in New York, USA, to find a more permanent home for the Institute. When he was contacted in June 1934 with an offer to begin the Institute anew at Columbia University, Horkheimer readily accepted. The Frankfurt School now became a neo-communist think-tank across the Atlantic that was protected from the fascist rise. They would come to influence the United States in ways no one could have predicted, and that was largely through one of their youngest students, a man named Herbert Marcuse (1898–1979).

Perhaps the strangest thing about history of the Frankfurt School is, back at that time, much of the world was completely oblivious to it—especially North America. The world was wrapped up in more pressing concerns during the 1930s, specifically with the onset of the Great Depression. The US saw unemployment rise to an estimated 25 per cent—the highest ever witnessed—while almost one in every five mortgages was foreclosed. Homelessness and joblessness were ubiquitous, and the government feared anarchy was imminent. Things had to be changed, and fast. Franklin D. Roosevelt brought in his New Deal in 1933, but the federal government couldn't have been sure of its success.

The average citizen in North America had no clue what was fomenting in one little, seemingly insignificant institute at Columbia University. The US was watching Europe's development like everyone else, where Hitler was re-activating his nation by defaulting on the heavy reparations of the Treaty of Versailles. This while reigniting the German economy with work projects like the Autobahn and rising industry. There were just too many concerns to stop and wonder if the tiny institute of Marxist thinkers invited over from Germany were a threat. At the time, the US public was still in the dark about the bloody goings-on of Stalinist Russia too. They had no idea of its death toll.

But the Frankfurt School wasn't communist, its theorists argued, because it was an attempt to revise Marxism with an altruistic aim of a cultural revolution. It was no longer about promoting class antagonism. However, that was a similar sort of emotional appeal Marx made when he claimed to be in tune with the suffering of the workers in Manchester, England. The goal for Marxism wasn't alleviation of suffering so much as it was the destruction of society. In fact, over time it would become clear that Neo-Marxism wasn't a new or stand-alone product but much more akin to a repackaging of Orthodox Marxism, with some deceptive new ideas added. New ideas with the old aim of destroying society. This attachment is made explicit when we examine the history of dialectical leftism. No single person is more responsible for the advancement of dialectical leftism as it related to Neo-Marxism than Herbert Marcuse.

HERBERT MARCUSE

Herbert Marcuse was one of the last additions to the Frankfurt School before its move to the US. Like many of his Frankfurt School predecessors, Marcuse was an upper-class German of Jewish descent. He graduated from the University of Freiberg with a doctorate in sociology and began his first work for the Institute during their time in Geneva. He would spend from 1934–1942 developing critical theory at Columbia University in New York, USA, where he emigrated and then acclimatized to his capitalist surroundings. Marcuse became a naturalized US citizen in 1940.

Reason and Revolution. One of Marcuse's most important early writings was his book Reason and Revolution: Hegel and the Rise of Social Theory, first published in 1941. In this book, Marcuse attempted to cut any existing ties between G.W.F. Hegel any Nazism, or any ties Marcuse had with his old professor and collaborator, Martin Heidegger (1889–1976). While Marcuse and Heidegger had worked together at the University of Freiberg from 1928–1932 to answer the failures of Orthodox Marxism, the resultant Heideggerian (or phenomenological) Marxism lent itself to Nazism. Moreover, Heidegger would officially endorse the Nazi party in 1933, so there was no uncertainty about his ideology. This led Marcuse to sever all ties with Heidegger and Heidegger's work. Reason and Revolution was Marcuse's attempt to show that Hegel couldn't be legitimately interpreted as promoting Nazism.

In this sense, Marcuse was attempting to save the Hegelian dialectic—the pattern of negative thinking, which, as we saw, addressed an (abstract) idea against its (negative) contradictions to result in a (concrete) synthesis. It was essential for Marcuse to overcome the idea that Hegel's dialectical process necessarily led to Nazism so that Marcuse could live with himself and his communist aspirations. This work also allowed him and the entire Frankfurt School, who were predominantly Jewish, to justify continuing the dialectic when it called to violently overturn society, similar to how the Nazis did beginning in 1933 under the *Enabling Act*. Importantly, violent revolution was something both Nazism and Marxism demanded. These two extremist ideologies are a great deal more related than most people realize.

In addition to his intelligence, Marcuse had a certain charm as part of an overall affable personality, so he frequently collaborated with Institute members on various projects. He was even asked to conduct work for the US's Office of War Information (OWI) beginning in 1943. He worked for OWI as an anti-Nazi propaganda specialist for a short period of time before he was transferred to the Office of Strategic Services (OSS), the precursor to the CIA. When the OSS was disbanded at the end of WWII, he shifted a third time to the US Department of State as an intelligence analyst on Nazism, where he eventually retired his analytical career in 1951.

After this began Marcuse's realization of his raison d'être: to teach his Neo-Marxist views to young Americans in colleges and universities. As a professor in America, he would be directly subverting Western minds, which was at the core of Marx's original dialectical materialism—to become the agent of revolution oneself. This might seem like an unbelievable contradiction, given all Marcuse's service to US intelligence from 1943–1951, but the US had not come to fully understand communism yet. Although it would have been difficult to remain some kind of communist agent during all that time employed by the US government, Marcuse demonstrated it was entirely possible to retain radical left ideology despite serving a right-leaning government. The US standoff against communism—the Cold War—had yet to begin. The US government was probably using the opportunity of his employment to study Marcuse's Neo-Marxism as an inroad to any ideological threats it might be able to expose, and not just to help them fight Nazism. It's serendipitous that Marcuse left his position in the US government just a few short years before McCarthyism would come to dominate US politics.

Eros and Civilization. Marcuse would teach political theory from 1953–1970 at several universities across the US, including Columbia, Harvard, Brandeis, and the University of California. During this time, he also developed theoretical treatises, such as an attempt to synthesize Marx with the approach of Sigmund Freud, which would critically represent the next step in dialectical leftism. This he published in Eros and Civilization: A Philosophical Inquiry into Freud in 1955. This was a particularly important work because it helped to explain the failure of Orthodox Marxism in several ways.

First, Marcuse believed Marx had been too narrow in defining the proletariat as only the working class. Although he agreed with Marx that the workers were oppressed, they weren't the only ones being imposed upon in capitalist society. Marcuse wanted to expand the definition of proletariat to include individuals who were repressed in capitalist society. Under this preface, he delved into the popular psychology of the day. Psychoanalyst Sigmund Freud's work provided a window into that repression and how it occurred within the individual. Freud had examined patients psychoanalytically and determined that various behaviours had surfaced thanks to repression of memories of unfortunate events. However, Freud didn't believe repression was always a bad thing.

To Freud, repression was a necessary evil to maintain society, but Marcuse further delineated the presence of different types of repression. He agreed with Freud that there was indeed a "basic repression" required within an individual's psyche to withhold the urge to satisfy themselves (Freud's pleasure principle) in ways that would infringe upon the rights of others. Extreme examples of this are rape and stealing to obtain the pleasure one desires without the consent of other citizens. But past that basic level of repression to keep people from infringing on one another's rights, Marcuse believed there was also a "surplus repression" imposed on members of society.

The existence of surplus repression was revealed from the hidden truth that advanced industrial societies had enough resources and food for everyone. The whole concept of "scarcity" was a falsehood promoted to compel workers in society to conduct "surplus work." The hidden reality was that they could do a lesser amount of work (or "basic work") and still meet all their needs and the needs of society. It was the capitalists who pushed for the illusion of scarcity because they controlled the means of production, so a surplus work would benefit them. It would leave them controlling a disproportionate amount of society's abundant wealth and resources as well as the means to produce them.

A second error Marcuse saw in Orthodox Marxism was its exclusion of imagination, culture, and art as tools of liberation. Marx had relied heavily on the misgivings the workers would have—the *emotional reasoning* and *dichotomous thinking* (see Chapter Fifteen)—to drive them into class warfare. While Marx's approach was centred on the workers' mistreatment as the motivation for slaughtering their oppressors, Marcuse had a much cleverer idea in mind: subversion. Through the Frankfurt School and connections to the works of Antonio Gramsci, Marcuse was aware of the methodological advances Cultural Marxism had made in subversion, so he promoted them in his Neo-Marxism.

In addition to this, Marcuse saw the seeking of pleasure itself (again, Freud's pleasure principle) as in direct opposition and suppressed by the performance principle (also Freud's).

The capitalists pushed for repression of human desires so that the average man would be focused on production and the maximizing of profit through work: the performance principle. For this to occur, men had to be convinced of the scarcity of resources, threatened for their survival on an instinctual level, and not want to challenge that thinking. They needed to believe that their life of servitude was the only option to support themselves and their families. Marcuse saw art, sex, cultural endeavours, and promoting other repressed desires for pleasure as a direct threat to the imposed performance principle. In this way, for Neo-Marxism, a cultural revolution became the goal instead of a class revolution. Too much pleasure engagement would effectively blow up capitalist society.

A third error Marcuse saw in Orthodox Marxism was its inability to predict the complicit nature of the proletariat. This directly challenged Marx's whole notion of class consciousness, which had to be reached among the proletariat before revolution could occur. The workers were not enraged at their mistreatment because they couldn't see that they were mistreated. Nor were they able to critically examine what was going on. Instead, as Vladimir Lenin had claimed, an elite (in Marcuse's case, the critical theorists, and for Lenin the vanguard party) were needed to show the proletariat how they were being mistreated and what to do about it. In this manner, Neo-Marxism came far too close to Leninism, where the elites are required to push the proletariat's consciousness and for violent revolution. This shows the inherently elitist (and violent) underpinning of Neo-Marxism as espoused by the Frankfurt School and Marcuse. Only they had the true solutions for liberation. Without the critical theorists to guide them, people would continue to think uncritically. Marcuse sometimes labelled this uncritical, complacent mentality as false consciousness. He called that consciousness "false" because it didn't align with the communist perspective, namely that the capitalist superstructure held workers down with a culture industry that turned their brains into mush.

One-Dimensional Man. This uncritical thinking, which Marcuse dubbed "one-dimensional thinking," produced what he called a one-dimensional man, explained in his eponymous work One-Dimensional Man, published 1964. In this depressing regurgitation of the Marxist dream of emancipation of workers, Marcuse lamented that capitalist society enforced and propagandized its way to a complicit, one-dimensional society. All the media, including news, advertisements, movies, and the like, were propaganda geared to reinforcing the uncritical thinking family in society. People would continue about their daily lives on a diet of capitalist propaganda, believing they must work hard to afford the latest gadgets and "keep up with the Joneses." That greedy and self-centred mantra was just another capitalist trope that kept the average citizen as a slave to the products they helped make and the few people who owned their means of production.

The answer to the problem of one-dimensional thinking was to hop up to the next stage: Marcuse and the Frankfurt School's ever-so-clever two-dimensional thinking. And what thinking had two-dimensions to it? You guessed it! The Hegelian dialectic, or what must now be thought of as dialectical leftism. It was necessary to uncover the hidden truths in society because these revealed contradictions that had to be dialectically addressed so that the communist state could synthesize them and create the correct solution.

Marcuse's favourite hidden contradiction in advanced industrial society was that it created wealth for just a few while keeping the vast majority in slave-like conditions. The hidden truth there is that the poor people were slaves; they just didn't realize it. This was the conspiratorial thinking at the heart of the Hegelian dialectic, and remains as evidence that dialectical leftism is a faith—a belief that society evolving through time, facing its contradictions, will produce paradise.

Marcuse's *One-Dimensional Man* was just another call to move forward using the dialectic as the only method possible to obtain the truth. He never stopped to consider that if the state faced its contradictions over and over again, it might not yield an ultimate truth like communism. All it might yield was a wasteland of ideas so bizarre and disconnected they could not be further pressed. Kind of like pulverized grapes that couldn't possibly produce any more wine.

Mai 68. We noted earlier that you can't kill an idea, and how dangerous ideas can be. Herbert Marcuse's Neo-Marxist ideology, built from the many years of writings of the Frankfurt School professors, wasn't esoteric musings for the few. In the spring of 1968, far-left radical students and teachers, many belonging to the New Left (see Chapter Three), took to the streets throughout France to protest the capitalist monster. This wasn't prefaced by some peaceful, carefully planned series of demonstrations. It was several months of academia battling back and forth with French police. Chaos that began relatively small-scale and escalated with unnerving speed.

French union leaders the country over pushed for their workers to join in solidarity with students and teachers by striking. No one could have been prepared for what happened next. That push by union bosses immediately and shockingly led to 11 million workers walking off the job. Over 20 per cent of the population of France suddenly went on strike. The entire economy came to a standstill. Protest sizes continued to increase, and the government began to fear revolution was imminent.

The violent attempts by the police to quell the earliest academic protests led to a nationwide backlash against the authorities. The President of France, Charles de Gaulle (1890–1970), the same man who as Brigadier General of the French Army epically fled before the Nazi occupation in 1940, would again run to the hills, this time in the face of the massive civil unrest. Only the French military command was able to convince him to return and fight for his country.

In an homage to the neo-Marxist ideas of Marcuse, French protesters created a massive amount of "protest art" designed to promote liberation from capitalist society, just as Marcuse theorized. Their signs and songs criticized factory conditions and employer demands as abusive. Another target of the protest art was the de Gaulle government, frequently compared with fascists and Nazis for their hardcore response to the original university protests. Those first few protests didn't require violence to control, as they were conducted by less than two hundred unarmed students and teachers. After they were attacked in later protests, the citizens did engage in some violence using rocks to throw and barricades to hide behind. The clumsy response by the French government enraged the public. One protest march saw more than a million French citizens shift through the streets of Paris, at which time the police were nowhere to be seen.

Somehow a small group of indoctrinated radicals, combined with a tiny minority of the French population who were armed militants, came very close to toppling France in May 1968. The New Left, including communists, socialists, and anarchists—an old-time collection of Antifa prototypes—came very close to taking down the de Gaulle government. All this from the simple protesting of class discrimination beginning at the Paris Nanterre University, one of the thirteen descendants of the University of Paris, the first university in Europe to be officially declared secular (see Chapter Five).

When the French government decided to use its brains instead of its brawn to solve the problem, things got better quickly. To quell the striking workers, which was the real reason the protests were effective, the government met with employers and unions to negotiate for wage increases. These were signed in late May 1968 as the Grenelle Accords. After this, the de Gaulle government created nationalist parades as a kind of propaganda to show solidarity among the French

PART III: THE VINE SUFFOCATES

people and that there would be peace. The solution was on the nose, as after this, a snap election was called to satisfy the wants of the people. de Gaulle's government won by a landslide. Just as had occurred in Germany of 1918–1919, a minority of radical leftists came close to overturning society but were in the end unable to control the larger population.

When it was all over, Marcuse washed his hands of the whole deal. He refused the moniker of "Grandfather of the New Left," although he clearly supported both what the people were doing and why they were doing it. The radicals had been indoctrinated to a significant degree by both Orthodox Marxist and Neo-Marxist ideology. They had incorporated Marcuse's new techniques to achieve liberation through the use of art and culture, which was unprecedented too. The entire ordeal had Marcuse's name all over it, no matter how much the old man denied it.

AN ESSAY ON LIBERATION

As if to prove that Marcuse really, really wanted to forcefully and finally achieve his desired revolution in a capitalist society, especially after the near-miss in France of 1968, he continued to write on new ways this might be achieved. From his life in the United States since the year 1934, he now had a very broad understanding of the socio-economic issues that were plaguing the land of the free and the home of the brave. And there was a not-so-hidden desire he'd been fostering for some time. The US represented the ultimate capitalist society, and Marcuse wanted to create enmity where others tried to find solutions. He was, after all, a clever old man. But more than that, he was a shyster. Much like the real personality of Marx before him, Marcuse's affable personality and friendly banter were a façade to his real hellbent intent on revolution. Revolution against inequalities that were often at best described as perceived and at worst described as a sad reality. Everyone in society is suffering from something, and to put that all on capitalism continues to be one of the most narrow-minded, myopic evaluations of the human condition.

Nevertheless, Marcuse wanted his communist revolution—a successful communist revolution—within advanced capitalist society. After witnessing France in 1968, he collected his thoughts on what would be necessary to achieve a more successful result in the United States. He saw that the Frankfurt School and his own Neo-Marxist writings had been successful at subverting academia, and that the dissatisfaction of the workers (class consciousness) could be achieved if pushed by critical theorists. Still, in the end that didn't prove to be enough to overturn France. So, especially for the bastion of capitalism in the West, he needed to add even more fuel to the fire.

To that end, he decided to begin playing up a new, American proletariat. People he thought he could manipulate to be the victims of indoctrination because they were already disenfranchised within society, and largely by the government. For that purpose, Marcuse chose what he referred to as "the ghetto population." In his book *An Essay on Liberation*, first published in 1969, he laid out the groundwork for how Neo-Marxism would use Black Americans as the new working class to foment revolution against the state.

> The ghetto population of the United States constitutes such a force. Confined to small areas of living and dying, it can be more easily organized and directed. Moreover, located in the core cities of the country, the ghettos form natural geographical centers from which the struggle can be mounted against targets of vital economic and political importance.
>
> (…)
>
> The long-range power of the black rebellion is further threatened by the deep division within this class (the rise of a Negro bourgeoisie) and by its marginal (in terms of the capitalist system) social function. The majority of the black population does not occupy a decisive position in the process of production, and the white organizations of labour have not exactly gone out of their way to change this situation. In the cynical terms of the system, a large part of this population is "expendable," that is to say, it makes no essential contribution to the productivity of the system. Consequently, the powers that be may not hesitate to apply extreme measures of suppression if the movement becomes dangerous. The fact is that, at present in the United States, the black population appears as the most "natural force" of rebellion.[2]

Although neither Marcuse nor Marx was responsible for any of organically grown Black liberation (Black power) movements in the US, Marcuse was making a blatant attempt to co-opt them for his own violent communist purpose. Some of the Black liberation movements had, through their own direction, come to

---

[2] H. Marcuse, *An Essay on Liberation*, first edition (Boston, MA: Beacon Press, 1971), 57–58.

adopt Marxist methodology and goals, and this would help assimilate them into the larger Neo-Marxist cause if they so chose. And many of them did choose to join the growing ranks of the New Left, which we will examine in the following chapter. The history of slavery provided a ready-made tension and disenfranchisement, which Marcuse selfishly and hatefully attempted to exploit, all for the glorious destruction of capitalist society. He set the stage for the next step in dialectical leftism, based largely on the "empirical" evidence he could see from France in 1968, which promised that revolution was indeed within his grasp.

CHAPTER NINE
MARXISM IS A THREAT TO PUBLIC SAFETY

AS INFLAMMATORY AS the writings of the Frankfurt school come across, not all of it was created with malicious intent. In fact, the good intentions of the Frankfurt School were driven by a fear of Nazism recurring, and it's understandable that professors of Jewish descent were particularly terrified of that possibility. The slaughter of six million Jews left an indelible mark on generations of Jew and non-Jew alike. The reality that such an atrocity occurred to anyone as a "solution" is the stuff of pure evil, and thus it might drive one to seek desperate measures to avoid ever having to face again.

Unfortunately, Marcuse and the Frankfurt School were pre-occupied with this fear because they believed that the only possible trajectory of an advanced industrial society was to morph into fascism like Nazi Germany. The transition to fascism would happen unless it was short-circuited by a revolution, which would knock society into communism and save the day. Importantly, this conclusion reveals dichotomous thinking, an unfortunate pattern we will discuss in Chapter Fifteen: Modern Marxist Methodology. It's an oversimplification clung to out of fear.

It's likely some of the neo-Marxists thought they were doing something good by recommending a violent revolution to stop Nazism. Having said that, the solution to evil cannot possibly be to become evil yourself. Communism and fascism are cut from the same extremist cloth.

In this chapter, we'll examine the impetus for violence in Neo-Marxism. The point is to show that the acceptable ideological underpinning of the New Left and critical theory was supposed to be their abandonment of Stalinist violence. Protests of the Vietnam War, for instance, bore witness to a pacifist stance among many in the New Left. But Marcuse finally and irrevocably admitted violence was a necessity in Neo-Marxism, just as it had been for Orthodox Marxism, in his 1965 work, *Repressive Tolerance*. He didn't just promote violence during revolution, either. Marcuse always called for violence against right-wing ideology, which he justified by saying that all right-wing ideology led to fascism anyway. This claim gave the Neo-Marxists carte blanche and opened the door right back to Stalinist measures. In *Repressive Tolerance*, Marcuse also promoted the removal of basic rights from individuals who supported right-wing ideology. This meant Neo-Marxists wanted to deny members of society both freedom of speech and the freedom of peaceful assembly, two freedoms that are absolutely critical to the stability of Western democracy.

Neo-Marxism's call for violence was embodied in a wave of Marxist-based terrorist groups that sprung up around the globe during the 1960s. The most famous of these was the Palestinian Liberation Organization (PLO), which was instrumental in destabilizing the Middle East. Canada witnessed its own rise in radical left insurgency too. Neo-Marxism combined with nationalism and xenophobia in the province of Quebec to form the terrorist organization called the *Front de libération du Québec* (FLQ). Over time, the ideology of the FLQ became increasingly violent, and this would inevitably force the government of Canada to invoke the *War Measures Act* during the October Crisis of 1970. The most famous ideologue defining the framework of the FLQ was undoubtedly Pierre Vallières, whom we examine in some depth.

In a speech discussing the codependent communist relationship of violence required to enforce lies, Alexsandr Solzhenitsyn brilliantly summarized their twisted harmony:

In his 1970 Nobel Lecture in literature, the famous Soviet dissident and writer Aleksandr Solzhenitsyn declared that the violence that is at the root of communist totalitarianism—the Stalinist labour camps and brutal violence that he experienced and chronicled in works like The Gulag Archipelago—is inherent to that system. "It is invariably intertwined with the lie," he said. "They are linked in the most intimate, most organic and profound fashion: violence cannot conceal itself behind anything except lies, and lies have nothing to maintain them save violence. Anyone who has once proclaimed violence as his method must inexorably choose the lie as his principle."[1]

But Neo-Marxism, and especially the New Left, were clamouring for a non-violent communism. Had they found it? By 1965, Herbert Marcuse, the so-called Grandfather of the New Left, would be forced to admit there was no such thing as non-violent Marxism.

REPRESSIVE TOLERANCE

In 1965, Herbert Marcuse published a thirty-seven-page essay called *Repressive Tolerance*, which gave a rare glimpse into the methodological development of Neo-Marxist ideology.[2] It had been almost forty years since Antonio Gramsci conjured up the tactic of subversion of bourgeois culture during the inter-war period. It was perhaps the most significant achievement of all Gramsci's work while writing his so-called Prison Notebooks. In *Repressive Tolerance*, Marcuse argued for another great leap forward for Neo-Marxism by exposing a necessity for the linked ideas of intolerance and violence. These were (and remain) warning signs, red flags if you wish, of radical ideology—the preference for violence and the inability to tolerate dissenting opinions. The potential for violence of radical ideology is especially critical for members of law enforcement and the judicial branch of government to recognize as potential threats to public safety. This potential remains in direct contradiction with the liberal values of a Western democracy, which Canada still clearly is. This development caught many leftists off guard in the latter half of the 1960s, as the whole big argument for Neo-Marxism was that it abandoned the murderous Stalinist (tankie) approach of communism. Neo-Marxism was originally in opposition to violence against the citizenry.

However, Neo-Marxism ultimately proved to be just as communist as Orthodox Marxism and necessitated just as much violence. It took a much more deceptive route to obtaining it, though. For all his faults, Karl Marx lacked the deceitfulness of the Frankfurt School, which was not beyond lying their way to

---

[1] C. Gershman, "The Coronavirus Exposes the Lie at the Heart of Communist China," *The Globe and Mail*, March 11, 2020, https://www.theglobeandmail.com/opinion/article-the-coronavirus-exposes-the-lie-at-the-heart-of-communist-china/

[2] Repressive Tolerance was part of the book *A Critique of Pure Tolerance* with co-authors Paul Wolff, Barrington Moore, and Herbert Marcuse, published in 1965 by Beacon Press.

whatever they believed was best. To the Frankfurt School's disciples, the ends could justify the means. They were willing to conduct evil acts, while claiming to be good guys, to prevent evil. *Repressive Tolerance* demonstrates this very clearly. Marx, on the other hand, had a much more transparent violent nature, which he wasn't afraid to embrace himself or let loose upon those around him.

For all Marcuse had witnessed up to 1965, he connected the very existence of law enforcement and the military as undeniable proof that there was neither authentic tolerance nor peace in democratic society. Instead, democratic society relied on the image of tolerance and the threat of violence to reinforce the status quo. He compared this fake tolerance in society to a universal tolerance, an unattainable ideal.

> In other words, tolerance is an end in itself only when it is truly universal, practiced by the rulers as well as by the ruled, by the lords as well as by the peasants, by the sheriffs as well as by their victims. And such universal tolerance is possible only when no real or alleged enemy requires in the national interest the education and training of people in military violence and destruction. As long as these conditions do not prevail, the conditions of tolerance are 'loaded': they are determined and defined by the institutionalized inequality (which is certainly compatible with constitutional equality), i.e., by the class structure of society. In such a society, tolerance is de facto limited on the dual ground of legalized violence or suppression (police, armed forces, guards of all sorts) and of the privileged position held by the predominant interests and their "connections."[3]

So the democratic society, or at least the society that claims it is democratic (a liberal value), is in fact not democratic. Although Marcuse's writings are purposefully covered in the obfuscating language of the radical left, he eventually makes his undemocratic belief explicit:

> Historically, even in the most democratic democracies, the vital and final decisions affecting the society as a whole have

---

[3] H. Marcuse, R. P. Wolff, and B. Moore Jr., *A Critique of Pure Tolerance* (Boston, MA: Beacon Press, 1965), 84–85, https://www.marcuse.org/herbert/publications/1960s/1965-repressive-tolerance-1969.pdf.

been made, constitutionally or in fact, by one of several groups without effective control of the people themselves.[4]

He uses this uncomfortable assertion to question those who are afraid of authoritarianism or dictatorships, showing that they're living in a society that's a lot closer to those regime types than citizens of a so-called democratic society might think. This fits in well with his idea that advanced industrial society will eventually transition into fascism, especially since two key values of the fascist regime type are that they are non-pluralist and non-democratic. Of course, communism fits those two values into its schema as well. Sure enough, Marcuse admits that "undemocratic means" are required to achieve liberation (read: communism).

> Surely, no government can be expected to foster its own subversion, but in a democracy, such a right is vested in the people (i.e. the majority of the people). This means that ways should not be blocked on which a subversive majority could develop and if they are blocked by organized repression and indoctrination, their reopening may require apparently undemocratic means.[5]

Marcuse then argues that the push for communism (or *liberation*, as he deceptively refers to it) necessitates violence and intolerance, because those means must be used to overcome the default path of advanced capitalist society: toward Nazism. Although we will define it more thoroughly in Chapter Fifteen, this is an example of dichotomous thinking, a cognitive pattern associated with mental illness that tries to force you into one "group" or another. In this case you must choose Nazism or communism because, according to the Frankfurt School's empirical (historical) data, those were the only possible outcomes of advanced industrial societies.

Of course, this was an overly simplistic way to think. It also clumsily avoided regime types that have come to prominence today, such as populist and (anti-capitalist) technocratic. The Frankfurt School seems to have been incapable of imagining such alternative regime types, ones that didn't fall in line with what they had already observed. This demonstrated another tangible weakness in

---

[4] Ibid., 104.

[5] Ibid., 100.

Hegel's historicism. Despite the fantastic application of the dialectic to society, critical theorists proved incapable of imagining some combination of what they had already seen.

That limitation to the confines of history cost them in more than one way. Another example of how short-sighted their obsession with historicism made them was that it convinced them societal patterns must recur. Because Marcuse's examination of history led him to the conclusion that violence was always present during regime-changes for the better (i.e., ones that he believed were more equitable and spread suffering and misery more equally), he assumed that violence should be promoted. In fact, he directly linked violence with progress:

> With all the qualifications of a hypothesis based upon an 'open' historical record, it seems that violence emanating from the rebellion of the oppressed classes broke the historical continuum of injustice, cruelty, and silence for a brief moment, brief but explosive enough to achieve an increase in the scope of freedom and justice, and a better and more acceptable distribution of misery and oppression in a new social system—in one word: progress in civilization.[6]

Does anyone want to tell Marcuse "progress in civilization" is three words? Right, a bit late for that.

Marcuse goes on to cite the revolutions that he equated with violently forcing through "progress" in the article, including the English Revolution, the French Revolution, the Chinese Revolution, and the Cuban Revolution. The problem with this list is, according to his own qualifier from the quote above of a "more acceptable distribution of misery and oppression," only the French revolution might fit the bill.

Of the remaining three revolutions he presents as evidence, the starkest failure to bring about a "more acceptable distribution of misery and oppression" for the working class was probably the Chinese Revolution (1949). In Marcuse's defence, a great deal of critical evidence against his claim was not readily available during his lifetime. It was very well concealed, even hidden from most of urban China. The atrocities committed under Chairman Mao, testified to by innumerable survivors, were only indirectly admitted by the CCP's limited release of records in the twenty-first century (see for example

---

[6] Ibid., 107.

Dutch historian Frank Dikötter's book *Mao's Great Famine*). Following the revolutionary ascension of the Chinese Communist Party in 1949, Mao's Great Leap Forward, conducted from 1958–1962, just a decade into the newly formed People's Republic of China (PRC), killed a conservatively estimated 30 million Chinese people, largely from starvation in the countryside. It also failed to industrialize China or increase its existing irrigation systems as promised. Following that, Mao's Cultural Revolution (1966–1976), a purge of right-wing ideology to re-assert communism, killed an estimated 1.6 million Chinese.[7] This can't in any way be evaluated as a "more acceptable distribution of misery and oppression." The number of Chinese people killed is far too great for any excuse of any magnitude to praise as "progress," even omitting the servitude that followed.

The Cuban Revolution (1953–1959) was a changing of authoritarian regimes and not some heaven-sent relief for the Cuban people. Even though he wasn't the same ideological breed as the corrupt Batista government he overthrew, Fidel Castro (1926–2016) was a dictator and a common thug. It was, ironically, in 1965 (the same year *Repressive Tolerance* was first published), after just six years under his leadership, that Castro told poor and starving Cubans they could leave the country under their own volition, via the port of Camarioca.

This turned out to be a deathtrap for some of the desperate Cubans, who launched into the Caribbean in poorly made rafts and other slipshod vessels to head for America several hundred kilometres north by sea. Many died of exhaustion or drowned, while several thousand ended up in Miami, Florida. Today, there are approximately 2 million Americans of Cuban descent in the US, with 1.2 million Cuban-Americans living in the Miami-Dade County alone, at the Eastern tip of Florida. They feared communism and Castro to such an extent that many risked death trying to get to a capitalist country.[8]

The English Revolution that Marcuse mentions doesn't refer to the bloodless one in 1689. Instead, like other Marxist historians—most notably Engels—Marcuse refers to the series of wars between 1639–1651 in which Charles I of the House of Stuart (1600–1649) was executed and a Commonwealth established. Of course, we know that "end" to the monarchy didn't last, and the Crown was

---

[7] M. De Witte, "China's Cultural Revolution Was a Power Grab from within the Government, Not from without, Stanford Sociologist Finds," *Stanford News*, October 19, 2019, https://news.stanford.edu/2019/10/29/violence-unfolded-chinas-cultural-revolution/.

[8] "Facts & Figures," Cubans in America, February 1, 2019, retrieved July 13, 2023, from https://cubansinamerica.us/web/facts-and-figures/#:~:text=There%20are%202%20million%20Hispanics,States%2C%20especially%20in%20South%20Florida.

re-established during the Stuart Restoration (1660). Marxists continued to harp on this as a significant revolution because they claimed it saw an end to feudalism and a shift into agrarian capitalist society. However, non-Marxist historians have noted that there is insufficient evidence to claim such a massive societal change can be attributed directly to the period from 1639–1651.[9] This Marxian claim remains, therefore, dubious at best.

Marcuse's excuse for violence is the "progress" it has created in places like Cuba, China, and England. However, those events only demonstrated tangible violence through casualties accrued during their respective revolutions, and not progress. Whether any one of them had resulted in a favourable transition of society to a "more acceptable distribution of misery and oppression" is highly in doubt. Then again, as we learned in Chapter Two, Marxism is based on lies. Marcuse was bold to try and make a concrete defence of his repressive tolerance, but boldness and truth are not the same thing.

Marcuse's solution to the (then contemporary) issue of tolerance and violence was promoting what he called liberating tolerance, which was actually intolerant. In the usual Marxian style of bafflegab, he admitted how it was necessary to silence the voices on the right of the political spectrum and treat them with complete intolerance. This meant no freedom of speech and no freedom of peaceful assembly. All these unacceptable removals of freedom are justified in the name of the oppression the right has enforced for centuries. Marcuse spells out just how he would treat the right if he was able:

> [W]ithdrawal of toleration of speech and assembly from groups and movements which promote aggressive policies, armament, chauvinism, discrimination on the grounds of race or religion, or which oppose the extension of public services, social security, medical care, etc. Moreover, the restoration of the freedom of thought may necessitate new and rigid restrictions on teachings and practices in the educational institutions which, by the very method and concepts, serve to enclose the mind within the established universe of discourse and behaviour—thereby precluding a priori a rational evaluation of the alternatives.[10]

---

[9] Wikipedia, s.v. "English Revolution," June 2, 2023 https://en.wikipedia.org/wiki/English_Revolution#cite_note-21.

[10] H. Marcuse, R. P. Wolff, and B. Moore Jr., *A Critique of Pure Tolerance* (Boston, MA: Beacon Press, 1965), 100–101, https://www.marcuse.org/herbert/publications/1960s/1965-repressive-tolerance-1969.pdf.

CHAPTER NINE: MARXISM IS A THREAT TO PUBLIC SAFETY

Marcuse wanted nothing to do with democracy or peace. Just as with Marx, if by some incredible miracle a utopia arrived on earth, Marcuse's violent revolutionary programming would be completely out of place. His true intentions of violence, suppression, and revolution were finally and undeniably described to the masses in *Repressive Tolerance*, and although this work may have served to inspire the May 1968 protests in France and elsewhere, his ideology had become too exposed. Like the red-hot lava we discussed in the second chapter, communism's weakness is being exposed to fresh air. The rapid cooling that takes place turns it into a brittle, smashable subject. This is one of the reasons it survives and thrives in a society uneducated as to its perils. You have to understand it before you can expose it to others. Then it can be hammered to bits.

LE FRONT DE LIBÉRATION DU QUÉBEC

Marcuse's sadistic thoughts, penned with overt malice, proved highly influential. Despite being hidden away in books bound for Marxian-sycophants and hapless undergrads, Marcuse's writings helped inspire direct action from numerous terrorist cells during the 1960s.[11,12] These were radical left movements that made the New Left look like kindergarten. They combined Neo-Marxism's cultural focus and Marcuse's call for violence with ideological elements such as nationalism and xenophobia to form a deadly cocktail.

That violence was acceptable according to scholarly literature emboldened terrorist cells in the US, including the Weathermen, the Black Panthers, and the Symbionese Liberation Army. Canada would not be spared such insurgency either. The teachings of Marcuse were combined with a younger generation of anti-Anglophone Quebec nationalists, and the result was increasingly radicalized terrorist cells in the *Front de libération du Québec* (FLQ).

The FLQ was a coming together of nationalist, socialist extremists in 1963, with the intent of using violence and terrorism until their demands for a sovereign socialist Quebec were met. This was a new nationalist movement at the time, one completely detached from the long-standing rural and religious nationalist inclination of the French-Canadian Catholic Church. The new nationalists

---

[11] The Marxist socialist terrorist organizations (and cells) formed in the 1960s include the Weatherman (USA), the United Red Army (Japan), the Black Panthers (USA), SWAPO (South West Africa), ALN (Brazil), Tupamaros (Uruguay), FLQ (Canada), PLO (Middle East), Montoneros (Argentina), ERP (Argentina), the Red Brigade (Italy), PFLP (Middle East), DPFLP (Middle East), Baader-Meinhof (Germany), Black September (Middle East), and SLA (USA).

[12] S. R. Hicks, *Explaining Postmodernism: Skepticism and Socialism from Rousseau to Foucault* (Brisbane, AU: Connor Court Publishing, 2019), 168.

aimed instead for a secular state as the ultimate authority to create a sovereign Quebec. Despite this new nationalist sentiment, there were approximately one million French-Canadians living outside Quebec in the 1960s, a significant portion compared with roughly five million Quebecers.

Many Quebecer's attitudes toward the French-Canadians who had emigrated from the St. Lawrence River area between 1830–1930 was that those emigres were anglicized and no longer truly French-Canadian. The only true borders defining French-Canada were now those of Quebec, where French language and culture were protected. This new wave of Quebec nationalists therefore wanted to affect their relationship with the federal government to promote the social, cultural, and economic sovereignty of Quebec. Anglicization, and especially "Anglo-Saxons," were the enemy, including those English-speakers from the US.

Before nationalist extremism had fully developed, many Quebecers supported an initiative that revealed a widespread, much more moderate nationalist sentiment. Beginning what was labelled the *Quiet Revolution* (1960–1966), the Quebec Liberal Party under Jean Lesage (1912–1980) defeated the incumbent Union Nationale in 1960, ending sixteen years of conservative government. Lesage saw socialist reforms implemented over the next several years to promote the independence of Quebec, including massively increased provincial bureaucracy, increased scrutiny of the federal-provincial government relationship, the nationalization of the hydro industry, and the secularization of hospitals and schools.

Despite all this social change, the reforms were too slow-working and ultimately insufficient for young extremists, especially those anxious over perceived English control of French-Canada. The loss of the French language was a particular fear of many extremists and remains a sensitive issue to this day.[13] Eventually, that anxiety overflowed into the formation of the terrorist FLQ. Over a period of ten years, the FLQ carried out numerous terrorist attacks in Quebec, including 144 bombings, 48 robberies, and 17 arson attacks.[14]

> Inspired by the FLN of Algeria and the Cuban Revolution, intellectually nourished by Marx, Marcuse, Mao, Che Guevara and Carlos Marighella, [the FLQ] had already claimed

---

[13] E. Morris, "Bloc Québécois Leader Sends U.S. Secretary of State Letter Defending French-Language Laws," CBC: Montreal, January 31, 2024, retrieved February 18, 2024, from https://www.cbc.ca/news/canada/montreal/blanchet-bloc-blinken-letter-french-1.7100343.

[14] C. Crouch, *Managing Terrorism and Insurgency Regeneration, Recruitment and Attrition* (Oxfordshire, UK: Routledge, 2010).

responsibility for bombings in all parts of the province but particularly Montreal, where six people had died, and for several armed robberies.[15]

These terrorist attacks exclude the most infamous incident perpetrated by the FLQ.

THE OCTOBER CRISIS

The October Crisis of 1970 was the nadir of the attacks conducted by the FLQ. On October 5, 1970, the FLQ terrorist Liberation Cell kidnapped British Trade Commissioner James Richard Cross (1921–2021) from his Montreal home. FLQ cells were involved in other plots to kidnap diplomats from both the US and Israel, perceived as bourgeois oppressors of Quebec. Imprisoning Cross in a secret location, the Liberation Cell contacted police and gave a list of demands focused on the release of "political prisoners." These prisoners were terrorists who had been arrested and imprisoned after the RCMP crackdown of the FLQ in the fall of 1966. The FLQ demands also included that their manifesto be read by the CBC.

The FLQ manifesto was broadcast over both Quebec's French- and English-speaking media outlets on October 8, 1970, in an attempt to buy the hostage more time. The appearance of inaction proved unsatisfactory for anxious FLQ members. Following the initial kidnapping of Cross, the FLQ terrorist Chenier Cell kidnapped Quebec's Minister of Labour, Pierre Laporte (1921–1970), on October 10. This second kidnapping spread terror throughout Montreal (even though the two separate terrorist cells remained unaware of each others' subsequent actions), and the Quebec government requested the military be brought in. Bringing the Canadian Armed Forces (CAF) into Ottawa, Quebec City, and Montreal for protection was entirely legal under the *National Defense Act*, and all levels of government agreed the deployment should proceed.

General Gilles Turcot (1917–2010), commander of all land forces in Canada, ordered the Royal 22nd Regiment into Montreal on October 12.[16] CAF soldiers were also sent into Ottawa to safeguard federal property and prominent individuals there. The presence of the military escalated tension to an unprecedented level. When CBC journalist Tim Ralfe questioned him about

---

[15] L. L. LaPierre, "White N- of America," *New York Times*, April 11, 1971, https://www.nytimes.com/1971/04/11/archives/white-niggers-of-america-the-precocious-autobiography-of-a-quebec.html.

[16] Note that General Turcot served in this same regiment in WWII.

the military presence and just how far he was willing to go, Prime Minister Pierre Elliot Trudeau (1919–2000) responded with the most unforgettable line of his career: "Just watch me."[17]

Unfortunately, the clever rhetoric did little to de-escalate the situation. After Trudeau's statement, numerous prominent Quebec citizens urged giving into the demands of the FLQ. The lawyer for the FLQ, Robert Lemieux (1941–2008), exacerbated matters by publicly urging students at the University of Montreal to ditch their classes and join an FLQ solidarity rally. He was successful in rallying approximately three thousand students at an indoor arena in Montreal. The rhetoric escalated further when a union boss, the Marxist socialist Michel Chartrand (1916–2010), implied shooting politicians would force them to give in: "We are going to win because there are more boys ready to shoot members of Parliament than there are policemen."[18]

It was nowhere near as clever as Trudeau's sound bite. It was simply disturbing. In addition, the rally in Montreal terrified Canadians across the country. It looked and sounded like a revolution.

After this escalation in tension, negotiations between the government and the FLQ were abruptly terminated. On October 16, at the request of the Quebec provincial government and the Montreal Police Department, Pierre Trudeau authorized the *War Measures Act*. Martial law came into effect across Canada. Police were given sweeping powers to detain and arrest citizens and to search houses at their discretion. They had the military for backup in Quebec.

In response to the Act, FLQ's Chenier Cell decided to reciprocate in the most violent way they could. They murdered hostage Pierre Laporte by strangling him to death and, after dumping his corpse, tipped off the authorities as to where Laporte could be found. At the same time, the Liberation Cell, who were holding James Cross hostage, communicated that they would not execute him unless the police attempted to discover their whereabouts. The Liberation Cell continued to push for the release of the "political prisoners" and for more reading of the FLQ's manifesto.

Having killed their hostage and without any leverage, the Chenier Cell was doomed to be captured. Pierre Trudeau would keep the *War Measures Act* enabled until all the terrorists were captured or killed. It took until December

---

[17] CBC, "CBC Archives: Just Watch Me, 1970," YouTube video, 7:33, December 3, 2008, https://www.youtube.com/watch?v=XfUq9b1XTa0.

[18] Wikipedia, s.v. "October Crisis," February 9, 2024, https://en.wikipedia.org/wiki/October_Crisis.

CHAPTER NINE: MARXISM IS A THREAT TO PUBLIC SAFETY

28 until all four of the terrorists in the Chenier Cell were rounded up to be tried for murder.

In a curious turn of events, the Liberation Cell eventually released James Cross after holding him captive for sixty days. He was ill-fed and had lost ten pounds during captivity. The terrorists successfully negotiated a plane to take them to communist Cuba, where Fidel Castro had personally assured their acceptance. They would eventually return to Canada and receive custodial sentences.

Following the October Crisis, the FLQ was effectively destroyed. Between the years of bombings and the murders of Laporte and several others, the leftist extremists became incredibly unpopular. Their evil deeds were now exposed, with faces put to them. The sentiment for a sovereign Quebec, however, would live on and even increase in the following years, without the need for extremist violence. But the question remained as to how and why the FLQ's tactics became so dramatically escalated after years of violent but very simple and repetitive bombings. Why was it elevated to the level of a crisis? The answer seems to lie with the FLQ's ideological mastermind.

PIERRE VALLIÈRES

Pierre Vallières (1938–1998) was born into poverty in the slums of Montreal in Ville Jacques-Cartier (modern day Longueuil). His father worked himself into an early grave trying to support the family, while his mother's distant and frugal nature kept their family alive. Pierre would later decry that his was a loveless and violent childhood that instigated his turn to Marxist literature, a choice he made to learn how Quebecers like himself could truly be freed from the bonds of what he perceived as slavery.

But we shouldn't get lost in Vallières' story of self-pity too easily because it's entirely reminiscent of every other hardcore Marxist ideologue, and that noticeable recurrence reminds us that neither hardship nor poverty necessarily breed criminality. Certainly neither poverty nor hardship is an excuse for criminal action. That's a hopeless, determinist belief to which we must not subscribe. It doesn't justify the murders committed by the FLQ or the plots constructed by Vallières.

In fact, Vallières had been offered a chance to lift himself out of the doldrums he claims were inescapable—through an extension of the Christian Church. He initially accepted an offer to join the Franciscan Order, a brotherhood with over half-a-million members to this day. He agreed to participate for a time, during which the church educated the underprivileged youth and gave him the literary skills he would use to build a fledgling career.

But these gifts weren't enough for him. They did nothing to eradicate Quebec's poverty and suffering under the Anglo-Saxon's boot as far as he could see. Instead of being thankful for the development of his skills and the opportunities they created, Vallières began to see the Church as complicit in the bourgeois oppression of Quebecers. The Marxist narrative of oppressor vs. oppressed took over Vallières' life, while he openly espoused a hatred for Christianity and the office of the priesthood.

His skills at reading and writing developed as he aged, but that did little to assuage his internalized angst. He struggled with depression and survived a suicide attempt. His skills saw him come to work for papers such as *Le Devoir* and *Cité Libre*, where he eventually became editor. It was a strange coincidence that the editor for *Cité Libre* before him would be the eventual prime minister of Canada and the most prominent opponent of the FLQ, Pierre Trudeau. Trudeau represented the French-Canadian bourgeoisie to the FLQ, a bourgeoisie who were not only complicit with the Anglo-Saxon oppressors but even bred with them.

At the same time as his skills were developing, Vallières' voracious appetite for reading became entirely focused on Marxist literature, including the latest musings of Herbert Marcuse. Marxist literature entirely captured any spirit Vallières had and left him with only resentment to live for. Despite eventually becoming a writer for the prestigious international newspaper *La Presse*, Vallières began conducting activities that would cost him his job. He was fired from *La Presse* after two years for engaging in what were described as "subversive" activities. After this experience, he decided to exclusively focus on the writing, editing, and production of only extremist media.

In 1965, along with his close friend, the sociologist and activist Charles Gagnon, Vallières took over publication of the FLQ's extremist newspaper, *La Cognée*. The following year, Vallières and Gagnon officially joined the FLQ as leaders of their own terrorist cell, and their contribution to the movement resulted in an immediate escalation in violence.

On May 5, 1966, a letter bomb was set off at a shoe factory experiencing an ongoing strike. Thérèse Morin, a sixty-five-year-old secretary at the factory, was killed by the blast. Just two months later, on July 14, an FLQ terrorist, Jean Corbo, was killed while arming explosives at a textile factory in Montreal.

In response to this escalation in violence, the RCMP aimed for an immediate takedown of the FLQ members under Vallières and Gagnon's leadership. A total of twenty FLQ members were arrested during police raids in the fall of 1966. These would be many of the militants that the October Crisis hostage-taking was plotted to free.

Although their terrorist cell was dismantled in 1966, neither Vallières nor Gagnon had been captured in the raids. They had fled to the US and turned up unexpectedly in New York City a few days after the mass arrests. In New York, they appealed to the United Nations to initiate a human rights case against their government. While protesting outside the UN building in the Big Apple, however, the pair were arrested and thrown in jail. They would spend the next several months incarcerated in New York jail cells before being extradited to Canada in January 1967 to face trial for the death of Morin.

It was during their incarceration in New York that Vallières began writing his infamous biography, titled *Negres Blancs D'Amerique,* which repugnantly translates to *White N- of America.* The book was published in May 1968 by *Parti Pris*, while Vallières remained behind bars. It was an effort to equate the struggle of Francophones in Canada with the African-American struggle for civil rights in the US and openly called for armed revolution against the state:

> It is by force and not by resignation, passivity, and fear that we will be free. The sooner the n- we are arm ourselves with our courage and with our rifles the sooner our liberation from slavery will make of us equal and fraternal men.[19]

The trial proceedings for Vallières commenced after his extradition, and although he was originally sentenced to life imprisonment for Morin's murder, he appealed, and a retrial was ordered:

> The first trial ended with a verdict of guilty and a sentence of life imprisonment both of which were quashed by an appeal court which ordered a retrial. "It seems possible that the appellant was condemned for his subversive ideas and his seditious writing rather than for his participation in the crime of which he is accused," said the court in its unanimous decision. In his

---

[19] P. Vallieres and C. Gagnon, *White N- of America: The Precocious Autobiography of a Quebec "Terrorist"* (New York, NY: Monthly Review Press, 1971), 288.

second trial, Vallieres however was once more found guilty, but this time sentenced to only thirty months.[20]

The result of the drastically reduced sentence was that Vallières was released on parole on May 26, 1970, after spending a total of forty-four months in prison. That the October Crisis happened just four months after Vallières' release was no coincidence. He provided the ideological motivation for the FLQ cells. There was clearly an inspiration from the act of his release that contributed to the FLQ's brazen crimes in the October Crisis. Vallières, whom journalist Adam Raphael for *The Guardian* equated as "the Herbert Marcuse of the FLQ," was a driving influence for violence and murder.[21] *The Guardian* article suggests Vallières might have had a desire for revenge after what he perceived as persecution by the Anglo-Saxon controlled criminal justice system: "The way in which the authorities prosecuted the Morin case against him has been a principal cause of this."[22]

In 1971, Vallières' culpability in the October Crisis was proven in a court of law. He accepted a plea deal and received a one-year suspended sentence on three charges of counselling kidnapping for political purposes. Although he publicly renounced violence at that time, it's most likely this was a stipulation of his plea deal and not some heartfelt change from all the years of agitating for armed rebellion. Like many Marxist writers before him, Vallières was not a hands-on killer capable of committing the most vicious and heinous acts his writing begged for. Like Marcuse before him, he was largely an ideologue, a generator of the violence-inducing ideas that would drive those more desperate to see the defeat of the Anglo-Saxon imperialists.

The ideological contribution of Marxism to the greatest domestic terrorist threat Canada has ever faced is a reminder to all Canadians that this ideology is a tangible threat to public safety. Marxism can contribute to escalations of violence, especially in modern cases, where terrorist acts can be conducted under salad-bar extremism. Marxism supplies a ready-made ideological component that both vindicates and emboldens those who seek to conduct violence, whether or not it contributes to initiating that desire.

---

[20] A. Raphael, "Murderers' Martyr," *The Guardian*, October 21, 1970, https://www.newspapers.com/newspage/259945352/.

[21] Ibid.

[22] Ibid.

CHAPTER TEN
CO-OPTING THE CIVIL RIGHTS MOVEMENT

WHEN WE ADD together the necessity for violence found in *Repressive Tolerance* in 1965 with the identification of the Black population of the US as the "most natural source of rebellion" in *An Essay on Liberation* from 1969, we can piece together the overarching theme of Marcuse's works. However, if we stop and think about it, a large segment of the Black population had its own ideas on how and what to achieve in society—a society that had treated them as either slaves or second-class citizens since its foundation. Their answer was the Civil Rights Movement (1954–1968).

In this chapter, the key to remember is that the individuals I discuss link Neo-Marxism to the co-optation of the Civil Rights Movement, as Marcuse planned.

Late in his life, Marcuse received a reprieve in his student Angela Davis, a Black feminist and communist. Under Marcuse's tutelage, Davis began learning about critical theory at UCLA, after which she was taught at the Frankfurt School, which had returned to Germany. Davis revealed her radicalization in a connection to the Black Panthers and a horrific courthouse hostage-taking that left several people, including a judge, dead. Davis had purchased the weapons used in that incident. She spent time in prison before continuing her journey in Neo-Marxism. Her work provided an essential critique of the patriarchy existent in Black liberation movements like the Panthers. She is a clear link between Neo-Marxism and the struggle for civil rights.

Next we come to the inception of critical race theory (CRT) and lawyer Derrick Bell. Bell is considered the founder of CRT. As a civil rights lawyer, Bell tried over three hundred cases centred largely around desegregation of schools under the key decision Brown vs. Board of Education of Topeka (1954). Trouble occurred when Brown began to question the whole initiative of desegregation. He had an existential crisis and concluded that racism would reassert itself even if the law was changed. He also decided that civil rights laws had been created not for the sake of equality but to appease Cold War criticism of America's racism by the Soviets. Bell's work as a teacher at Harvard, beginning in 1969, would lay the groundwork required to share his ideas, which are considered the basis for CRT today. They would be picked up by Kimberlé Crenshaw, whom we cover in Chapter Twelve.

THE CIVIL RIGHTS MOVEMENT

The Civil Rights Movement was non-violent civil disobedience. It included Black bus-riders not relinquishing their seats for White passengers. It included Black youths staging a sit-in at a "Whites only" lunch counter. It included marches and walks, arm-in-arm in solidarity. They did not promote violence, nor did they hope to destroy capitalism. The calm and courageous demeanour in which they protested was critical to achieving equal rights under the law for Blacks in the US. It was a righteous movement espoused by everyday African Americans like Claudette Colvin and Rosa Parks. But it also had more prominent figures in the Black community, like Martin Luther King Jr. and, later, Malcom X. It was not beholden to Marxist ideology. It was not beholden to communism. It certainly did not require the direction of radical liberal academics like Herbert Marcuse, who simply wanted to use Black people for his own desire for revolution. Given all the turmoil of the late sixties, and the incredible advancements in civil rights for the Black population of the US, why did Marcuse think he had anything to add to the movement?

As mentioned, Marcuse had become a naturalized US citizen in 1940. He witnessed changes the Civil Rights Movement brought from its inception in 1954 under *Brown v. Board of Education of Topeka*, which saw segregation in public schools struck down as unconstitutional, all the way through to the assassination of Martin Luther King Jr. on April 4, 1968. Marcuse witnessed the Black population, under its own volition, gaining equal rights under the law, which included voting, education, integration, and housing. The US courts had been instrumental in beginning to turn around centuries of prejudice, and this must have lifted the hearts of many of those who were truly oppressed.

But Marcuse didn't think, for whatever reason, that such changes were enough. Perhaps, as he hinted in *Repressive Tolerance*, there hadn't been enough violence in the Civil Rights Movement for him to classify it as one of the "successful" historical revolutions—revolutions that resulted in a better distribution of misery and suffering. Like today's breed of radical leftist, he decided what was best for the Black population by his own faculty of reason.

Considering the timing of *An Essay on Liberation*, published in 1969, it becomes clear that Marcuse was trying to goad the Black population into violent, full-scale revolt. It was first published just a year after the assassination of Martin Luther King Jr., after all. It probably took that year to write and get published. In it, Marcuse referred to Black people as the "ghetto population," a stinging reminder that despite all the rights they had attained during the fifties, the vast majority still lived in poverty. Blacks were still being treated unacceptably by many people, particularly in the deep South. Changing the law didn't magically make the US into a country of tolerance overnight. It was just the first step.

Marcuse knew this. He had witnessed the bumps along the road during the Civil Rights Movement, including widespread riots throughout the US from 1963–1967, fueled by explosive racial tension. Over a hundred people were killed. He witnessed the riots following the assassination of Dr. Martin Luther King in 1968 too. These were particularly damaging to the case for non-violence—a case King adamantly defended during his life. Many in the Black community began to argue that non-violence clearly didn't work if it was being met with violence, especially the violent assassination of Dr. King.

This was Marcuse's chance for his acrimonious Marxist sales pitch.

His voice did not go unheard.

ANGELA DAVIS

Angela Davis (1944–) first witnessed Marcuse speak at a rally in 1962, during the Cuban Missile Crisis. By 1969 and the end of the Civil Rights Movement, she was a radical Black feminist and Neo-Marxist communist. She personified the intense dissatisfaction with the treatment of African Americans that Herbert Marcuse badly wished to co-opt.

Davis was born in Birmingham, Alabama, a city permeated with violent anti-Black racism, including in 1963, when Martin Luther King Jr. was jailed there for protesting segregation in department stores. An assassination attempt was then made on Dr. King's brother by bombing a hotel. That same year, a church was bombed by the Ku Klux Klan (KKK), resulting in the death of four young Black girls.[1] Davis was no stranger to violent racism. She was born into the thick of it. Birmingham existed in long-standing infamy for anti-Black racism and terrorism, including bombings of homes of Black residents in the 1950s to try and force them out of historically "White" neighbourhoods. Davis, an unfortunate witness to this evil, was raised in an atmosphere of hatred, fear, and violence.

Davis's mother was a member of the Southern Negro Youth Congress, supported by the Communist Party of the United States of America. Despite this, Angela was raised as a regularly practicing Christian. As a young student, Angela was awarded a scholarship for Brandeis University, and upon sitting in on one of Herbert Marcuse's classes, she was drawn into his use of the Hegelian dialectic. She explains the beginning of her adoption of Neo-Marxist ideology from Marcuse from an interview in 2014:

> I attended his lecture course when I was a first-year student, a freshman, and I was drawn by the way he was able to put history and philosophy together in a context that allowed us to think about the future as history. […]
>
> I went to him, and I told him I was really interested in studying philosophy, but I didn't know where to begin and I hadn't had any formal training. I had read Sartre and Camus and I had read a lot of the French philosophers in connection with my French studies and so, I mean—he didn't know me from whoever—but he said "Okay, well let's spend the first semester doing independent study, which will be an intensive engagement with the history of western philosophy." So, we started with the pre-Socratics, and I met with him a couple of times a week and, you know, managed to get a sense of the history of western philosophy in one semester.[2,3]

That beginning in Neo-Marxism led to a full-fledged commitment to the school of critical theory, including Davis attending the University of Frankfurt

---

[1] Wikipedia, "16th Street Baptist Church bombing," June 30, 2023 https://en.wikipedia.org/wiki/16th_Street_Baptist_Church_bombing.

[2] Exploration in Black Leadership, "Brandeis University: Herbert Marcuse—Angela Davis," YouTube video, 6:06, May 28, 2014, https://www.youtube.com/watch?v=zqMG_iZF50c.

[3] "Reflections on Brown. Explorations in Black Leadership," University of Virginia, retrieved December 13, 2023, from https://blackleadership.virginia.edu/transcript/davis-angela.

and studying under critical theorists Max Horkheimer and Theodor Adorno (1903–1969). The Frankfurt School had officially returned from Columbia University to the Goethe University Frankfurt in 1951, although Marcuse continued to live in the US.

After her time in Frankfurt, Davis returned to the States at the University of California in San Diego (UCSD), following Marcuse's switch from Brandeis. There she earned her master's degree and took up a position of (acting) assistant professor in 1969 at the University of California in Los Angeles (UCLA). During her time at UCLA, Davis continued her activism and gave speeches that echoed the dichotomous thinking of Marcuse and the Frankfurt School. In one speech, she warned that America's racial inequality and government bias could mirror the rise of Nazi Germany:

> The signs of a conspiracy are cropping up. A conspiracy whose present goal appears to be the destruction of the very possibility of education in this state. Now, I think it's significant—as I've said before—that the Regents chose me as a target of their attack. I think it's symbolic because Black members of the Communist Party are far, far from being the only Black people who are beginning to see that this society must be thoroughly transformed if we're going to solve these basic problems. [...]
>
> We have to ask ourselves whether we are going to make an effort now towards individual fulfillment or whether we're going to wage a fight for a more humane society. Whether we're going to create a strong defensive against what may very well become a mirror of fascism.[4]

After witnessing her activism firsthand, UCLA decided to part ways with Davis. The "Regents" to which she refers in her speech were UCLA's Board of Regents who, under advice from then California governor Ronald Reagan, implemented a policy banning professors with communist affiliations. They originally tried to fire Davis on the basis of her communist beliefs, but she appealed, and they were deemed to be insufficient grounds. The Board of Regents then changed tack and cited Davis's use of inflammatory speech as alternate grounds for dismissal. That approach stuck, and 1970 would be Davis's last year at her position.

---

[4] AfroMarxist, "Angela Davis and the Soledad Brothers (1971)," YouTube video, 56:31, November 9, 2019, https://www.youtube.com/watch?v=t_rKEP6cmcs.

Angela Davis and the Black Panthers. Later in 1970, Davis gained notoriety for being connected to a hostage-taking in a California courthouse.

During the trial of one James McClain, a Black Panther accused of stabbing a guard at San Quentin State Prison, a heavily armed Black youth burst into the courtroom carrying several guns. He tossed weapons to some of the defendants, including McClain, who were all prisoners from San Quentin. Together they took the presiding judge, the District Attorney, and three female jurors hostage. The armed youth demanded authorities release the so-called "Soledad brothers," three Panthers awaiting trial for murdering a White prison guard in Soledad State Prison. Despite the hostage situation, the police refused to negotiate.

The youth then led the defendants and hostages outside to his getaway van, where they attempted to flee. A shoot-out ensued. The young hostage-taker, Jonathan Jackson, sibling to one of the Soledad brothers, was shot dead by police, along with two of the defendants he tried to free. The judge for the trial, Harold Haley, was also shot dead during the melee.

Jonathan Jackson had used several firearms in the hostage-taking later discovered to have been purchased by Angela Davis. At just seventeen years of age, Jackson was too young to purchase the weapons, but at that time Davis was twenty-six. Davis was also already known to be affiliated with the Black Panthers. A warrant was issued for her arrest in connection to the crime under California law. In response, she suddenly disappeared. This led her to being posted on the FBI's most wanted list, which many of her supporters thought ridiculous given her academic background.

In a short time, she was found and captured in New York City. She was incarcerated in a woman's detention center, where she remained sixteen months. Her trial, which had been moved from Marin to Santa Clara County under a request for change of venue, included an all-White jury that found her not guilty.

Davis was lionized in the thriving New Left subculture of the time for having the guts to actively protest injustice in the prison system. Her disappearance, capture, and trial brought her instant stardom. For the remainder of her life, she was particularly vocal about the injustice toward Black prisoners, and in 1997, co-founded the Critical Resistance movement, dedicated to abolition of the Prison-Industrial Complex (PIC), a popular Black Lives Matter demand today. Davis's career continued in academia in various professorial roles.

Angela Davis is an absolutely critical link in the chain for Marxist development, both ideologically and methodologically. She was both directly taught in the Frankfurt School and directly involved in Black feminism and Black power movements on the street. This was the step "forward" Marcuse desired so badly, using what he called the "ghetto population," as we saw in *An Essay on Liberation*, realizing that after the near-miss in France 1968, communism's best chance in the United States would be to co-opt the more fringe aspects of the Civil Rights Movement. What Marxism really needed, what it really didn't have in the United States, was legitimacy. By stealing the fight for equality and the struggle for fair treatment from the Black population, Marxism could live on well past its expiry date.

Despite the significance of Davis to dialectical leftism, the direct line through Marcuse and the Frankfurt School was not the only way Marxist indoctrination reached American minds. That brings us to our next subject, a lawyer who would greatly influence critical legal studies and is considered the founder of critical race theory, Derrick Bell.

DERRICK BELL

Derrick Bell (1930–2011) was born in Pittsburgh, Pennsylvania and raised Christian (Presbyterian). The first of four children in a Black working-class family, Bell was also the first in his family's history to attend college. He enlisted in the armed forces in 1952 and served in Korea for a year as an Air Force servicemember. Although President Truman had issued the order to desegregate the armed forces in July 1948, all-Black units were still used during Korea. After returning, Bell completed his studies at the University of Pittsburgh (PITT). He was the only Black person to graduate with a Bachelor of Laws at PITT in 1957.

During his twenties, Bell watched the Civil Rights Movement with intense interest, especially the cases supervised by Thurgood Marshall (1908–1993), lead counsel for the National Association for the Advancement of Colored Persons (NAACP). Marshall represented the Brown family in *Brown v. Board of Education of Topeka* (1954) and was consulted for *Browder v. Gayle* (1956), two landmark cases of the Civil Rights Movement. Unfortunately, by the time Bell expressed his interest in becoming a civil rights lawyer, he was advised that he'd missed the boat.

> When I graduated law school in 1957, I went up to see Judge William Hastie, the first black federal judge—a very sophisticated man—and I told him my interest of being a civil rights lawyer. He said, "Derrick, praise-worthy, but you were born fifteen years too late. The Brown decision has been

decided. There is some mopping up to be done." What happens throughout history though [...] is that during economic good times or during national crises the recognition of the need for blacks to have basic rights increases. During economic bad times it goes down.[5]

Bell's analysis (from an interview in 1994) may be difficult to apply to the future. The George Floyd riots in 2020 did not occur during an economic good time but during one of the greatest contractions of the US economy in history, caused largely by the pandemic. That could instead be considered a crisis, which would fit Bell's model. Since that time, the economy in North America has struggled to find its footing and, in accordance with what Bell says above, there has been a marked shift of focus from rights for Blacks to the backburner by mainstream media.

Bell didn't typify a radical left activist. He spoke softly and concisely and was known for being very tolerant of opposing views. He didn't reveal any obvious sort of Neo-Marxist indoctrination, certainly nothing like Marcuse's repressive tolerance.

Though a generation late to litigate the key cases of the Civil Rights Movement, Bell did the next best thing. With further promotion of civil rights on the top of his agenda, Thurgood Marshall, who would eventually become the first African American appointed to the Supreme Court of the United States, hired Bell on as a member of the NAACP's Legal Defense Fund (LDF) in 1960.

Bell's job was to try desegregation cases in Mississippi, yet another state in the deep South notorious for anti-Black racism and violence. A great number of the school boards in the South were simply refusing to heed the ruling in *Brown* and continued to operate segregated schools. Bell was warned the job might cost him his life, and proceeded with a measure of caution. His civil rights legal career would include a total of over three hundred cases for the LDF, where he fought for the desegregation of schools. He was a civil rights lawyer in the clearest sense of the term, fighting the day-to-day struggle African Americans needed. There was ample proof that segregation in schools was harmful to Black children and their opportunities in the long term, although, according to Bell, that wasn't the real reason the *Brown* case succeeded.

---

[5] CUNY TV, "The Urban Agenda: Derrick Bell on Racism," YouTube video, 29:08, September 12, 2012, https://www.youtube.com/watch?v=RVy8w0Sz9LY.

CHAPTER TEN: CO-OPTING THE CIVIL RIGHTS MOVEMENT

After his time as a civil rights lawyer, Bell switched to academia, teaching law to others. He began a long but tumultuous career at Harvard Law School in 1969. He authored several books in which he shared his experience with racism as teaching aids to his courses, the most famous of which was *Race, Racism and American Law*, published in 1970.

It was around that time, when looking back at all the cases he tried on desegregation for the LDF, that he had an existential crisis. It seemed to Bell that despite all his efforts to enforce them, the legal and societal changes of the Civil Rights Movement were not changing attitudes toward Blacks. Over time, Bell came to believe that racism would reassert itself no matter what legal and societal changes occurred, and that the US was an irredeemably racist nation. He despaired that all the cases he had tried were in vain. He believed White families forced to go to school with Blacks had simply fled from those geographic areas where multi-racial schools existed, a cultural phenomenon colloquially labelled *White flight*, to try to reassert segregation insidiously.

The conspiratorial and permanent nature of racism that Bell perceived didn't come from just his experiences in the courtroom or from the Black families he worked with. Something Bell witnessed from outside those personal experiences affected him so deeply that he began to believe the US Civil Rights Movement emerged not as a result of an awakening to racism but as a pragmatic answer to the Cold War. He believed this so firmly that he wrote an article titled *"Brown vs. Board of Education and the Convergence Dilemma,"* published in the *Harvard Law Review* in 1980. Within that article, he explained three key reasons he believed were the real explanation for the success of the Civil Rights Movement in the courts. Among these, his discussion of the pragmatic decision to alleviate pressure from Russian propaganda, which had been pointing out America's racism before and during the Cold War, was paramount.

> First, the decision helped to provide immediate credibility to America's struggle with Communist countries to win the hearts and minds of emerging third world peoples. At least this argument was advanced by lawyers for both the NAACP and the federal government. And the point was not lost on the news media. Time magazine, for example, predicted that the international impact of Brown would be scarcely less important than its effect on black children: "In many countries, where US prestige and leadership have been damaged by the fact of

US segregation, it will come as a timely reassertion of the basic American principle that 'all men are created equal.'" ⁶

Although he believed the propagandists from the Soviet Union had shamed the US into the decision of *Brown*, Bell didn't seem to realize that it was instead possible that *he* was the one affected by that propaganda and not the US government. Why did he use that propaganda as part of his justification for the heavy criticism and devaluing of something as resoundingly good as the Civil Rights Movement?

In his article on the interest-convergence dilemma, he blames White people's greedy desire for industrial development in the South as one of the two other factors contributing to the Civil Rights Movement's success. The third he lists as addressing the hypocrisy coming out of WWII that Blacks who served were coming home to a racist country—a country that was not free to them, even though they were willing to die defending it.

It seems likely that Bell had been deeply affected by Soviet propagandists, who made a point of continually reminding those in the United States that they were hypocrites. Did he not realize that the whole purpose of Soviet Cold War propaganda was not to shame the US into bettering itself but to turn US citizens against each other, and especially against their government? Did he not realize he might be played in this fashion and performing a critical function of Soviet propaganda? It's clear that propaganda was specifically designed to inflame tensions by highlighting the biggest failures in US race-relations and to stymy any unification the Civil Rights Movement promised. An article remembering that sustained propaganda attack was published in the *New Yorker*:

> Armed with images of American racial hypocrisy, the Soviet Union had a damning counter to American criticism of its behavior in Eastern Europe. (As early as the 1931 Scottsboro trial, in which nine African American teen-agers were wrongfully convicted of raping two white women, the Soviets publicized examples of American racism internationally; the tactic became more common after the start of the Cold War.) ⁷

---

[6] D. A. Bell, "Brown v. Board of Education and the Interest-Convergence Dilemma," *Harvard Law Review*, 93(3), 518–533. 524, 1980, https://doi.org/10.2307/1340546.

[7] J. Cobb, "The Man Behind Critical Race Theory," *The New Yorker*, September 13, 2021, https://www.newyorker.com/magazine/2021/09/20/the-man-behind-critical-race-theory.

In fact, Bell's school of critical race theory (he is considered to be the founder by its current adherents) followed Marxist tenets from its very inception. The Soviet Union in the latter half of the 1950s was a Marxist-Leninist government under Nikita Khrushchev, and although he was no Stalinist, Khrushchev and the KGB did run the gamut of Marxist-Leninist subversion techniques, which they had discussed in concert with the Frankfurt School for some time: "While never officially supporting any party, the Institute entertained intensive research exchanges with the Soviet Union."[8]

We will discuss this in Chapter Thirteen, where we'll rely on the works of a defected KGB informant to explain the ins and outs. Propaganda is incredibly effective because it skirts laws and subverts the unwitting, whether they're brilliant like Bell or dull as dishwater. These techniques that might influence people, namely subversive actions that have not been clearly defined as threats to public safety, remain difficult to pin down in today's morally relativistic society.

When asked directly if he was Marxist, Bell claimed to have limited interest in such ideology. His works contain a different story, however, as they are—in the Marxist tradition—clearly focused on ruthless criticism:

> Criticism, as we in the movement for minority rights have every reason to learn, is a synonym for neither cowardice nor capitulation. It may instead bring awareness, always the first step toward overcoming still another barrier in the struggle for racial equality.[9]

Bell's application of the ruthless criticism of critical theory to matters of race would be amplified in a coming generation of his students. In the meantime, that criticism left the problem of destroying all the hard work of the Civil Rights Movement by reducing it to no more than virtue signalling. All this apparently conducted by a White elite, who pragmatically decided they'd better be able to show something was happening or be called out for who they were. It's hard to imagine that the deconstruction of the Civil Rights Movement by Bell (and then others) didn't also already demonstrate an adherence to the growing trend of postmodernism.

---

[8] C. Corradetti, s.v. "The Frankfurt School and Critical Theory," Internet Encyclopedia of Philosophy, retrieved November 5, 2023, from https://iep.utm.edu/critical-theory-frankfurt-school/.

[9] D. A. Bell, "Brown v. Board of Education and the Interest-Convergence Dilemma," *Harvard Law Review*, 93(3), 518–533. 533, 1980, https://doi.org/10.2307/1340546.

CHAPTER ELEVEN
CRITICAL LEGAL STUDIES VS. POSTMODERNISM

DERRICK BELL MAY have been the founder of critical race theory before it even received its name, but since his time, many lawyers and academics have carried on his work. Before CRT clearly emerged from those legal scholars, however, there was a radical movement developed in the US called critical legal studies (CLS), which materialized in 1977. It was a movement first constituted of legal activists who had lived through the Civil Rights Movement and joined in the anti-Vietnam protests along with the New Left.

In this chapter, the key focus is on the addition of postmodernism to dialectical leftism, which had stagnated. The end of the 1970s brought about the death of Marcuse and the New Left. Advanced industrial capitalism persisted, and society did not disintegrate.

The 1970s saw the shock and anger after the assassination of Martin Luther King fade into a series of incredible successes for Black Americans: the first Black university president was elected in 1970 (Dr. Clifton Wharton Jr.); the first Black Pulitzer Prize winner won in 1970 (Charles Gordone); the first Black player was inducted into the Baseball Hall of Fame in 1971 (Satchel Paige); the first Black person campaigned for the Democratic presidential nomination in 1972 (Shirley Chisholm); the first Black mayor of LA was elected in 1973 (Thomas Bradley); the first Black manager in Major League Baseball was hired in 1974 (Frank Robinson); and the first Black president of the American Historical Association was elected in 1975 (John Franklin). The Black community clearly didn't need Marxism to succeed.

But Marxism trudged on. A new breed of thinkers amalgamated in the lawyers and academics of the critical legal studies movement to apply the ruthless criticism of Marx to the law and subvert the state through legal means. This approach ended up being combined with new subcategories of postmodernism, including social constructivism and deconstructionism.

Postmodernism is well-represented in the unstable radical Michel Foucault, who began his academic career under Marxist training. Foucault's erratic personal life mirrored his intellectual activity, with increasingly unstable ideas being matched by increasingly dangerous behaviour. The postmodern focus on power relationships above all—even above truth—allowed Foucault to excuse his mad fantasies as normal. Foucault would die at an early age from AIDS and his constant throwing of caution to the wind. His contributions to postmodernism remained and provided the door to pass through the barrier of reality. That door was holding back Neo-Marxism from moving any further.

CRITICAL LEGAL STUDIES

Critical legal studies was an attempt to bring the Hegelian dialectic to bear on existing US law. It was the kind of ruthless criticism Marx was famous for, tearing through US state and federal law, looking for opportunity to revolutionize society. All in an apparently legal manner. This begs the question of why on earth anyone would willingly allow the angry, critical approach of Marx to burn up the law. What good would that do? Why didn't anyone stop CLS lawyers and their legal activism? Those activists wanted to overturn legal precedent to pit the citizenry against one another and especially against the government.

But that's not the "official" premise CLS was brought in with. CLS lawyers didn't have a giant banner saying, "Burn down the legal system!" But that's what they wanted to do. When CLS first began, however, nobody outside it would dare to suggest that lawyers, using Marxist ideology, were attempting to subvert the law. Instead, lawyers promoted CLS as a kind of saviour, used only to correct unjust laws. It was the law that was flawed—not Marxism. Remember what civil rights lawyer Derrick Bell said about the critical Marxist approach. It's so implicating it's worth repeating:

> Criticism, as we in the movement for minority rights have every reason to learn, is a synonym for neither cowardice nor

capitulation. It may instead bring awareness, always the first step toward overcoming still another barrier in the struggle for racial equality.[1]

Now it becomes clear what Bell was saying.

He was adamant criticism was useful in law because he didn't trust the law at all! He believed the law was "still another barrier in the struggle for racial equality," as it didn't address all people as equal in his eyes. He also believed that even if the law was changed in the best way possible, society would remain racist.

So the CLS lawyers came in under the false pretense that they would only attack laws that clearly promoted inequality. In reality, they would arbitrarily label one law or another as "unjust" or "racist." It's the same false pretense as calling people Nazis when they are clearly not, so you're justified in physically assaulting them. When CLS lawyers arbitrarily defined a law as unjust, they were then justified in overwriting or repealing that law. They could attack it without reserve.

The façade of CLS as a legitimate way to address inequality convinced many. It was easy enough to point to old laws, especially Jim Crow laws in the southern US, that were clearly racist, after which it wasn't hard to imagine that there was more racism to be rooted out. CLS lawyers were courageously aiming for the re-evaluating and re-writing of outdated, racist laws only. That's all. They were heroes. From the outside, that's what they were hoping to be viewed as. On the inside, they knew better.

Right now, Canada is going through this same Marxist revisionism, with legal activists and criminal defence lawyers claiming that parts of Canada's Criminal Code are outdated.[2,3] A recent Liberal bill also made bail hearings less onerous for Indigenous peoples, whose background judges must now bring into consideration when deciding bail.[4] While there are some older laws that clearly

---

[1] Ibid.

[2] K. Harris, "Experts Urge Liberals to Update 'Embarrassingly Bad' Criminal Code," CBC News: Politics, November 18, 2016, https://www.cbc.ca/news/politics/criminal-code-outdated-justice-discrimination-1.3853810

[3] "Canada's Criminal Code Is Outdated," Kruse Law: Criminal and DUI Lawyers, retrieved April 3, 2024 from https://www.kruselaw.ca/library/canada-s-criminal-code-is-outdated-kruse-law/.

[4] "Charter Statement - Bill C-75: An Act to Amend the Criminal Code, Youth Criminal Justice Act and other Acts and to Make Consequential Amendments to other Acts," Government of Canada, September 1, 2021, retrieved November 7, 2023, from https://www.justice.gc.ca/eng/csj-sjc/pl/charter-charte/c75.html.

did cause problems, the lack of concern about overwriting the Criminal Code is disturbing. Creating a two-tiered justice system based on race was a terrible idea and will hopefully be corrected soon. The law must not be a mechanism used to achieve equality of outcome.

The real intent of Marxist revisionism isn't to revise the law to make it more equitable. It's to overturn society, the same goal of all Marxist-based ideologies. CLS is no different. It's just the most docile-appearing attempt yet. There are no people smashing things on the streets. There are no vicious fights in schools and churches. If CLS reached its desired goal, it would be entirely legal to overturn society, and there wouldn't be anything we could do about it.

Marxists understood the ulterior motive to pushing forward with CLS. These CLSers were generally well-educated, linguistically gifted lawyers who knew the history of dialectical leftism inside and out. They realized CLS was another way to try and get to the revolution that had historically eluded Marxism. Trying to subvert a capitalist state had failed under Orthodox Marxism, as there was no uprising of the workers to overturn society. Neo-Marxism appeared like it would do better, as the takeover of culture or the cultural institutions, such as after the sexual revolution, caused incredible damage to institutions of civil society, especially the family, the Church, and marriage. But it didn't result in revolution. Marxists desperately needed a new method to try to achieve their goal.

That's not what any of them are going to admit, however.

Besides the US, the CLS movement saw a similar inception point within the United Kingdom just a few years after its American precursor began. Wherever it festered, CLS rejected the assumption of neutrality of the law, because that neutrality only reinforced the status quo. The status quo was bad, CLSers argued, because it was biased against minorities and therefore sustained inequality. The law, they believed, was not immune to politics. It had been created by rich White men during a time when slavery was widely accepted—and so it *must* be biased. Maintaining such an unequal law in today's day and age reinforced oppression. That oppression kept the poor and suffering in misery while keeping hierarchy of establishment in place.

CLSers saw the law as yet another tool of oppression. It was up to the activist lawyers to help citizens achieve a "critical legal consciousness," whereafter they would recognize the co-optation of the law (that the law was systemically racist) and seek its transformation. This entirely mirrors Marx's dialectical materialism, where the one pushing for revolution was the individual communist in a capitalist society. In the case of CLS, it would be a Marxist lawyer pushing to overturn the law. Professors Peter Fitzpatrick and Alan Hunt explain the Marxist purpose of CLS in the *Journal of Law and Society*:

> The central focus of the critical legal approach is to explore the manner in which legal doctrine and legal education and the practices of legal institutions work to buttress and support a pervasive system of oppressive, inegalitarian relations. Critical theory works to develop radical alternatives, and to explore and debate the role of law in the creation of social, economic, and political relations that will advance human emancipation.[5]

There it is, spelled out with some precision by the Critical Legal Conference, the mirror-movement formed in the UK. The British version of CLS was focused on a core of Marxism, feminism, and the critical theory of the Frankfurt School. The US movement also had those ideologies but additionally included concerns of legal activist lawyers focused on race, which caused further splits in critical legal theory as it grew. The different groups in CLS are explained by Harvard professor of law (emeritus) Mark Tushnet:

> At present one might describe the political location of critical legal studies as occupied by certain feminists ("fem-crits"), certain theorists concerned with the role of race in law (critical race theorists), a group influenced by recent developments in literary theory (postmodernists), [and] a group that stresses the role of economic structure in setting the conditions for legal decisions (political economists).[6]

SOCIAL CONSTRUCTIVISM

A postmodern influence was clearly and immediately evident in CLS, just as it was in the later writings of both Marcuse and Bell. Although a comprehensive discussion of postmodernism is far too involved and lengthy to be included herein, we will discuss it briefly in the next section of this chapter. We can also reveal that one of the most important and dangerous aspects sired by postmodernism was social constructivism.

---

[5] P. Fitzpatrick and A. Hunt, "Introduction," *Journal of Law and Society*, 14(1), 1–3. 1-2, 1987, https://doi.org/10.2307/1410292.

[6] M. Tushnet, "Critical Legal Studies: A Political History," *The Yale Law Journal*, 100(5), 1515–1544. 1518, 1991, https://doi.org/10.2307/796697.

Social constructivism is a philosophy that tends to believe nature and especially biology don't tell us anything about who we are. It also tells us that biological observations—such as "I have a nose"—don't count as knowledge gained. So, for example, social constructivism would suggest that just because a man has male genitalia doesn't prove he's a man. Instead, social interactions within society are how we learn about things, and this process of interaction between people constructs our very reality. In our example, that would mean that even if a man had male genitalia, we could make him a woman by talking about him as a woman and allowing him to refer to himself as a woman too. In social constructivism, the biological reality of the male genitalia is secondary to the power to control the narrative and force people to believe the man is a woman.

If you think about it, this is equating reality with a belief system—and could be used to argue for such ideologies as transgenderism—which believes that biology doesn't dictate what you are, and that gender is socially constructed. Social constructivists claim that many of the noticeable differences in gender are socially engineered as opposed to evidently attached to biology, anatomy, or chemistry.

Social constructivism is like moral relativity on steroids, because it really suggests there is no such thing as an absolute truth, since truth is secondary to power. Consider, for example, the coronavirus pandemic. During the pandemic, an attempt was made by those in authority to present a unified front on "the science," regarding both the danger of the coronavirus and the safety and necessity of the vaccine. It was a very dangerous thing to question "the science" at this time, because any individual who did so was attacked in mob-like fashion by leftists, medical technocrats, and the government, often through the existing legal framework.

The truth of the matter was that these authorities were pushing their knowledge with very limited and sometimes no scientific basis, largely because of the lack of time for appropriate testing and a lack of verifiable information. What was important during the pandemic proved to be listening to the authorities and not really listening to "the science," because scientific information lacked its hallmarks of hypothesizing, experimentation, and repeatability. The scientific method was abruptly streamlined. The coronavirus vaccine was clearly rushed through to completion, without the typical clinical trial time of five to ten years for vaccines.[7] A great deal of people got stuck in this postmodern trap, gladly

---

[7] "Vaccine Research & Development," Johns Hopkins University & Medicine, retrieved November 8, 2023, from https://coronavirus.jhu.edu/vaccines/timeline#:.

sucking up whatever the government told them, even if it was entirely opaque, authoritarian fearmongering.

Critical legal studies displays an obsession with the value of power over the value of the truth, one we also find in postmodernism and social constructivism. They're just like the example of pandemic management, where power to control people was more important than the truth of what they were being given. In fact, postmodernism is in direct contradiction (an *antithesis*) to Neo-Marxism and Marxism in general. Why is this so?

As we saw in previous chapters, Marxists believe that throughout history, there is indeed an absolute, unchanging truth, hidden in the organization of the state. That is the communist utopia they seek. That's why Hegel's dialectic remains so important to them: it continues critical thinking by addressing an ideology's contradictions. It transcends those contradictions during a synthesis process (or *aufgehoben*) to move one step closer to the golden nugget of truth at the end of the rainbow.

POSTMODERNISM IS A LEPRECHAUN

For postmodernists, every path claiming it leads to the truth, whether it's Marxism, capitalism, Christianity, etc., is like the rainbow that leads us to a pot of gold. It's a complete waste of time. If you've ever chased a rainbow, you'll understand why. In chasing a rainbow, you'll quickly learn that it changes when you move too much, often disappearing entirely. It's impossible to get to the end of a rainbow. Postmodernists likewise look at all sorts of ideologies and theologies as promising to lead you to the truth, but upon approaching that truth, never finds it.

What postmodernists really believe in is the power ... of the leprechaun. That's because the leprechaun actually buried the pot of gold, and that means it's in a fixed location somewhere on the ground that only he knows. Trying to get to the pot of gold by the rainbow never works. You must capture the leprechaun to find the pot of gold, because only he knows where it's really buried. The leprechaun has all the power in this situation and thus controls what the truth is and if you will ever find it, or if it will remain buried.

Within CLS, there was a contest to see whether the Marxist or postmodern approach would be used as CLS progressed. The battle between Marxism and postmodernism was summarized as far back as 1987 by Fitzpatrick and Hunt: "A rough characterisation of this controversy is that of the issues joined between 'critique,' drawing heavily on Marxism and critical social theory, and 'postmodernism' drawing on Foucault and deconstruction, for example."[8]

They also point out that approaching the 1990s, it wasn't clear who was going to "triumph" between Neo-Marxism and postmodernism: "It is far too early to summarize this engagement, let alone to announce the triumph of one side or the other or to celebrate a successful synthesis."[9]

MICHEL FOUCAULT

The postmodern philosopher Michel Foucault (1926–1984), who is strongly connected to the social constructivism we're concerned with, was steeped in dialectical thinking from his youth. Although he would never be classified as an Orthodox Marxist, many of his beliefs stemmed from the approach of historicism. Foucault's tutor during university, the Hegelian and Marxian expert Jean Hyppolite (1907–1968), clearly influenced Michel toward Marxist studies. With Hyppolite as his supervisor, Foucault's master's thesis was titled *The Constitution of a Historical Transcendental in Hegel's Phenomenology of Spirit*.

As well as his interest in Hegel, Foucault read for himself the works of Nietzsche, Marx, Kant, and Heidegger. Foucault's influencers therefore fell strongly in line with those of Herbert Marcuse. After completing his thesis with Hyppolite, Foucault began tutoring under Marxist philosopher Louis Althusser (1918–1990), who tried to convince Michel to become a communist in word and deed by joining their official party in France. Although Foucault joined the French Communist Party and remained a member for three years, he eventually left because of the party's blatant hatred toward Jews and homosexuals. That sounds very much like another totalitarian regime of which the average individual is abundantly more aware.

Foucault was very openly homosexual (long before it was generally socially acceptable), and he had many partners with whom he didn't practise safe sex. He frequently experimented with mind-altering drugs and sadomasochism. From a young age, he had a disturbing penchant for violence and was given to fits of self-harm that required psychiatric treatment. Foucault's carefree lifestyle eventually caught up with him. He died of complications due to AIDS at the age of fifty-seven.

---

[8] P. Fitzpatrick and A. Hunt, "Introduction," *Journal of Law and Society*, 14(1), 1–3. 1–2, 1987, https://doi.org/10.2307/1410292

[9] Ibid.

Some of his most controversial ideas included signing a depraved application to the government of France attempting to lower the age of consent for sexual intercourse, as he believed children could consent to adults in this manner. Foucault's social constructivist beliefs had no limits. He believed you could make whatever reality you wanted by creating the social interactions that would materialize it, beginning at the smallest possible level, between two people. His belief in social constructivism was probably to some degree a coping mechanism to help him deal with his obvious fondness for violence, sadomasochism, and other deranged fantasies he possessed. His personality and beliefs were so off-putting they often surprised others.

After participating in a televised debate against Foucault in 1971, where they argued over the nature of humanity, the popular intellectual Noam Chomsky (1928–) confessed: "He struck me as completely amoral, I'd never met anyone who was so totally amoral [...] I mean, I liked him personally, it's just that I couldn't make sense of him. It's as if he was from a different species, or something."[10]

Let us return to the pitched battle between Neo-Marxism and postmodernism within CLS. Of course, those who understand the dialectic will know there is never really a clear winner in a synthesis, but Fitzpatrick and Hunt believed it was still possible that one of the two—Neo-Marxism or postmodernism—might triumph unabated. As we learned, a synthesis involves taking aspects from both preceding ideologies, while also containing aspects of neither. If it took absolutely none of the tenets of one of the ideologies, it wouldn't be a synthesis—it would be a wipeout. An obliteration perhaps not recorded in the annals of history because it was too brief or too insignificant to mount a resistance. Yet the battle between postmodernism and Neo-Marxism hasn't seen a wipeout of one or the other, and, at least according to Dr. James Lindsay, a synthesis occurred in something called the theory of intersectionality, which we will discuss in just a moment. Intersectionality turned out to be based on a synthesis of Neo-Marxism and postmodernism, and thus is the ultimate "winner" (if one had to be chosen) in the tension between those two ideologies within the CLS movement.

---

[10] Wikipedia, s.v. "Michel Foucault," July 2, 2023, https://en.wikipedia.org/wiki/Michel_Foucault.

CHAPTER TWELVE
WOKE IDEOLOGY

IT WAS A student of Derrick Bell's, ironically during his self-imposed absence from Harvard University in the early 1980s, who would take on the reins of the dialectic and officially synthesize the ideologies of Neo-Marxism and postmodernism, blowing the whole CLS movement out of the water.[1] After all, many of the original scholars involved in CLS were White males, and the growing focus in the US on feminism, civil rights, poverty, and especially race made them completely at odds with a rising critique from Black feminists.

Enter Kimberlé Crenshaw, a critical legal theorist with cunning and a particular understanding of propaganda. She was able to take the next step on the dialectical journey and help foment a revolution where none was warranted.

In this chapter, the most important take-home points are that Neo-Marxism and postmodernism synthesized to make the most current form of dialectical leftism, known as the woke ideology. That synthesis was officially conducted by critical legal theorist and lawyer Kimberlé Crenshaw. The reader should make it a point to have an at least cursory understanding of the two theories that drive the woke ideology.

Crenshaw was instrumental in the creation of the woke ideology's two biggest theories, which are used as the basis for pursuing dialectical leftism within the institutions of civil society today. The first, known as intersectionality, argues for multiple dimensions of oppression to be recognized by the law. In this

---

[1] Bell left Harvard in 1980 to be the dean at the University of Oregon law school, and resigned his position at Harvard officially five years later in protest. J. Cobb, "The Man Behind Critical Race Theory," *The New Yorker*, September 13, 2021, https://www.newyorker.com/magazine/2021/09/20/the-man-behind-critical-race-theory.

fashion, it's possible to subvert the law by rewriting it to enforce equality of outcome for all marginalized groups, including those groups suffering compounded oppression (marginalized in multiple categories, especially including race, gender, sexual orientation, and wealth).

The second, called critical race theory, was a continuation of Derrick Bell's seminal work and created the theoretical basis for identity politicking—a favourite weapon of politicians and activists today. Under Crenshaw's guidance, critical race theory is a weapon to use in courts, government, and schools to indoctrinate the newest generations into those who believe systemic oppression is everywhere. This is a way to subvert civil society, as CRT posits White supremacy permeates its institutions, which were set up to maintain the status quo to enforce hierarchy. The law is not neutral as many claim it to be but keeps rich White males in power, just as Jim Crow laws did.

KIMBERLÉ CRENSHAW

Today, Kimberlé Crenshaw is a professor of law at Columbia University and a distinguished professor of law at Harvard. She taught law at UCLA from 1986–2017 (for thirty-two years!), where she developed a great deal of the theory she's known for today. She's been the director for the Center for Intersectionality and Social Policy Studies since 2011, and the executive director for the African American Policy Forum since 1996, both at Columbia University. She's been a guest speaker at numerous events and had a TED talk in 2016 titled "The Urgency of Intersectionality."[2] Despite all these rather fantastic sounding credentials, Kimberlé Crenshaw is, above all, a simple propagandist.

Crenshaw was born in Canton, Ohio on May 5, 1959. Even as a youth, she was able to confound her parents when they made simple demands, such as that she share her daily learning experiences with them. Even in tidbits about her life she reveals, Crenshaw aims to push Black feminist propaganda, making herself a victim. Consider one of her stories as related in *The Guardian*:

> Crenshaw knew from a young age that she wanted to be a lawyer. When she was six, she was sent to church with her 14-year-old brother. It was summer and her dad told them to stay together.

---

[2] "Kimberlé Crenshaw: The Urgency of Intersectionality," TED, November 14, 2016, https://www.ted.com/talks/kimberle_crenshaw_the_urgency_of_intersectionality?language=en.

But her brother wanted to leave early and use their collection money to buy sweets. They took their time walking home, enjoying the goodies, not realising their parents would go to the church to pick them up. When Crenshaw got home and saw her parents were not there, it was clear there would be trouble. But, she says, "it never occurred to me in a million years that I would get in trouble, because I was following his orders." She argued to her dad that this was in a lose-lose situation for her: she was in trouble for following her brother's rules, but she would also have been in trouble if she had not gone with him. In the end, her father told everyone: "'Don't let her get a word in edgewise. When she starts to talk, you will not know what you were trying to say.' And that's when they started calling me a lawyer." [3]

It's telling that Crenshaw blames the patriarchy—even in her own childhood story. She learned early on what playing-up victimhood does, and she regularly omits the most contradicting alternative in her stories: to take accountability for one's own actions.

A childhood story is perfect propaganda material because a child must be a victim in an anecdote containing only adults and older siblings. Crenshaw's deterministic view that we are slapped into our circumstances under a brutal patriarchy (usually a White supremacist patriarchy, but her dad and brother in this example) is oppression-centred Marxist thinking. To her, it's the reason society is so corrupt: there's just so much inequality, especially when it's compounded like in Crenshaw's circumstance, born both Black and female. That means the deck is stacked against her. She therefore doesn't want to play with the cards she's been dealt. She doesn't want a re-deal either. She wants an entirely new deck and, perhaps, a change of dealer. Jane Coaston, a political reporter for *Vox*, sums it up thusly: "… Crenshaw isn't seeking to build a racial hierarchy with black women at the top. Through her work, she's attempting to demolish racial hierarchies altogether."[4]

---

[3] A. Mohdin, "Kimberlé Crenshaw: The Woman Who Revolutionised Feminism—and Landed at the Heart of the Culture Wars," *The Guardian*, November 12, 2020, https://www.theguardian.com/society/2020/nov/12/kimberle-crenshaw-the-woman-who-revolutionised-feminism-and-landed-at-the-heart-of-the-culture-wars.

[4] J. Coaston, "The Intersectionality Wars," Vox. May 28, 2019, https://www.vox.com/the-highlight/2019/5/20/18542843/intersectionality-conservatism-law-race-gender-discrimination.

PART III: THE VINE SUFFOCATES

Demarginalizing the intersection of race and sex. Crenshaw was responsible for one of the most significant contributions to the culture of victimhood ruling today. As a Black woman, she was able to officially put a name to the compounded oppression she and other Black females were suffering. She called it "intersectionality," because it was an intersection—like where two streets cross— of being oppressed as a woman (street number one) and of being oppressed for being Black (street number two).

In her paper *Demarginalizing the Intersection of Race and Sex* (1989), Crenshaw used legal examples to argue that it was on many occasions insufficient for a Black woman to make allegations of discrimination under the premise of *either* womanhood *or* being Black. Instead, there must be an ability for the courts to assess allegations of discrimination that are intersectional, such as the concomitant racism and sexism that occurs against those who are Black *and* female.

Problems with her approach are revealed in her chosen cases for supporting evidence in the paper, which were *DeGraffenreid v. General Motors* (1976), *Moore v. Hughes Helicopter* (1988), and *Payne v. Travenol* (1982). We will look at each example briefly, in turn.

At the time her paper was published, her most important case, *DeGraffenreid*, was over a decade old. It's now approaching the fifty-year mark but remains her most important case citation (see her 2016 TED talk, for example, where she still uses it).[5] Throughout this section, we will discuss why citing cases of racial injustice in perpetuity is problematic.

In *DeGraffenreid*, General Motors (GM) had not hired any Black females at a plant they owned during the 1970s. In fact, GM as a company had only begun hiring Black women in 1964. At the time of the case, they had hired both Black men and White women at the plant in question, so they met antidiscrimination laws that individually specified hiring for those marginalized groups (women and Blacks). However, they did this without actually hiring anyone who was both marginalized groups at the same time. They had never hired a Black woman.

The first and biggest problem with this case is that it aims for equality of outcome for marginalized groups because it assumes that before concerns of qualification are addressed, a company should be hiring marginalized groups in amounts that reflect the current society. Those who instead argue for meritocracy (aiming for equality of opportunity) would instantly be met with vociferous

---

[5] "Kimberlé Crenshaw: The Urgency of Intersectionality," TED, November 14, 2016, https://www.ted.com/talks/kimberle_crenshaw_the_urgency_of_intersectionality?language=en.

criticism from the left and mainstream media. Political-left stances purport that a Black woman is at a huge disadvantage in modern society because a hierarchy of White males dominate business and share their business with each other exclusively, if unchecked.

Today, that paranoid conspiracy theory is spouted as *White supremacy*, which finds limited popular support in a country like Canada but has obtained significant traction in the US. That's because despite creating abolitionist laws before Canada (the British Empire) did in the North, the American South held on to slavery for a long time, and even made it a serious point of contention in the American Civil War (1861–1865). That history of slavery and racism has branded the US, and despite its age, is recalled frequently in the name of equity. Crenshaw wants to specifically open a new dimension on that call for equity, a call she believes is forgotten for Black women. To get equity, she makes claims of victimhood in perpetuity.

The word "perpetuity" is used because a lot of the worst incidents of racism that Derrick Bell, Kimberlé Crenshaw, Patricia Williams (1951–), and other critical race theorists cite have no expiration date. There is no statute of limitations on racism to these theorists and the activists who support such causes. Their argument for perpetuation relies on the conspiracy theory that there is an implicit goal of White supremacy, which doesn't have to be in writing, that sees to it that rich White males support each other and ensure their hierarchy continues uninterrupted. This they do by maintaining the status quo in law (as we discussed with critical legal studies) because that law was written by rich White men during a time when slavery was socially acceptable.

How critical race theorists effectively maintain such claims in perpetuity—without people losing interest in them—is by linking traumatic events, however old and out-of-touch with today's reality they might be, through the emotions they illicit. This is why you can't read an interview on Crenshaw without her mentioning an incident like the lynching of Emmet Till (1941–1955), who was murdered, mutilated, and dumped in a river, all apparently for offending a White woman at a grocery store in Mississippi. Crenshaw resurrects this hideous racist incident in her *Guardian* article cited above.

This is why critical theorists often minimize the Civil Rights Movement. They would rather focus on violent and divisive incidents, like the lynching of Till, to promote their cause. The Civil Rights Movement was non-violent, successful, and didn't allow for claims of victimhood in perpetuity. If you believe the Civil Rights Movement made progress in its form of non-violent revolution, you're saying that there's a resolution that doesn't fit G.W.F. Hegel's historicism or Karl Marx's lust for violence. That's why Herbert Marcuse tried to undermine the Civil Rights Movement by writing *An Essay on Liberation* in 1969, wherein he attempted to goad Black people into a violent revolution he thought would result in "real" change. That's why critical race theorists like Derrick Bell and Kimberlé Crenshaw attempt to minimize the effects of the Civil Rights Movement whenever they speak about it. It's a direct affront to their whole violent, revolutionary way of thinking: that the system is so corrupt, it must be completely torn down before it can be rebuilt.

As we saw in the quote above from *Vox*, Crenshaw is "attempting to demolish racial hierarchies altogether." Marcuse, of whose Neo-Marxist work Crenshaw was a student in CLS, insisted this revolution would necessarily be a violent process. How exactly does Crenshaw plan to "demolish" hierarchy? Has she found some secret, non-violent adaptation of Marcuse's method she's not sharing with us?

Crenshaw's second legal example in *Demarginalizing*, *Moore v. Hughes Helicopter (1988)*, brings to light one of the most disturbing implications of CRT. In that case, we can see exactly how CRT replaces the value system of meritocracy with intersectional claims of victimhood.

In *Moore*, the plaintiff, a Black woman, claimed that her employer demonstrated both racist and sexist discrimination in promotion choices. Her attempt to obtain a certification order as a representative of her class, which is required for a class action lawsuit in the US, fell apart in court. Crenshaw attempted to blame this failure on discrimination by the court. What really prevented the plaintiff from obtaining a certification order, however, was that she presented her original complaint to the Equal Employment Opportunity Commission (EEOC) as discrimination against Black women. She was therefore implying a need to be certified as a class representative of Black women in court.

When the plaintiff went before the court, however, she suddenly wanted to change to addressing the company's discrimination against *all* women, not just Black women, as she originally complained to the EEOC. The company's bias against all women promised her the highest chance of a favourable verdict in a class action suit. Her approach of changing her class representation suggested a level of opportunism where the ends justified the means (winning a suit against the company however she could). Despite this, the court didn't believe she could simply switch from aiming for certification as a class representative for Black women to a class representative for all women because she had changed this suddenly and not approached with it from the outset.

Like any good propagandist, Crenshaw cleverly works her way around this reality by claiming that it was the court's fault (not the plaintiff) for being unable to see that a victim in two classes (Blacks *and* women) should be able to represent and be certified for either of those two classes (Blacks *or* women), which the court would have allowed had they adopted Crenshaw's theory of intersectionality. In her attempt to change class representation, the plaintiff appeared inconsistent and dishonest before the court, thus tripping herself up to the point where both the certification and her subsequent appeal were denied.

To Crenshaw, the plaintiff's inconsistency and opportunism don't make a lick of difference. Because the plaintiff was Black, Crenshaw believes she should have been given more leeway to change class representation. This represents Crenshaw's desire for a two-tiered justice system, which would completely subvert a legal system that is supposed to view all as equal.

This case also points out the double-standard in Crenshaw's ideology. Crenshaw's beliefs are completely at odds with her claim that the critical feminist (fem-crit) perspective is centred around White woman only and can't possibly represent all women. She doesn't believe a woman plaintiff who is "White" should be able to represent all women, particularly women of colour. Why is it that, according to Crenshaw, a Black woman's perspective should be acceptable to represent all women, while a "White" woman's perspective should not? Again, it has to do with power relationships. The White supremacy conspiracy theory makes Blacks into a subordinated (oppressed) group, and that means "Whites" can't represent Blacks. That's a double standard that says it's acceptable to Crenshaw to give more power, or weight, to the person who is classified higher on the victimhood scale by having more classes that are subordinate.

The final case Crenshaw cites is *Payne vs. Travenol* (1982). In this case, two Black women came forward to sue a pharmaceutical plant they claimed demonstrated racist hiring practices. They sought certification as class representatives for all Blacks but were denied by the court. The court explained that statistical disparity between Black males and Black females, particular to the case, meant that Black females couldn't accurately represent the class of Black males. When the plaintiffs learned this, they requested to represent only the class of Black females, which the court granted certification for. The plaintiffs went on to win their suit, and backpay for Black women at the plant, as the court found substantial evidence of discrimination against the class of Black women had been conducted by the pharmaceutical company.

This ruling irked many, including Crenshaw, because she believes that Black women automatically have a right to represent Black men as part of the overall class of *all Blacks*. She believes the findings of discrimination should have been projected onto the class of Black men, and that they too should receive backpay. Such an outcome is acceptable to her because she ranks Black women higher on the victimhood scale than Black men, because they have two oppressed classes to represent versus the Black man's one. This is a problem for Crenshaw's whole theory of intersectionality, because she wouldn't allow Black men to represent all Blacks, because they wouldn't adequately represent the class of Black women, who suffer more oppression.

The citations Crenshaw makes in her seminal paper on intersectionality, as important as they must be considered for their exposition of racism, are rendered as spin-doctored propaganda by the theory of intersectionality. The first and most egregious fiction is the existence of White supremacy, a paranoid conspiracy theory based on historical racism and historical racist incidents cited in perpetuity. To be sure, racism exists today, but to assume it exists implicit in the law and other institutions as some grand conspiracy that keeps down Blacks is simply not true. Racism exists today on the margins of society, not as a mainstream movement or framework. It is rightly exposed and chastised where it is found. Some people simply believe it can be found under every rock.

The second problem with *Demarginalizing* is the new hierarchy Crenshaw's theory of intersectionality wishes to create, in hopes of overtaking the current supposed White supremacist patriarchy. Even if temporary, it would be a very large problem to impose—because people do not exist in the categories of privilege she presupposes. She argues that people who dare to critique intersectionality are simply buying into it, since it must mean they are White supremacist males at the top of the patriarchy who are afraid to lose their positions. Let's look at how she explains it:

> "When you're going to sign on to a particular critique by rolling out your identity, exactly how was your identity politics different from what you're trying to critique?" Crenshaw said. "It's just a matter of who it is, that's what you seem to be most concerned about."
>
> [...]

To Crenshaw, the most common critiques of intersectionality—that the theory represents a "new caste system"—are actually affirmations of the theory's fundamental truth: that individuals have individual identities that intersect in ways that impact how they are viewed, understood, and treated. Black women are both black and women, but because they are black women, they endure specific forms of discrimination that black men, or white women, might not.[6]

Crenshaw's counterargument to critiques of intersectionality is essentially: *if you critique my system, you are buying into it*. While that is clever lawyering, it's not true at all. In fact, people who already exist outside of the fantasy of White supremacy and realize that they don't have special privileges have a right to be concerned at losing whatever equal standing they currently have under the law.

For instance, affirmative action can result in discrimination and was recently found by the Supreme Court of the United States (SCOTUS) to be unconstitutional.[7] This is not playing into identity politics, as Crenshaw cleverly suggests, but is asking to maintain equality. In the SCOTUS case referenced above, it's asking to remove race from consideration in college admissions. Critiquing intersectionality can be based on a difference in underlying assumptions. Crenshaw's White supremacy assumption is the biggest, most problematic one of all. Crenshaw reduces and dehumanizes individuals to class relations so that they can be pigeonholed as either oppressor or oppressed, sometimes in multiple classes, and be used to further her agenda. The oppressed are then given the value and power to affect the courts more dramatically from their ability to represent multiple classes of oppression to which they belong. It's an attempt to literally turn society on its head, if it were really ruled by White supremacist patriarchs, as opposed to the rich and powerful of today. It relies on the fiction of White supremacy to validate its illogical and unfair approach.

The final problem with this work is that we see the ends justify the means. She was perfectly okay in the example of *Moore* with having the court forced to overturn its procedure to fit the highest chances of success for the Black woman

---

[6] J. Coaston, "The Intersectionality Wars," Vox. May 28, 2019, https://www.vox.com/the-highlight/2019/5/20/18542843/intersectionality-conservatism-law-race-gender-discrimination.

[7] D. Mangan, "Supreme Court Rejects Affirmative Action at Colleges as Unconstitutional," CNBC. June 29, 2023, from https://www.cnbc.com/2023/06/29/supreme-court-rejects-affirmative-action-at-colleges-says-schools-cant-consider-race-in-admission.html.

plaintiff. She avoided discussing her motivation in her advocacy, which was the success of the class action suit, instead hiding under the premise that the existing law was racist. Crenshaw believed a racist law was why the case went the way it did, as opposed to the law seeking consistency in procedure.

While each of the cases cited had legitimacy and advanced in some sense the understanding of the law and race-relations, they were each propagandized to promote the "greater good" of having Crenshaw's theory of intersectionality more widely accepted. The greater good must be advanced. The ends justified the means, and Marcuse is happy that message wasn't lost on his student.

Mapping the margins. In the Canadian Parliament, often televised live, viewers moan and groan when we witness yet another identity politicking foray by the Trudeau Liberals. It's a tired MO, where the grits attempt to either defame a group they claim has mistreated minorities or raise their own profile, ostensibly for having aided such minorities. The most infamous of these identity politic attempts is to cry "racist!" Identity politics is not just the most current and divisive tactic of the Canadian government, either. It's among the most dominant conversations in Western governments right now.

How did identity politics get to be so prominent?

If Crenshaw's seminal paper on intersectionality rocked the boat of identity politics, her second effort, two years later, would capsize it. "Mapping the Margins" (1991) is a fifty-nine-page journal article drowning in citations, chock-full of conjecture, and near void of statistics or eye-witness reports. It's a popular paper, cited over 1,400 times. You'd think it therefore had some ground-breaking addition to the overall discussion on intersectionality.

Yet, in truth, the content of Mapping the Margins is at least half-comprised of repetition and rewording of what Crenshaw stated in *Demarginalizing* back in 1989. The focus remains on tearing away from perspectives and policies of anti-racism and feminism, two classical liberal ideologies, since, according to Crenshaw, neither is capable of addressing the intersection of two dimensions of victimhood at the same time. The primary victim remains "women of colour" who, as subordinates in two classes (race and gender), are doubly oppressed. Crenshaw explains:

> Because women of colour experience racism in ways not always the same as those experienced by men of colour, and sexism in ways not always parallel to experiences of white women,

dominant conceptions of antiracism and feminism are limited, even on their own terms.[8]

The new spin promised in "Mapping the Margins" is to expound upon the experiences of women of colour. That might be a good thing if considered in a broad, humanizing context. As wide a range of experience as anybody can have in life, however, in her work Crenshaw reduces individuals through a Marxist lens, always defining a person as oppressor or oppressed. For women of colour, this means Crenshaw attempts to dive into the most extreme negative experiences imposed upon those women, specifically rape and battery. These are particularly poignant choices because such extreme examples illicit emotions, which often distorts rational thinking, a thought process we explain in more detail in Chapter Fifteen under the heading "Emotional Reasoning."

Despite the hefty length of the paper, Crenshaw proved unable to provide any statistics on rape and battery, a failure she conveniently passed on to both the police (a White supremacist institution, to her understanding) and the communities of colour she believes to be ruled by patriarchy. Here is how she passed the buck:

> I attempted to review the Los Angeles Police Department statistics reflecting the rate of domestic violence interventions by precinct because such statistics can provide a rough picture of arrests by racial group, given the degree of racial segregation in Los Angeles. L.A.P.D. however, would not release the statistics. A representative explained that one reason the statistics were not released was that domestic violence activists both within and outside the Department feared the statistics reflecting the extent of domestic violence in minority communities might be selectively interpreted and publicized so as to undermine long-term efforts to force the Department to address domestic violence as a serious problem. I was told that activists were worried that the statistics might permit opponents to dismiss domestic violence as a minority problem and, therefore, not deserving of aggressive action.[9]

---

[8] K. Crenshaw, "Mapping the Margins: Intersectionality, Identity Politics, and Violence against Women of Color," *Stanford Law Review*, 43(6), 1241–1299. 1252, 1991, https://doi.org/10.2307/1229039.

[9] Ibid.

There was another reason those police service members didn't want to release sensitive information on the lives of people of colour. It's important to realize that the July 1991 publication of "Mapping the Margins" couldn't have been more apropos. In March of that year, a local Los Angeles television studio, KTLA, played amateur footage they had received of African-American Rodney King being brutally beaten by a group of LAPD officers. The grainy footage of King being beaten to a pulp lasted several minutes.

King had been speeding down the interstate in San Fernando Valley, Los Angeles, driving drunk with two of his friends as passengers. When the California Highway Patrol (CHP) saw him speeding, they gave chase and attempted to pull him over. King refused to stop his vehicle because he was drunk. He also had several priors, including assault, battery, and a robbery, for which he was on parole. He knew a DUI would be a violation of his probation. His foolhardy attempt to outrun the police only resulted in a cavalcade of CHP and then LAPD cars chasing him down the interstate. Eventually, a police helicopter joined the chase, putting a searchlight on King's car.

When King was finally forced to pull over, he was the last of the three to exit his vehicle. He was instructed to lie on the street, after which one of the most vicious assaults by police ever recorded immortalized him being tased, beaten savagely with billy clubs, and kick-stomped in what looked like a modern-day lynching. The officers attacking King were all either White or Hispanic and were surrounded by over a dozen officers standing and watching the horror show.

In March 1991, at the time of the Rodney King beating in Los Angeles, Crenshaw was an acting professor at UCLA, where she had been teaching for five years. By July of that year, the same month "Mapping the Margins" was published in the *Stanford Law Review*, she was promoted to full professor. When Crenshaw asked the LAPD for a contribution to her 1991 paper, it's entirely possible it was during the very sensitive time after March, when the release of the King video had minority communities up in arms, but before July, when "Mapping the Margins" was first published. In fact, the typical academic paper requires only about three months from written completion to be reviewed and printed, and that's very close to the exact time between the beating of Rodney King and the publishing of the article.

Though she doesn't mention it in her paper, it's possible that the police rejected her request for statistics for fear of further inflaming racial tensions

CHAPTER TWELVE: WOKE IDEOLOGY

between the LAPD and minority communities, in addition to the reasons she supplies (or instead of them). Police brutality was a long-standing issue in Los Angeles, associated with the push against gangs since at least the mid-1980s.

Four of the LAPD officers directly involved in the beating were charged with excessive force. They were tried in the spring of 1992, approximately a year after the incident. Racial tensions remained high, and although the LAPD had anticipated trouble once a verdict was released, they weren't adequately prepared for what happened next. All four of the accused police officers were acquitted of all charges. Within several hours, South Los Angeles erupted into anarchism. It got so bad so quickly that the National Guard was called in.

> Residents set fires, looted and destroyed liquor stores, grocery stores, retail shops and fast food restaurants. Light-skinned motorists—both white and Latino—were targeted; some were pulled out of their cars and beaten.
>
> [...]
>
> During the five days of unrest, there were more than 50 riot-related deaths—including 10 people who were shot and killed by LAPD officers and National Guardsmen. More than 2,000 people were injured, and nearly 6,000 alleged looters and arsonists were arrested.[10]

It was an incredible coincidence that Crenshaw's paper popped out almost exactly three months, the time required to bring a written piece to publishing, after King's savage beating. Yet as far as propaganda goes, that would be as quick a timing as possible for Crenshaw to get her paper out after witnessing the terrible event and trying to capitalize on the emotional damage it spread. It's entirely possible that was the impetus for her publishing of "Mapping the Margins," as she makes clear in a footnote on its very first page that the paper had already existed for some time and was being used in her workshops: "Earlier versions of this article were presented to the Critical Race Theory Workshop and the Yale Legal Theory Workshop."[11]

---

[10] A. S. Krbechek and K. G. Bates, "When LA Erupted in Anger: A Look Back at the Rodney King Riots," NPR. April 6, 2017, https://www.npr.org/2017/04/26/524744989/when-la-erupted-in-anger-a-look-back-at-the-rodney-king-riots.

[11] K. Crenshaw, "Mapping the Margins: Intersectionality, Identity Politics, and Violence against Women of Color," *Stanford Law Review*, 43(6), 1241–1299. 1252, 1991, https://doi.org/10.2307/1229039.

Despite claiming to focus on women of colour's experiences with rape and battery, the paper contains just a single anecdote on that subject, with absolutely no broader statistics on rape or battery researched by Crenshaw herself—none. That's an incredibly glaring hole in a work that's supposed to represent experiences of coloured women. But the paper isn't about science or law; it's about propaganda and identity politics—spreading the narrative of victimhood.

We get this propaganda in Crenshaw's assessment of other people's words—people that disagree with her theory—not from the victims of rape and battery. In the paper she demonizes Senator David Boren for some ill-chosen phrases that demonstrated his subtle racism by "othering" women of colour. She criticizes the CBS investigative program *48 hours* for their exposé on domestic violence, because they marginalize a woman of colour's experience in her view. She criticizes the feminist perspective of rape as inadequate to represent women of colour in her view. She criticizes the media for sensationalizing interracial crime, claiming it negatively affects people of colour in her view. She recounts racial injustices, including Emmett Till and the Scottsboro Boys, nine African American teenagers who were wrongfully convicted of raping two White women in 1931.[12,13] She cites the celebrity rape case example of Desiree Washington against Mike Tyson, opining how a woman of colour is marginalized in relation to a man of colour because of the patriarchy in coloured communities, in her view.[14] She even spends several pages analyzing why rappers 2 Live Crew were arrested in Florida for their violent, misogynist lyrics.[15] That was racist in her view. All this endless propaganda, her views, with very little words and absolutely no statistics from her own work regarding the women of colour Crenshaw claims to represent in the paper.

The purpose of "Mapping the Margins" is ultimately subtly revealed right from its outset, but one can only assess this after completing the entire slapdash effort. Right from the get-go, Crenshaw advises that it's essential to "embrace identity politics." Recall, if you can after all this bafflegab, that is exactly how we began discussing "Mapping the Margins."

---

[12] Wikipedia, s.v. "Emmett Till," June 28, 2023, https://en.wikipedia.org/wiki/Emmett_Till.

[13] Wikipedia, s.v. "Scottsboro Boys," July 11, 2023, https://en.wikipedia.org/wiki/Scottsboro_Boys.

[14] Wikipedia, s.v. "Mike Tyson," July 10, 2023, https://en.wikipedia.org/wiki/Mike_Tyson#Rape_trial_and_prison.

[15] Wikipedia, s.v. "2 Live Crew," June 24, 2023, https://en.wikipedia.org/wiki/2_Live_Crew.

Right from the beginning of the analysis, we asked "How did identity politics get to be so prominent?" We now have a significant contribution to the answer. Crenshaw's paper, perfectly timed in the wake of the Rodney King beating, was designed for the promotion of identity politics. That's really what this paper—the entire paper—is about. While it drifts in and out of its focus on women of colour between broader antiracism and feminist issues, it's always pushing identity politics instead of facts. The entire article contains a single (just one!) anecdote from a woman who was possibly battered and was Hispanic but was denied admission to a shelter because she couldn't speak English. Even though that example had not been from Crenshaw's own research, it was perfectly valid in the context of her paper purporting to address violence against women of colour. If she had included a few more anecdotes like it, the paper may well have been worth reading. Instead, Crenshaw slipped us a hint, right at the beginning, of the paper's true nature:

> Drawing from the strength of shared experience, women have recognized that the political demands of millions speak more powerfully than the pleas of a few isolated voices. This politicization in turn has transformed the way we understand violence against women.
>
> [...]
>
> This process of recognizing as social and systemic what was formerly perceived as isolated and individual has also characterized the identity politics of African Americans, other people of colour, and gays and lesbians, among others. For all these groups, identity-based politics has become a source of strength, community, and intellectual development.[16]

An apt conclusion to our analysis of "Mapping the Margins," a paper rammed through the works to capitalize on the raw emotions of the Rodney King beatings. The "few isolated voices" to which Crenshaw derogatorily refers would have lent this paper substantial meaning and value. Instead, while presenting no statistics from her own research (an omission for which she blamed White supremacy and the patriarchy), Crenshaw claimed to represent all women of colour and to speak with a magnified voice of millions. It's hard to imagine how someone with absolutely no statistics and just a single

---

[16] K. Crenshaw, "Mapping the Margins: Intersectionality, Identity Politics, and Violence against Women of Color," *Stanford Law Review*, 43(6), 1241–1299. 1241–1242, 1991, https://doi.org/10.2307/1229039.

anecdote claims in her work to have such a powerful voice for the communities of coloured peoples.

WHAT IS WOKE IDEOLOGY?

The woke ideology of today is chiefly comprised of ideas from the CLS movement that contain both postmodern and Neo-Marxian ideologies.

There's no doubt the woke ideology dominating North American culture today includes Crenshaw's theory of intersectionality. Intersectionality has been analyzed by Dr. James Lindsay in his book *Race Marxism* and found to contain aspects of both Neo-Marxism and postmodernism. Intersectionality clearly displays the Marxist victim-centred approach, complete with a need for forcibly overturning society. Intersectionality also has a postmodern component in the way that Crenshaw used deconstructionism to selectively devalue all categories of oppression as secondary to race. Crenshaw's intersectional theory provides an entirely new way to quantify inequality in society, inequalities that had existed for a long time, according to Crenshaw, but had never been put into words. Now compounded (intersectional) categories of oppression create a wider-than-ever list of victims in society and offer to redistribute power and wealth to those on the margins of society, like Black women.

Another powerful Marxist social justice theory is critical race theory. As we saw, CRT was originally formed by Derrick Bell. Crenshaw, a student of Bell's in his Harvard classes on critical theories of race, became the most widely known face of CRT, and its chief advocate today. CRT contains Neo-Marxist aspects in that, using the ruthless criticism of Marx, it focuses on identity-based oppression and aims at revolution to solve society's ills.

Dr. Lindsay explains that CRT is:

1. Calling everything you want to control "racist" until it is fully under your control
2. A Marxian conflict theory of race (i.e. Race Marxism)
3. A belief that racism created by white people for their own benefit is the fundamental organizing principle of society.[17]

Now, we might protest, "I'm not racist!" and we may well not *overtly* be, but CRT has an answer for such denialism. What we don't realize is that we *are*

---

[17] J. Lindsay, *Race Marxism: The Truth About Critical Race Theory and Praxis* (Independently Published, 2022), 1.

indeed racist, we're simply just not conscious of that fact, and, as we shall see, this unfounded accusation is what caused a gigantic ideological rift within the radical left. It broke apart CLS and its professors, beginning in 1985. Lindsay explains this unconscious racism, which was first presented as unconscious bias:

> A fundamental assumption of Critical Race Theory, then, is that systemic racism is upheld by people who don't realize they're upholding it, often unconsciously. This follows necessarily from the fact they are being characterized as participating in racism merely by the racial group they belong to happening to outperform some other racial groups in something. The idea is key to the formulation of racism as 'systemic' by Critical Race Theorists.[18]

CRITICAL RACE THEORY

Critical race theory originated from the critical legal studies movement, and Kimberlé Crenshaw was a vital part of that eventual transcendence. Scholars of colour within CLS had raised the possibility with their colleagues of race being an issue to address but were "often frustrated by the currency of arguments that cast doubt on the viability of race as a unit of analysis."[19] Those scholars of colour felt that it was the unconscious racial bias of "Whites" within CLS preventing them from seeing that race was an essential dimension to achieving revolution by overturning the White supremacist patriarchy. So those scholars of colour moved out on their own and left their unconsciously racist CLS colleagues behind, for failure to achieve "racial consciousness." They left a radical organization, essentially, for not being radical enough. Just as Lindsay reveals in his three points defining CRT, the proto-CRT crowd, then referred to as "race-Crits," called what they wanted to control—CLS— "racist," trying to control it. When enough of the voices opposing the race-Crits had disagreed with their accusations of racism, the race-Crits decided to create their own path. Crenshaw recounts the time when the race-Crits staged an intervention of a feminist conference and turned CLS upside-down.

---

[18] Ibid., 13–14.

[19] K. W. Crenshaw, "Twenty Years of Critical Race Theory: Looking Back to Move Forward," *Connecticut Law Review*, 43(5), 1264, 2011, https://doi.org/http://shain003.grads.digitalodu.com/blog/wp-content/uploads/2014/09/Twenty-Years-of-Critical-Race-Theory-Looking-Back-to-Move-Forward.pdf.

Race approached center stage in CLS during the 1985 Fem-Crit conference where a small group of fellow-traveling people of color agreed to lead a working session on race. Taking seriously the CLS commitment to workplace engagement, we organized our session around the provocative question: "what is it about the whiteness of CLS that keeps people of color at bay?" This was long before "whiteness studies" came on the scene, so the challenge posed by the question—to think about race not within the traditional terms of uplifting the "Other," but through interrogating racial power from the inside out—was to some a discordant, uncomfortable and even shocking experience. Several of the usually erudite and cool CLSers became angered by the framing of the debate leading one to denounce the session as simple "Mau-Mau-ing" that threatened to tear the organization apart.[20]

In truth, that professor who denounced accusations of racism proved absolutely correct. CLS, which still exists today in some capacity, was left in the dust compared to CRT. What dialectical leftism was doing here was something we've been studying throughout the book. Two ideologies, with significant contradictions, were elevating tension between them through scholarly discourse (or something akin to scholarly discourse), and a synthesis was about to occur. Lindsay explains that it was Crenshaw who advanced dialectical leftism to its newest synthesis. This she did by combining the neo-Marxist school of critical thinking, especially focused on invasion of the cultural institutions (CLS invaded the law), with postmodernism. The postmodern element she was after was the ability to deconstruct and devalue everything except race, which would be the only remaining—absolute—identity marker.

Neo-Marxist ideology, or critical theory, couldn't be used to obtain revolution by itself because that system had failed. It failed first under Marx, then under Marcuse. Its barrier was elements of reality itself, like the reality that industrial capitalism, however corrupt, helped raise much of the world out of abject poverty. The reality that the force required to impose communism automatically made it violent and authoritarian, and those murderous forces could never be avoided. The reality that groups on the fringes of society can't simply form a coalition of the disenfranchised and aim for liberation through a "Great Refusal" of the

---

[20] Ibid., 1290–1291.

culture imposed by a capitalist society. That wasn't possible because a great deal of that culture was not, in fact, created for the purpose of enslaving humanity to capitalism. A great deal of civil society in the West, which housed those cultural institutions, continued to exist because it specifically represented the interests and needs of the average man and woman in families, churches, marriages, businesses, clubs, and the like.

Although an entire discussion of the synthesis of postmodernism and Neo-Marxism won't be covered here, we can offer a synopsis from Dr. Lindsay that explains just enough for us to proceed into his book, *Race Marxism*, for those who want to have a fuller understanding of dialectical leftism.

> The key point to take away from this long and difficult section, then, is that the Cultural Marxists and Neo-Marxists wanted to remake humanity and society according to their Critical Theory, but they were unable to because they were constrained by reality itself, which their Theories wouldn't abandon even though they wanted to change it. Horkheimer and Marcuse were both quite clear that only by stepping out of the existing society (or "sensibility") could it be possible to achieve liberation from the existing society. This is where postmodernism came in and changed everything by characterizing every understanding of reality as just another application of political power. In fact, it went further, framing anything like a "common sensibility" we might share about the world as a falsehood—specifically an illegitimate and shortsighted abuse of power. Once a common understanding of reality, or the ability to have common ground about [how] we might ascertain truths about reality, was recast as part of the power-based superstructure of society, developing a new, almost hyper-Critical perspective that would engender a "new sensibility" became possible. Intersectionality became the tool that filled in the space, and the Critical Theories of identity, including Critical Race Theory, became the tools to implement it.[21]

Kimberlé Crenshaw is the shining beacon of dialectical leftism today that promises it will continue for some time to come. Although her ideas aren't

---

[21] J. Lindsay, *Race Marxism: The Truth About Critical Race Theory and Praxis* (Independently Published, 2022), 140.

widely accepted, they are definitely widely discussed. Identity politics remains a powerful tool used by leftist and radical politicians attempting to subvert normal channels of law and order through social unrest. It's a deceptive approach because it subtly forgoes the ranting and raving Karl Marx did surrounding revolution. Crenshaw also eschews the typical begrudging acknowledgement Marcuse offered his interviewers and critics when they asked if he believed revolution must be violent. The Grandfather of the New Left would somberly point out that all the historical advancements he saw as improving equity were drenched in blood, and although he didn't agree with that approach, he therefore assumed violence was necessary. Crenshaw is hardly a woman who lusts for violence. Her appearance as a gentle, grandmotherly type is compounded by her soft voice and caring demeanour. She's the latest iteration of dialectical leftism, and so has abandoned the overtly aggressive stance that defines either Orthodox or Neo-Marxism. Instead, Crenshaw plays possum. She attributes violence and brutality to the police and makes authorities appear racist by recalling traumatic events in perpetuity, whether they were racist or not and whether they were recent or not. The big, violent threat in the room is the White supremacist male, for whom she has set a trap in the name of achieving equity. The real question is: If her inversion of hierarchy was actually applicable to society (unlikely, because its assumptions are incorrect), what would really happen before total equality was achieved and the racial hierarchies she believes exist were destroyed? Would it be a peaceful, loving transition? Or would it cost everyone just to fix a problem that doesn't exist?

PART IV
THE WHEAT AND THE TARES

CHAPTER THIRTEEN
THE CBC'S LEFT-LEANING BIAS

HELLO AGAIN, DEAR reader. For this chapter, and this one alone, I'd like to return to the first person to relate my experiences. Follow along with me as I recount the many blessings and curses of attempting to engage the broader public through social media in Canada. This has been a long and uneven road, with little in the way of relief. A reward exists in sharing these stories with you, for which I'm thankful.

One of the things I find most interesting about running a small media site online, with just a few hundred and then later several thousand followers, is when a bigger, much more popular media outlet takes notice of you. I don't know if I find it necessarily flattering, but I certainly appreciate the chance to make an impact by telling the truth. For individuals like me, the impact that can be made through social media would be very difficult to achieve in the absence of the online world, the powerful digital network that connects us all. This is one of the reasons why internet censorship is currently so hotly contested. Some politicians would rather have only those they approve of on the bullhorn.

In this chapter, using the experiences of my online Facebook site, Woken Promises, over the past three years, I recount interactions with the Canadian Broadcasting Corporation. These interactions involve no direct conflict but rather CBC's articles, amendments, and responses, the timing of which reveals that they were likely affected by Woken Promises' posts and videos. This isn't a bad thing, because it demonstrates a willingness to correct misinformation. However, the CBC also tends to defame individuals they don't ideologically align with, sometimes without bothering to address the arguments of those individuals. That was certainly the case for Yuri Bezmenov.

I examine the very special case of Yuri Bezmenov and his 1983 lectures on Marxist-Leninist subversion. The CBC decided to tackle him by creating a hit-piece in 2022. Despite being sourced from heavily redacted documents, their article tears the deceased KGB-informant to shreds and leaves neither him nor his family with much dignity in its wake. I argue herein that Bezmenov should be lauded for having the courage to reveal the information he did. He was warned repeatedly by the RCMP and CIA that it could cost him his life to remain in the public eye. I will also refer to Bezmenov's Marxist-Leninist techniques to construct a model explaining the attempt to collapse civil society in the penultimate chapter. There is ample evidence that his ideas are being applied today.

The key point to take away from this chapter is that the CBC is highly critical of right-wing ideologies such as conservatism and populism, but much less so of left-wing ideologies, such as Marxism and socialism. This is problematic in that they claim to conduct "impartial and independent" reporting.[22] As a state-funded media outlet, the CBC is generally more a representative of the interests of the state than that of the people.

Evidence for my personal impact on larger media surfaced almost immediately in 2020, when I had just created my Facebook page before even completing the related website.[23] It was surprising because I quickly found out that I had rattled the cages of some employees at the Canadian Broadcasting Corporation (CBC), and I had not so much as mentioned them.

Woken Promises' first video. Several people were instantly angered by the ad for my very first Facebook video, titled "Why Teachers have F'd Up so Badly."[24] Keep in mind that this was at the very beginning of the pandemic in February 2020. Elementary and high school teachers were raising the ire of Ontarians with threats of yet another strike, with four separate teachers' unions participating.

Of course, the pandemic proved some teachers really are worth their salt. It's like any other job—some dedicated, some less dedicated. I think they had to be very dedicated to take the strain during the pandemic. I'm not saying I've ever

---

[22] CBC/Radio-Canada, CBCRC (@CBCRadioCanada), "Our journalism is impartial and independent. To suggest otherwise is untrue. That is why we are pausing our activities on," Twitter, April 17, 2023, https://twitter.com/CBCRadioCanada/status/1648033861152960531.

[23] See wokenpromises.ca.

[24] Woken Promises, "Why Teachers Have F'd Up so Badly," Vimeo video, 38:53, February 9, 2020, https://vimeo.com/manage/videos/394786566.

witnessed evolution, but maybe survival of the fittest finally did happen, behind teachers' desks, throughout North America.

The purpose behind "Why Teachers have F'd Up so Badly" was to demonstrate that teachers throughout Canada had been reproducing Marxist propaganda, whether they knew it or not. They'd been teaching Marxism in classrooms from kindergarten, beginning with European shaming, all the way through university, culminating in critical race theory.

Teachers in Ontario were also creating problems for civil society with their frequent, drawn-out strikes. They always had something to publicly justify their strike action, whether it was problems surrounding class sizes, distance education, or even special education. What they rarely admitted in public was that they were almost always striking over compensation, whether that was salary to match inflation or for increases in benefits or both.

It turns out, however, that when Ontario teachers' strikes occurred, they caused significant economic problems throughout Ontario (cost of missed work, daycare, or alternatives), but often didn't end up costing the teachers themselves. We know this because the Ontario teachers' unions were investigated in 2016 and found to be re-imbursed for their time on strike:

> Ontario's auditor general [Bonnie Lysyk] says $80.5 million has been given by the Liberal government to teachers' unions and the Ontario Teachers' Federation since 2000. She said giving government funds to teachers' unions is "unusual" but "within the government's authority." Lysyk said there is "no evidence" of the government reimbursing bargaining costs of other Ontario public sector unions, and no other province gives payments to teachers for bargaining costs.[25]

Now all the vitriol started to make sense.

When there is money involved, things get ugly real fast. One CBC technician on Facebook called me all sorts of names and made threats to harm me. I know he was a CBC technician because he listed it as his occupation, and that was publicly available information on his Facebook profile. Others incessantly mocked me. Some called me an agent for Doug Ford (then Premier of Ontario),

---

[25] "Liberals Have Given Ontario Teachers' Unions $80.5M for Bargaining Since 2000: AG.," City News, May 18, 2016, https://toronto.citynews.ca/2016/05/18/liberals-have-given-ontario-teachers-unions-80-5m-for-bargaining-since-2000-ag/.

which I am not and will never be. It was all a bit much, and for a moment, I closed the entire site. I wasn't sure what to do next.

Then I discovered the "block" button.

I reopened the site and began blocking a host of angry leftists: teachers, CBC technicians, union reps, and every other furious radical you might imagine who came after me with brutal verbiage. One lady, a small-time drama teacher and actress from downtown Toronto, began bombarding my Facebook ads with line after line of angry spam, to "pay me back" for my ad having popped into her feed. *Another twit.* Block. Problem solved!

One thing I did take away from this early experiment was to choose my episode titles more carefully. The media in Canada don't let you see this side of radical leftists. To see their unfortunate behaviour, you must go to American news sites to witness video of how such ideologues behave, or take to the street yourself (I don't advise that, especially in Toronto or Montreal). Vocal, self-identified representatives of the left are among the most hateful, intolerant, and threatening bunch of people you will ever meet online. Perhaps they only act dangerous when they're on the other side of a computer screen. Perhaps not. Don't count on the mainstream media in Canada to show you this side of things.

The CBC really should do a story on radical leftists, instead of pretending the only problem Canada has is right-wing extremists.

Take the following example, where the government of Canada funds research at a UK think-tank, which then accuses Canada of a rise in right-wing extremism online:

> A report released Friday on Canadian involvement in right-wing extremism online should serve as a "wake-up call" about the widespread nature of the movement and highlights a growing shift toward the use of less regulated platforms, says an expert on the phenomenon.[26]

The chain leading to this assessment is important to trace. The federal Liberals, through Public Safety Canada, pay for a study in the UK from a left-leaning think-tank to present using the left-leaning CBC, as statement of fact.

This doesn't seem like fair or balanced reporting.

---

[26] T. Daigle, "Canadians among Most Active in Online Right-Wing Extremism, Research Finds," CBC News, June 19, 2020, https://www.cbc.ca/news/science/canadian-right-wing-extremism-online-1.5617710.

Looking to the federal Ministers behind Public Safety Canada brings up Marco Mendicino, who falsely accused the Freedom Convoy of arson, and former Toronto Police Chief Bill Blair.[27] Blair was investigated for possible interference in the wake of the Nova Scotia massacre after publicizing the weapons used in an effort to promote the Trudeau government's firearms ban in May of 2020.[28] Blair was also questioned for his inability to check his email when he was electronically alerted to foreign threats to a Canadian MP but missed the warning.[29] Although he escaped these debacles unscathed, one of Blair's subordinates did not, which we will discuss in Chapter Sixteen on police.

It's unlikely the CBC will ever complete an unbiased story on radical leftists, because those ideologues are a significant portion of their viewership.

I wanted to present my material to the world, if possible, but found out that because it focused on social and political issues, Facebook limited advertising to Canada. This policy was likely in line with Canadian law, and that was perfectly okay with me. There were also people who came to the site of their own volition, looking for information to use.

In addition to whatever numbers of video viewers Facebook allowed me to see, it became clear that individuals from other news sites were willing to take both my ideas and criticism to help better their own efforts. This was also fine with me, provided they cited my work. I'm still waiting on those credits, however.

Tommy Douglas was a eugenicist. At the very beginning of creating a social media presence, I was my usual hot-headed self. I was ready to immediately begin talking about what I had studied regarding Marxism. I felt that this was an incredibly important topic because Canada had been badly victimized by socialist thinking throughout its history, and this was largely, if not entirely, left out of school curricula. Kids from my generation (X) had no idea what kind of a character Pierre Elliot Trudeau really was. The Millennials seemed even more lost. As an example of why we were all so lost, we were typically taught that

---

[27] H. Faulkner, "Trudeau Minister Repeats False Claims about Convoy during Inquiry Committee," *True North News*, April 28, 2022, https://tnc.news/2022/04/28/trudeau-minister-repeats-false-claims-about-convoy-during-inquiry-committee/.

[28] C. Tunney, "Blair Says He Never Interfered in N.S. Shooting Investigation, as More Allegations Emerge," CBC News, June 29, 2022, https://www.cbc.ca/news/politics/blair-lucki-guns-firearms-nova-scotia-1.6505604.

[29] C. Tunney, "Blair Says CSIS Could Have Picked up the Phone to Alert Him to Chong Intelligence," CBC News: Politics, June 14, 2023, https://www.cbc.ca/news/politics/blair-csis-chong-text-1.6876183.

PART IV: THE WHEAT AND THE TARES

Tommy Douglas was a saint for "inventing" health care, not realizing that he would have used that health care to sterilize many Canadians, given the chance:

> Tommy Douglas—the father of socialized medicine in Canada and one of the country's most beloved figures—once supported eugenic policies. In 1933, he received a Master of Arts in sociology from McMaster University for his thesis, "The Problems of the Subnormal Family." In the thesis, Douglas recommended several eugenic policies, including the sterilization of "mental defectives and those incurably diseased."[30]

And what did Canada's CBC think of Tommy Douglas? Surely they knew the truth.

> In 2004, Tommy Douglas was voted "the greatest Canadian of all time" as part of a CBC television series. The fact that he beat out famous Canadians such as Terry Fox, Pierre Trudeau, Wayne Gretzky, and Frederick Banting demonstrates the importance of public healthcare to Canadians.[31]

Voted the greatest Canadian? A eugenicist?

I had to help address the pattern of CBC-induced ignorance in Canada.

A target audience member for my videos might include, for instance, a close relative of mine who claims to be a socialist but who has a striking lack of knowledge about the history of socialism. I wonder if they even realize what kind of a man Tommy Douglas really was. My show would focus on such verifiable information, with appropriate citation, which was the sort of uncomfortable truth oft overlooked. You can guess how popular such an approach is among a thoroughly indoctrinated audience.

Despite a solid grounding, in the beginning I likely didn't have enough knowledge to really go in-depth to all the avenues within the ideology of Marxism itself. But I really hadn't over-thought my approach beforehand. I had read the challenges to Marxism by psychologists Jordan Peterson and Jonathan Haidt, and I understood the widespread history of communism. I was working through

---

[30] T. De Bruin, "Tommy Douglas and Eugenics," *The Canadian Encyclopedia*. June 7, 2019, https://www.thecanadianencyclopedia.ca/en/article/tommy-douglas-and-eugenics.

[31] Ibid.

a monstrous volume by William D. Gairdner at the time as well. I supposed that should be sufficient.

It turned out to be just the tip of the iceberg. As you've seen in the preceding chapters, the history of Marxism is not only long, but it has many branches—too many to cover in one book.

YURI BEZMENOV: THE PROPHET OF DOOM

Enter a friend of mine in the know, who immediately became frustrated that I dared to begin publishing material on Marxist ideology without a thorough understanding of its methodology. To him, the history of Marxism was only the branch of the ideology, not the *root*. My friend thus introduced me to the online remnants of the work of Yuri Aleksandrovich Bezmenov (1939–1993), alias Thomas Schulman.

Bezmenov was a former KGB informant who defected from the Soviet Union while living in India in 1969. He first moved to Canada in 1970 with the help of the Central Intelligence Agency (CIA) and eventually began work with, of all institutions possible, Radio-Canada International (RCI), broadcasting news stories in Russian for the CBC.

This might seem like a confusing position for a Soviet defector to take up in society, and apparently both the CIA and the RCMP advised him to instead hide himself. Yet it's possible Bezmenov felt that being under the public eye as much as possible was in his favour. The KGB, NKVD, Stasi, and other historical communist thugs weren't known for allowing their enemies to live peacefully.

A striking example of this Marxist-Leninist unwillingness to be openly challenged can be seen in the assassination of writer and journalist Georgi Markov (1929–1978). Markov defected in 1969, the same year Bezmenov defected from the KGB, and it's noteworthy that both Bezmenov and Markov became involved in broadcast journalism in their new countries. Markov and Bezmenov also both went on to reveal secrets about the regimes they had been forced to work under. Markov was assassinated in 1978 by a little poke of a poisoned umbrella-tip into the back of his leg. The story was related in an interview with American intelligence historian Keith Milton on the Netflix series *Spycraft*:

> Now Markov was a dissident but was also a commentator for BBC's Bulgarian Service. And between 1975 and 1978, he did a devastating series of reports that pointed to the ineptitude,

the corruption, of then Bulgarian President Todor Zhivkov. Zhivkov wanted him dead, and the idea was to create a pneumatically fired device that would shoot a tiny pellet, a little larger than the head of a pin. That pellet would be cross-drilled and inside would be filled the poison ricin.[32]

It was only because of a slip-up that the method of assassination eventually became known. Markov had survived longer than he was supposed to. Before he died, he was able to tell the story of being poked in the leg with an umbrella by a well-built foreigner.[33] The optimal Soviet goal was to have Markov die and leave no trace at all.

Ironically, Bezmenov died alone of a heart attack in Windsor, Ontario on January 5, 1993, according to the newspaper *The Windsor Star*.[34] That reported reason for death would not match up with a later revelation, however.

The lectures of Bezmenov from 1983, my friend advised, uncovered the root of the Marxist plague that engulfed North America almost forty years after they were recorded. That was hard to believe.

However, today's Marxist-based groups, like Black Lives Matter and Antifa, both of which revealed domestic terrorist components, were on the rise in North America. In the United States, they were tearing apart and burning down cities like Portland and Minnesota, all apparently in the name of social justice.

I followed a link to a YouTube site, and there it was. Over two hours of captivating lectures by Yuri Bezmenov from way back in 1983, explaining the Marxist-Leninist subversion tactics applied against the United States under then leader of the Soviet Union, Yuri Vladimirovich Andropov.[35] This was par for the course during the Cold War. There were also the proxy-battles they fought in other countries. I worked carefully through Bezmenov's Marxist-Leninist subversion methodology and came to two important conclusions:

The first and most alarming conclusion was that the subversion process was underway, and the markers of that, such as riots (BLM and Antifa), strikes

---

[32] Jon Loew, Martin Kase, Keith Melton, Max Serio, Maria Berry, and Danny Wilk, "Deadly Poisons," *Spycraft*, Netflix, 2021 https://www.netflix.com/.

[33] L. Mackie, and J. Andrews, "The Poison-Tipped Umbrella: The Death of Georgi Markov in 1978—Archive," *The Guardian*, September 12, 1978, https://www.theguardian.com/world/from-the-archive-blog/2020/sep/09/georgi-markov-killed-poisoned-umbrella-london-1978.

[34] Wikipedia, s.v. "Yuri Bezmenov," July 6, 2023, https://en.wikipedia.org/wiki/Yuri_Bezmenov.

[35] Oaken Embers Memoryhole, "Yuri Bezmenov Full Interview & Lecture," YouTube video, 2:51:35, March 20, 2017, https://www.youtube.com/watch?v=pzeHpf3OYQY.

(teachers), foreign influence (Russia and China), and economic blockades (the Wet'suwet'en Pipeline protest) were not abstract theory but evidence of the demoralization of society in 2020. North America had literally begun eating away at itself. Canada was experiencing it in a slightly different way than the US, but there it was, in both countries.

My second conclusion was that even though subversion was underway, it was likely not being perpetrated solely by Russians, and not necessarily by Russians at all. In today's world, the idea was then no longer to pin these Marxist tactics to some hidden Russian agents (historically called "sleepers") but to realize that Marxist subversion was well underway in academia across North America in the fields of sociology, political science, and even history. This reflected the culture of the New Left that had abandoned the streets at the end of the 1970s and moved into academe full-time.[36]

How could this be verified?

We know this today because of professors like Gad Saad, Jordan Peterson, and Jonathan Haidt. They have provided firsthand, evidence-based accounts of the persecution they and others have faced within the halls of academia. Gad Saad's book *The Parasitic Mind* is a must-read explanation of this very subject, and he calls these perpetrators "the enemies of reason."[37] Saad, Peterson, and Haidt have all helped to expose universities as the modern-day peddlers of Stalinism they have become. The Marxists attack today from the cover of a victim stance, or under the cover of the "victimhood Olympics," as Gad Saad might say—a term he uses to describe hierarchy within intersectionality—a Marxist based ideology, which, as we discussed in previous chapters, also contains a significant postmodern component.

That close relative I mentioned earlier has a university-level degree in history, is very intelligent and talented, but is clueless about the violent history of socialism and communism. I wanted badly to affect them and others who I worried are victims of propaganda and subversion, as opposed to recipients of truth.

Bezmenov refers to such people as "useful idiots" because they're often well-intentioned individuals who serve a purpose they're unable to fathom. They apply Marxist-Leninist subversion techniques, often without realizing it. They teach others not to think critically, for instance, but to rely largely on emotional

---

[36] As discussed in Chapter Three: The New Left

[37] G. Saad, *The Parasitic Mind: How Infectious Ideas are Killing Common Sense* (Washington D.C.: Regnery Publishing, 2020).

reasoning and faux victimhood. They believe existence to be deterministic and spread such crippling belief as a matter of course. Bezmenov explains:

> The useful idiots, the leftists who are idealistically believing in the beauty of the Soviet socialist or Communist or whatever system, when they get disillusioned, they become the worst enemies. That's why my KGB instructors specifically made the point: never bother with leftists. Forget about these political prostitutes. Aim higher. [...] They serve a purpose only at the stage of destabilization of a nation. For example, your leftists in the United States: all these professors and all these beautiful civil rights defenders. They are instrumental in the process of the subversion only to destabilize a nation. When their job is completed, they are not needed any more. They know too much. Some of them, when they get disillusioned, when they see that Marxist-Leninists come to power—obviously they get offended—they think that they will come to power. That will never happen, of course. They will be lined up against the wall and shot.[38]

Now, of course, there is no longer a Cold War. During that time frame (1947–1991), the Soviet Union aimed to undermine the United States with the application of Marxist-Leninist subversion. During the Cold War, Bezmenov's Marxist-Leninist subversion model—with the goal of communist revolution—was repeated successfully in countries including Korea, Vietnam, Cuba, Nicaragua, and Grenada. Subversion was attempted in India as well but failed. Then the Soviet Union collapsed in 1991.

There's no reason to think that these techniques aren't being used to destabilize the West again, especially in the face of the violent protests in the US by both Antifa and Black Lives Matter groups in the past few years. Subversion techniques have resulted in Marxist control of academia throughout North America, as evinced in the presence of critical race theory, intersectionality, repressive tolerance, and other postmodern nonsense that has flooded halls of learning. Then there are the more concrete threats recently identified.

---

[38] Tool Theory, "Yuri Bezmenov on the Future of 'Useful Idiots' Leftists; Marxist, Communist Political Prostitutes," YouTube video, 4:38, November 5, 2020, https://www.youtube.com/watch?v=D8Ybgw9hGSM.

Today, the Canadian Security Intelligence Service (CSIS) reports there are concrete threats to North America from China, a country under communist rule.[39] Russia, no longer ruled by the Communist Party of the Soviet Union, has also recently been listed as a threat by CSIS. This assessment was verified when Russia invaded Ukraine on February 24, 2022. There has also been a slow but continuous escalation of tension between the West and China, beginning around November 2012, when Xi Jinping came to power. The threat is serious enough that it has been shared directly in a public speech by the director of CSIS:

> In a rare public speech, David Vigneault singled out Russia and China, saying that Beijing was engaged in "activities that are a direct threat to our national security and sovereignty."
>
> "You may think to yourself, 'I'm not a national security person. I'm a scientist, a business person, an academic and so on. I'm not interested in geopolitics,'" the Canadian Security Intelligence Service director said.
>
> "Well, I can say with some confidence that geopolitics is interested in you. And it's important that you know how you can be at risk and how you can protect your interests."[40]

Is China involved in the application of subversion techniques against Canada? Whether they are or not (CSIS believes they are through, for example, Confucious Institutes), they are directly linked through history as the originators of such clever ideas.[41] I use the verb "apply" whenever I talk about ideological subversion because it rarely involves the use of force or violence. Ideological subversion is something that follows in the footsteps of Sun-Tzu, a Chinese General from the fifth century B.C., whose very existence is uncertain according to conflicting historical records. Nevertheless, he's usually credited with writing one of the most influential military texts in history.

---

[39] C. Tunney, "Spy Agency Warned Trudeau China's Tactics Becoming More 'Sophisticated ... Insidious,'" CBC News, December 7, 2021, https://www.cbc.ca/news/politics/csis-trudeau-china-media-1.6270750.

[40] S. Bell, "China and Russia 'Aggressively' Targeting Canadians, CSIS Director Warns," Global News, February 9, 2021, https://globalnews.ca/news/7629494/china-and-russia-targeting-canadians-csis-director/.

[41] R. Boudjikanian, "Some Canadian Schools see China's Confucius Institute as a Handy Teaching Tool. Others Reject It as Propaganda," CBC Edmonton, December 1, 2019, https://www.cbc.ca/news/canada/edmonton/confucius-institute-schools-funding-1.5370858.

PART IV: THE WHEAT AND THE TARES

Sun-Tzu's approach shunned open conflict. He wrote a treatise on how to make war aimed at promoting state policy, called simply *The Art of War*, in which he proposed that the best technique to defeat an enemy was to use their own momentum against them. By subverting an enemy, manipulating it until it was misaligned within its own ranks, it was possible to defeat a powerful foe with very little force or loss of life. It was a brilliant but malicious treatise. It's now considered standard military education throughout the world, although, as Bezmenov mentions in his lectures, during the 1960s, 70s, and 80s, it was conspicuously absent from Canadian and American public libraries. Bezmenov had a lot of interesting and pertinent things to say, considering that his lectures were filmed almost forty years ago. But not everyone was happy that Bezmenov's lectures had suddenly resurfaced amid the current culture war.

CBC'S JORGE BARRERA PENS HIT PIECE ON BEZMENOV

What really rattled the CBC's cage was that people (and I say "people" because there must be others besides me) were apparently frequently citing the works of Bezmenov online, and the CBC saw this as fake news. So they did what they often do when they dislike someone's point of view: they attacked the person, not the argument. They released a massive, selectively researched hit-piece on Bezmenov on February 5, 2022, titled "Chaos Agent."[42] The article was written by journalist Jorge Barrera.

Peeling through the article to remove its bias is a strangely enjoyable experience. Jorge Barrera seems to be a very honest reporter, so when he confesses the CBC obtained thousands of heavily redacted documents from CSIS, it means we should be very careful about the article he has written. While we might feel Barrera is reporting honestly because he has confessed the documents are heavily redacted, we should also realize that means he is missing a certain amount of critical or sensitive information. Barrera's entire article is thus going to be biased in favour of what CSIS has already deemed unimportant. What we really need in order to find the truth about Bezmenov is unredacted or declassified information, not heavily redacted documents. The reason Barrera doesn't need declassified information, however, is that this is a hit-piece. It's designed to dissuade others from listening to Bezmenov. It's not quite as focused on truth as the author leads us to believe.

For the construction of the article, the CBC felt it necessary to contact Bezmenov's Canadian ex-wife and daughter. It's clear that they both had severely

---

[42] J. Barrera, "Chaos Agent," CBC News, February 5, 2022, https://www.cbc.ca/newsinteractives/features/yuri-bezmenov-soviet-defector-canada.

strained relationships with the man, and that despite claiming she has forgiven him, Bezmenov's daughter is struggling with bitter memories.

Barrera proceeds with the negligent father angle. He begins by calling Bezmenov "toxic" right from the get-go. He then highlights what he can from the redacted documents and combines this with firsthand testimony from one of Bezmenov's ex-wives, who lives in Montreal to this day. Of course, she's not his only ex-wife.

Barrera also paints the picture of Bezmenov's other poor, abandoned, Russian wife, whom he left in India, along with a lone infant, when he defected in 1969. It's confusing because Barrera explains that Bezmenov later receives letters from that same Russian wife, which were analyzed by the RCMP and evaluated as fake. The RCMP then warned him that his cover was blown and he could be in danger from the KGB. Did Barrera not consider that the life of a spy might involve fake marriages? Maybe Bezmenov didn't want to be married to the Russian woman in India, which was quite possibly part of his cover. The implication in the article is that he instead wanted to save his own skin.

As Bezmenov explains in his lectures, his official job for the Soviet Union was working as a reporter for *Novosti Press Agency*. His unofficial job was a KGB informant who must account for all people of influence in the government of India. These were people who the KGB would interact with to achieve subversion success. Explaining anything like this, however, wouldn't make Bezmenov out to be the bad guy. So Barrera harps on the destroyed families he left behind in Canada and India, implying at the end of the article that Bezmenov committed suicide by drinking methanol (a container of antifreeze). Barrera supports this suicide story by explaining that Bezmenov was an unusually heavy drinker.

What Barrera does reveal that may be of some use, which might actually address what happened to Bezmenov are found in the following quotations: "… the fallout with the federal government over his decision to go public with his story."[43] Ask yourself: Would the federal government be mad if Bezmenov ran around telling everyone fake news? Would they even care?

"Much remains unknown about Canada's role in the Cold War … because unlike the U.S. and the U.K., the Canadian government still lacks a proper declassification framework."[44] This is an indictment of Barrera's own research, because those heavily redacted documents greatly limited his report.

---

[43] Ibid.

[44] Ibid.

"That September, one of his RCI colleagues met with the RCMP and suggested Bezmenov was a Soviet spy."[45] Little wonder that Bezmenov was so agitated at work when people treated him in this fashion. Barrera does mention that this created problems for Bezmenov, but he uses it as a part of the story arc leading to his deterioration and suicide.

Instead of addressing the arguments that Bezmenov presented, specifically the steps of Marxist-Leninist subversion and whether they are occurring in Canada, the CBC went headlong into a character assassination of the KGB defector. Why address the ideas of a man when you can simply write him off as a depressed liar?

It's important to note that the KGB did the exact same thing with Bezmenov after he defected, claiming he was of "little importance." That doesn't gel with the RCMP warning him he could be in danger from the KGB. A final question to ask is: If Yuri Bezmenov is a source of fake news, why is the CBC spending so much time defaming him? Wouldn't it be easier to just address the fake news posthumously arising from him?

The CBC's approach to journalism is often vexing to those who don't share their ideological perspective. With my own media initiative, I have attempted to keep them honest, and called them out whenever they are being either inflammatory or untrue. I have so far had four encounters with the CBC in which they have reacted to my site.

My first encounter was that angry technician on Facebook I mentioned earlier, making threats against me in early 2020. He is now on my banned list. That first encounter might be construed as meaningless, but I have since discussed numerous issues with CBC fans, and they often seem hyper-aggressive. It's possible that the promotion of division over the last several years, especially during the pandemic, is something the CBC inadvertently pushed. Fear makes people do silly things.

CBC'S *DEADLY FORCE* DATABASE

The second encounter with the CBC was much more significant. It was on July 23, 2020, just six months into my online venture with Woken Promises. I had recently run an episode called "Bending to Marxism: Part 1," in which, among many other things, I criticized BLM member and activist Robyn Maynard for making an unsupported claim about police killings. Maynard had cited the

---

[45] Ibid.

CBC's online *Deadly Force* database.[46] At the time I reviewed their database, it presented data from the years 2000–2017 (it has since been updated). Maynard, then a PhD student at the University of Toronto, made the following claim in the BLM book *Until We Are Free* (which I researched for my episode): "I'm thinking about the recent studies that just came out showing—no surprise here—that Black and Indigenous people are far more likely to be killed by the police[.]"[47] I accessed the CBC study that Maynard cited in the book to support her claim.[48]

Even briefly examining the graph, it was as clear as day that Maynard's statement was false. You're much more likely to get shot by police if you are Caucasian/White. I showed the statistical interpretation error to two professionals, including a PhD/statistician, and they agreed with me. In my episode, I suggested what Maynard could have said to tell the truth: "Now if Robyn had said: 'for their percentage of overall population, Black and Indigenous victims are greatly over-represented in police killings from 2000–2017,' then she would have been correct."[49] The original air date of the episode "Bending to Marxism: Part 1" was June 25, 2020.

Just about a month later, on July 23, 2020, the CBC demonstrated that it had heard my criticism—which is, by the way, firmly lodged over half-an-hour into my program—and issued the following correction on a thumbnail for its new link to the Deadly Force database: "Black and Indigenous people over-represented in fatal police encounters in Canada, CBC research shows."

I wasn't overly impressed at the time, because this wasn't a retraction but an overwrite. But at least the CBC, or whoever oversaw the *Deadly Force* database, was trying to be more truthful. In this instance, they did what was correct. While it's possible they came to this decision entirely on their own, the fact it was within striking distance of my video's release is curious to say the least.

---

[46] J. Marcoux and K. Nicholson, "Deadly Force," CBC News, 2017, retrieved July 13, 2023, from https://newsinteractives.cbc.ca/longform-custom/deadly-force/.

[47] R. Diverlus, S. Hudson, and S. M. Ware, *Until We Are Free: Reflections on Black Lives Matter in Canada* (Regina, SK: University of Regina Press, 2019), location number 1425.

[48] Due to copyright laws, we can't include the graph here. Thankfully, CBC has archived the 2000–2017 version, which can be found at https://newsinteractives.cbc.ca/longform-custom/deadly-force/. The graph in question is the second one from the top of the article, labelled "Race and Ethnicity: Victims Vs. Population, Canada 2000–2017.

[49] Woken Promises, "Bending to Marxism: Part I," Vimeo video, 35:51, June 25, 2020, https://vimeo.com/manage/videos/432702719.

PART IV: THE WHEAT AND THE TARES

CBC'S CATHERINE TUNNEY OVERESTIMATES *EMERGENCIES ACT*

My third encounter with the CBC was on that dreaded day, February 14, 2022. That was the day Canadian Prime Minister Justin Trudeau invoked the *Emergencies Act* to bring the Freedom Convoy, then only left occupying downtown Ottawa, to an end. I had ironically been examining the *Emergencies Act* just weeks before because it had been suggested by a study done at Queen's University as something Trudeau could have used during the pandemic.[50]

To my surprise, a CBC report made the following statement the day the *Emergencies Act* was put into effect: "The law gives the federal government carte blanche to cope with a crisis."[51]

The term "carte blanche" of course means the freedom to do whatever you want to do—without repercussion. The article had been written by Catherine Tunney, and unfortunately her statement was false. I also worried that it was inflammatory because it made it sound like under the *Emergencies Act*, the federal government could do whatever they wanted without question. That might be very bad for the protesters. It might cause them to panic or act irrationally in the face of perceived danger. I had studied the *Emergencies Act* enough to know that it didn't allow carte blanche but tied the government to an automatic inquiry once the declared emergency was ended. I thought this would therefore be fantastic, because I had yet to see Trudeau's government be held accountable for the over-reach they had conducted during the pandemic.

I posted about how the statement was incorrect and—bang—the CBC instantly corrected the article by removing the sentence, "The law gives the federal government carte blanche to cope with a crisis." They also put a new tagline on the article, stating: "Act permits special temporary measures that may not be appropriate in normal times."[52]

Now, I'm uncertain if Catherine Tunney is an experienced reporter, and citing the law is usually not easy, because you really must know it well. Yet

---

[50] K. L. Brock, "The Impact of Covid-19 on the Future of Governance in Canada," White Paper, 2020, https://doi.org/https://www.queensu.ca/sps/sites/spswww/files/uploaded_files/publications/3%20The%20Impact%20of%20COVID-19%20on%20the%20Future%20of%20Governance%20in%20Canada.pdf.

[51] C. Tunney, "Federal Government Invokes Emergencies Act for First Time Ever in Response to Protests, Blockades," CBC News. February 14, 2022, https://www.cbc.ca/news/politics/trudeau-premiers-cabinet-1.6350734. They also changed the subheading of the article to "Act Grants Cabinet Ability to Take 'Special Temporary Measures That May Not Be Appropriate in Normal Times.'"

[52] Again, I have a copy of this thumbnail, but due to Canadian copyright laws, I am only allowed to have it for personal use and not to put in this book.

journalists have a responsibility to not post inflammatory rhetoric, especially *false* inflammatory rhetoric. There is evidence that the CBC and its journalists were reacting to events during the Freedom Convoy in a knee-jerk, inflammatory manner. They weren't just a little angry about the protesters. They were livid.

CBC'S DAVID COCHRANE MOCKS CHRISTIANS
David Cochrane, a long-time, award-winning CBC journalist, said live on-air during the final police takedown of the Freedom Convoy blockade, on February 18, 2022: "This protest is due to the two C's: Christ and conspiracy theories." It's one of the most bigoted, anti-Christian attacks I've heard anywhere on television. The CBC was involved in the conflict, and their bias showed in stunning fashion. Their behaviour during the entire ordeal was reprehensible.

My final surprising involvement with the CBC is, of course, when that story on Bezmenov popped up rather suddenly on February 5, 2022. The article reveals that the CBC used an *Access to Information Act* (ATIA) request to obtain documents from CSIS, so I'm uncertain how far back they began investigating Bezmenov and his history. It's a sad irony that the publisher of that story was Radio-Canada/CBC, who employed Bezmenov for a short time in the 1970s.

Bezmenov described four steps of Marxist-Leninist subversion in detail, and his lectures really are worth watching to understand what's happening to civil society and the state today.[53] Just because the CBC and other mainstream media in general refuse to deal with the arguments contained within those lectures doesn't invalidate them. If he were really peddling fake news, it wouldn't take long to analyze the few hours of Bezmenov's lectures online and debunk them—but that's not so easy to do. In fact, the *New York Times* produced an opinion piece called "Meet the KGB Spies Who Invented Fake News," which cited Bezmenov's lectures as authentic KGB techniques.[54] Bezmenov was featured along with fellow KGB-defectors Ladislav Bittman (1931–2018) and Stanislav Alexandrovich Levchenko (1941–).

DEMORALIZATION: FIRST STAGE OF MARXIST-LENINIST SUBVERSION
The first stage of Marxist-Leninist subversion, within which North America is hopefully still fighting, is called *demoralization*, a process that is supposed to

---

[53] The four steps of Marxist-Leninist subversion are: 1) Demoralization; 2) Destabilization; 3) Crisis; and 4) Normalization.

[54] The New York Times, "Meet the KGB Spies Who Invented Fake News | NYT Opinion," YouTube video, 15:37, November 19, 2018, https://www.youtube.com/watch/h5WjRjz5mTU?app=desktop.

take between fifteen to twenty years. The range specified is the time required to subvert a single generation.[55] The idea behind *demoralization* is self-evident: to demoralize the populace and thus have them looking for anti-societal beliefs and practices. This will pit them against the state.

According to Bezmenov, subversion to create demoralization is applied to six fields within a target country: religion, education, social life, power structure, law and order, and labour relations. It wouldn't be difficult to compile enough material for an entire book on the subversion of any one of these six fields and how they are under threat from Marxist ideology today. Legacy media like the CBC, CTV, CNN, MSNBC, NYT, and many others actively, perhaps inadvertently, contribute on all these fronts. They could be considered Bezmenov's "useful idiots." They promote values completely at odds with those that historically sustained civil society and secured some level of independence from the state.

My experiences with the Canadian Broadcasting Corporation have taught me that they have a clear left-leaning bias. They promote views that are both statist and anti-democratic when they aim to defame ideologies they do not agree with, such as the "populist" ideology of the Freedom Convoy.[56,57] They also tend to dramatize the threat posed by right-wing extremists while minimizing the threat posed by left-wing extremists.[58,59] The CBC does demonstrate some willingness to correct its mistakes, which is a good sign, I think, but sometimes they won't make a correction until long after damage has been done. This was certainly the case for their story claiming Alberta premier Danielle Smith's office had improperly contacted Crown prosecutors. Although proven false,

---

[55] For example, the millennials are a generation born from 1981–1996, a span of sixteen years. That fits within Bezmenov's specified range of fifteen to twenty years required to subvert a single generation.

[56] A. Wherry, "Populist Rage Demands Leaders Who Listen—and Choose Their Words with Care," CBC Politics, February 23, 2022, https://www.cbc.ca/news/politics/convoy-vaccine-pandemic-trudeau-populism-1.6360519.

[57] CBC News, "Protest Convoy Had 'Worst Display of Nazi Propaganda in this Country,' Anti-Hate Advocate Says," YouTube video, 4:47, January 30, 2022, https://www.youtube.com/watch?v=50kHdAumXvA.

[58] H. Caruk, "Manitoba Chapter of Proud Boys Disbanded, Local Anti-Fascist Group Says," CBC Manitoba, January 14, 2021, https://www.cbc.ca/news/canada/manitoba/manitoba-proud-boys-facist-free-treaty-one-1.5872253.

[59] S. Zhou, "'Antifa' Vs. the 'Alt-Right': Comparing Anti-Fascists to Those They Oppose Is Unfair," CBC Manitoba, September 23, 2017, https://www.cbc.ca/news/canada/manitoba/opinion-steven-zhou-antifa-alt-right-1.4302851.

the CBC did not retract their claims until after the Alberta provincial election, held on May 29, 2023.[60] The story served as a deterrent to Smith's potential voters. Although the CBC can't be all things to all people, they surely could expand to address more Canadians' perspectives, instead of focusing on only the Canadians who share their ideology. They may have to do this, and soon.

---

[60] D. Bennett, "CBC News Retracts Report Alleging Email Interference by Danielle Smith's Office," *National Post*, July 5, 2023, https://nationalpost.com/news/politics/cbc-retracts-report-on-danielle-smith-interference

CHAPTER FOURTEEN
STATISM AND MILITANT ATHEISM

In this chapter, the most important idea to remember is William Gairdner's "political sandwich" model for a free society in Figure 4. In that model are three distinct layers. The top layer of the sandwich is equated with the state, which has a monopoly on force. The middle layer is equated with the institutions of civil society, including marriages, clubs, churches, families, corporations, etc. Civil society has no monopoly on force and so must rely on moral authority for control and cohesion. Finally, the bottom layer is comprised of the autonomous individuals who populate a free society. Individual citizens are only autonomous if they're separated from the top layer of the state by the middle layer of civil society. Without a layer of civil society to keep citizens free, totalitarianism ensues.

Using Gairdner's model to understand how a free society is threatened, we move into examples of when a government pushes for atheism to increase control over its citizens. This aims to remove an institution of civil society—the Church—and thus bring the state one step closer to totalitarianism. This attempt to destroy civil society was seen in Stalin's purge of Christianity in the Russian Orthodox Church (1932–1938) and in China during Mao's Cultural Revolution (1966–1976). Being caught as either priest or parishioner in these horrific purges meant public shaming, re-education camps, or death.

From there, we look at how atheism is promulgated in a free society today. Many Canadians were appalled to witness the speech by former Governor General Julie Payette in November 2017 where she openly mocked people of faith. That stunt allows comparisons with Josef Stalin's "museums of atheism," which were also used to mock people of faith, through comparison with science. We explore why the Church, an essential institution of civil society, and its continuance, especially during times of persecution, display evidence of effectively providing an anti-communist bulwark.

WILLIAM D. GAIRDNER'S POLITICAL SANDWICH MODEL

Theories of subversive Marxist threats against civil society aren't limited to ex-spies from the KGB. A Canadian who closely reflects such understanding—independent from Bezmenov—is William D. Gairdner, whose book *The Trouble with Canada ... Still!* (2nd ed., 2010) explains the threats to institutions of civil society at length. The difference Gairdner presents is the attempt by the state to make civil society collapse, to control people directly. He explains this in his book with an analogy to a "political sandwich," a very useful mnemonic to imprint into our thinking. See Figure 4 below, explained in Gairdner's own words:

Figure 4: Political Sandwich Model of a Free Society (William D. Gairdner)

STATE

Executive, Judicial, Legislative, Police, Military

(Monopoly on Force: coercive)

CIVIL SOCIETY

Churches, Clubs, Families, Charities, Corporations, etc.

(Moral Authority: voluntarily accepted)

AUTONOMOUS INDIVIDUALS

Citizenry

(Self-control)

All free nations (distinctly not unfree ones) may be visualized as forming a kind of three-layered structure, a political sandwich, so to speak, each layer distinguished by its form of control.

At the top is the State, the only layer with a monopoly on force. Its form of control is coercion and power, and it is therefore authoritarian by definition.

In the middle is civil society, a community of countless voluntarily formed human associations such as families, clubs, sports teams, corporations, churches, charities, and so on, which has no monopoly on force and so must rely for cohesion and control on the various forms of moral authority it naturally generates by means of religion, parental instruction and obligation, employment contracts, rules of conduct, the natural leadership of the highly esteemed, and so on. This authority is voluntarily accepted by members of society who choose to live, work, and play within such groupings, or it is rejected at a price. But for adults at least, social and moral authority is never coercive because no one is forced by law to join or to leave a family, a church, a team, a university, a charity, or a company, and so on, except for misconduct, malfeasance, terms of contract, and the like.

At the bottom is the mass of autonomous individuals whose natural form of control (or lack thereof) is self-control.

[…]

I will be speaking more about the natural tendency of the coercive State at the top to undermine and weaken the freely formed middle layer of civil society so as to garner the allegiance of and achieve increased control over the millions of autonomous individuals in the bottom layer. It does this by taxing the citizens at increasingly heavy rates over time, and with the funds substituting sweet-sounding government goods and services for as many possible of those goods and services that the members of civil society once provided for, or offered voluntarily to, or sold to, each other. In this way, over time, the regulatory, or welfare, or cradle-to-grave Nanny State substitutes itself for civil society as the origin of human security and happiness.[1]

It's important to differentiate Gairdner's political sandwich analogy from Bezmenov's model for Marxist-Leninist subversion a bit here, but we'll do this even more carefully and clearly using diagrams in Chapter Seventeen. These are

---

[1] W. D. Gairdner, *The Trouble with Canada … Still! A Citizen Speaks Out* (Bastian Publishing Services Ltd., 2010), 16–17.

two separate attempts to achieve two separate goals, but, critically, both target and attack civil society, albeit utilizing differing methods.

Marxist-Leninist subversion pits the state against civil society so that they will *both* collapse, and a third party can invade and control people directly. The difference seems subtle, but it's significant. In Gairdner's model, the government survives and becomes the tyrant. In the Marxist-Leninist model, the government does not survive, and a new tyrant comes in. In both cases, civil society is a primary target and is pushed to collapse. In both cases, the aim is for some power (either an existing or foreign government) to achieve a totalizing system over the individuals in a geographic region or country.

Now retired, Gairdner was a successful businessman, an academic who taught at York University in Toronto, an author of several books, and an Olympic-level athlete in his youth. Gairdner describes himself as libertarian when it comes to economics, and Burke-ian when it comes to his values, referencing Irish statesman and Christian, Edmund Burke (1729–1797).

The CBC would be hard pressed to create the kind of hit-piece against Gairdner they constructed against Bezmenov.

CBC's Peter Gzowski snubs Gairdner. It turns out the CBC did their best to avoid Gairdner altogether back in 1990, when he published the first edition of The Trouble with Canada. We'll let Gairdner explain directly from his personal blog, from a post where he talked about how he eventually cajoled an interview out of Peter Gzowski's producer:

> Well, I found this original 1990 CBC Radio Interview on an old-style tape, and had it transferred so I could upload it to YouTube. The backstory, as they say, is that I had been pestering his Producer for months to do an interview about this book. She kept refusing because she didn't like anything I argued in the book. But when the book hit #1 in Canada on the Globe and Mail Bestseller List, and had sold about 50,000 copies, she finally relented, and we did this interview. After his genteel opening, Gzowski jumps in and begins to fire questions at me. You can hear how he is sort of trying to write a book of his own here, rather than to express any genuine interest in my book. At the end of the interview, which was quite steamy, I extended my hand to thank Gzowski, who was,

after all, Canada's Public Radio Servant #1. But he refused to shake hands with me.²

It's difficult to imagine such an erudite renaissance man as Gairdner being treated like that. That treatment and the producer's ignorance suggest petty politics have existed within the CBC for a long time. Remember too, back in the mid-1970s, Radio-Canada International treated Bezmenov rather poorly as well, accusing him of being a spy. Thank goodness such treatment didn't dissuade Gairdner from publishing more material, and especially updating *The Trouble with Canada … Still!* in 2010. It was the 2010 edition in which he added that *… Still!* part onto the title.³

Gairdner/Gramsci model for civil society. In *The Trouble with Canada … Still!*, Gairdner explains his understanding of civil society in terms very similar to those defined by the Albanian-Italian Cultural Marxist Antonio Gramsci, whom we examined in some detail in Chapter Seven. As we saw above, Gairdner's explanation of civil society is made using a sandwich model. The top slice of bread of the sandwich is the "state," which includes the branches of government and the military and police (that legitimate the power of the state). The bottom slice of the sandwich is the "autonomous individuals," and that autonomy is reliant on being kept away from the top piece of bread. In between the two slices of bread is the layer of "civil society." The institutions comprising civil society are equated with all the goodies in a sandwich: meat, cheese, lettuce, tomato, condiments, etc. Civil society thus contains various institutions, including families, marriages, churches, clubs, corporations, and anything else populated with the autonomous individuals below that doesn't involve direct control of the state above. Gairdner's model is similar (but not identical) to that conceptualized by the Marxist Antonio Gramsci, perhaps as much as seventy years before it was adapted by Gairdner.

Gramsci developed the concept of civil society as containing Marx's class struggle, viewing it as a level of society that could be occupied by different classes. Gramsci believed that when it was occupied by the bourgeoisie, it was a tool of oppression to maintain control over the working class below. He postulated that

---

² W.D. Gairdner, "My Original Feisty Interview with Peter Gzowski, Host of CBC's Morningside Radio Show," William D. Gairdner Blog, August 31, 2018, https://williamgairdner.ca/my-original-feisty-interview-with-peter-gzowski-host-of-cbcs-morningside-radio-show/.

³ Gairdner's newest release, *Beyond the Rhetoric: A Collection of In-Depth Essays Published in the Epoch Times* (2021), reveals a sharp clarity in well-thought-out and fresh ideas. This book is well-worth spending time on.

civil society housed the ideological and cultural hegemony of the bourgeoisie, and that was the level that needed to be contested by the proletariat. The state above could then be affected by civil society occupied by the proletariat. This differs from Marx, who viewed civil society as the private sector and a sphere of bourgeois economic influence, topped by a corrupt state that enforced bourgeois laws. Marx believed it all had to go. That's why in Marxist-Leninist theory, as explained by Bezmenov, the target isn't just civil society, but civil society and the state together must be brought to crisis.

Gairdner clearly sees it from a different standpoint. To Gairdner, civil society consists of beneficial institutions of the free (autonomous) people in modern society—*all people*. Not just those entitled by power and wealth. Unlike Gramsci, Gairdner sees the potential for a hegemony in the state instead of in civil society. This is because Gairdner doesn't consider citizens divided into economic and cultural classes but divided by influence of the state. To Gairdner, a healthy and robust civil society firmly protects the autonomy of all the people from the influence of the state. Gairdner basically views the concept with Gramsci's understanding, but as Gramsci was a radical leftist, Gairdner is clearly somewhere on the opposite end of the ideological spectrum.

Gairdner's point is that those who favour totalitarian regimes, whom he cleverly refers to as "statists," push to have the institutions of civil society replaced with government-controlled equivalents. That means instead of churches and religion, statists push for atheism and appropriate buildings of worship (as we will see below, Stalin did this). Instead of traditional marriages of a man and woman, supported by the community and churches, statists push for civil unions between unspecified genders and sexual orientations. Instead of clubs where people get together and hang out to relax, statists have government-controlled organizations and clubs where you are registered and must submit a digital ID. Instead of businesses that are independent of government control, the government has a powerful say in the direction of the business and may tax and regulate the life out of it (such as in communist China). Statists push for the elimination of civil society institutions because they feel that "big government," informed by atheistic beliefs and operating with government-equivalent institutions, is best suited to the interests of humanity.

Statists are content living within the nihilism that militant atheism forces onto most people because they find their meaning in power. Remember Josef Stalin's Five-Year Plan for Atheism pushed by The League of the Militant Godless? To enforce that push for atheism and absolute power, Stalin had to kill hundreds of thousands of Christians.

CHAPTER FOURTEEN: STATISM AND MILITANT ATHEISM

"What would we have to do today to get rid of Christian beliefs?" a statist might ask.

JULIE PAYETTE AND A WHIFF OF MILITANT ATHEISM

It's important to carefully consider the words that Julie Payette, engineer, astronaut, and the former Governor General of Canada, delivered in her speech at the Canadian Science Policy Conference in Ottawa, in November of 2017:

> And we are still debating and still questioning whether life was a divine intervention or whether it was coming out of a natural process let alone, oh my goodness, a random process. And so many people—I'm sure you know many of them—still believe, want to believe, that maybe taking a sugar pill will cure cancer, if you will it![4]

What kind of person would push militantly for atheism in today's day and age? Surely Payette wouldn't indulge in the kind of open mockery Stalin did, such as his effort to turn religious buildings into museums of religious barbarity:

> [S]acked churches, synagogues, and mosques were transformed into anti-religious "museums of atheism," where dioramas of clerical cruelty sat alongside crisp explanations of scientific phenomena. Icons and relics, meanwhile, were stripped of their mystique and treated as ordinary objects.[5]

Perhaps Payette would approve of such mockery in the name of "science." Surely this comparison of Payette to Stalin is ridiculous.

Well, there is no way anyone in Canada would be given the power Josef Stalin held in Soviet Russia, but it's important to see what people do with the amount of power they do possess.

In January 2021, just over three years after her public attack on people of faith, Julie Payette would be forced to resign as Governor General of Canada due to accusations that she ran an abusive workplace environment. Those accusations

---

[4] R. Urback, "In What Universe Is It Appropriate for a Governor General to Deride People for Their Beliefs?: Urback," CBC News, November 2, 2017, https://www.cbc.ca/news/opinion/governor-general-speech-julie-payette-climate-change-1.4384481.

[5] N. Frost, "Why Stalin Tried to Stamp Out Religion in the Soviet Union," History.com, April 23, 2021, https://www.history.com/news/joseph-stalin-religion-atheism-ussr.

were verified via third-party investigation. Payette's behaviour ultimately cost the Canadian taxpayer a big chunk of change, as her office at Rideau Hall paid out a total of $277,592 in five separate, confidential settlements, along with a legal bill of approximately $170,000.[6] The workplace review conducted by that third party concluded that Payette "belittled, berated and publicly humiliated Rideau Hall staff" and "created a toxic, verbally abusive workplace."

Payette was invested as Governor General of Canada on October 2, 2017, under Prime Minister Justin Trudeau. Before appointing Payette in 2017, Trudeau disbanded a non-partisan appointments committee that could have reviewed her nomination. When accused of poor vetting and allowing workers at Rideau Hall to suffer in 2021, Trudeau refused to apologize for his choice. Instead, he attempted to spin the embarrassment as a Liberal Hallmark moment.

> "I think as a government, we've demonstrated time and time again how important it is to create workplaces that are free and safe from harassment and in which people can do their important jobs in safety and security," Trudeau said.[7]

Though he attempted to distance himself from his militant atheist choice for Governor General after her resignation, Trudeau has demonstrated ideological connections that tie him to like-minded, totalitarian thinking. Before he came to power, Justin Trudeau revealed his own statist beliefs as far back as 2013, during a "ladies' night" Liberal fundraiser, when he spoke the following immortal words:

> There's a level of admiration I actually have for China. Their basic dictatorship is actually allowing them to turn their economy around on a dime and say, "We need to go green, we want to start investing in solar."[8]

---

[6] R. Tumilty and C. Nardi, "Exclusive: GG's Office Paid $277,000 in Secret Settlements the Year Julie Payette Resigned," *National Post*, January 28, 2022, https://nationalpost.com/news/politics/ggs-office-paid-out-277k-in-settlements-the-year-julie-payette-resigned-but-wont-give-details.

[7] C. Nardi, "Trudeau Refuses to Apologize or Take Any Responsibility for Decision to Nominate Julie Payette as Governor General," *National Post*, January 22, 2021, https://nationalpost.com/news/politics/trudeau-refuses-to-apologize-or-acknowledge-any-responsibility-in-decision-to-nominate-now-former-governor-general-payette.

[8] Toronto Sun, "ADMIRING A 'BASIC DICTATORSHIP': Trudeau's Bizarre Praise of China," YouTube video, 4:19, March 1, 2023, https://www.youtube.com/watch?v=sLTGbtfkh_s.

What Justin Trudeau may have accidentally let slip was his admiration that the state, unfettered by civil society (as in a "basic dictatorship"), was able to impose its initiatives immediately onto the people. He used the happy circumstance of "going green" as an example, but statist initiatives have rarely been so benign. Let us digress for a moment to investigate what kind of initiatives a basic dictatorship has conducted in the most populous country on the planet.

XI JINPING OPPRESSES HONG KONG
Ruled by dictator Xi Jinping and the Chinese Communist Party (CCP), China's Marxist-Leninist regime recently executed a dictatorial initiative "on a dime," which Hong Kong's citizens were unable to stop.

In February 2019, Hong Kong's government introduced the *Fugitive Offenders and Mutual Legal Assistance in Criminal Matters Legislation (Amendment) Bill*. That legislation allowed those deemed criminals to be extradited from Hong Kong to mainland China. In response to the passing of that bill, the people of Hong Kong poured into the streets in protest in the hundreds of thousands in June 2019. Chaos ensued as unarmed citizens were brutally beaten and arrested. China's way of handling the protests was to crackdown, passing the *Hong Kong National Security Law* in June of 2020, granting the state widespread powers to arrest dissidents:

> The national security law established four particular crimes of secession, subversion, terrorism, and collusion with foreign organisations; any open speech, verbal promotion or intention of Hong Kong's secession from China is considered a crime as well. The implementation of the law entitles authorities to surveil, detain, and search persons suspected under its provisions and to require publishers, hosting services, and internet service providers to block, remove, or restrict content which the authorities determine to be in violation thereof.[9]

Xi and his communist subordinates also rewrote the democratic process in Hong Kong's elections to ensure that "patriots" were installed in key positions.

---

[9] Wikipedia, "Hong Kong National Security Law," July 8, 2023, https://en.wikipedia.org/wiki/2020_Hong_Kong_national_security_law.

Trudeau had to eat the words he foolishly let loose in 2013. He condemned China's imposition of the *National Security Law* in 2020.[10] Regardless, it's horrific that Trudeau would believe that a "basic dictatorship" was ever a successful method of government, as the entire history of the CCP is rife with human rights abuses. Let's take a brief look at some of the carnage.

MAO ZEDONG'S WAR ON RELIGION

The CCP first came to power in 1949 under Mao Zedong, when the People's Liberation Army defeated Chiang-Kai-Shek and the Kuomintang in a long, drawn-out civil war. The People's Republic of China (PRC) was formed. By that time, Zedong had already adopted a Marxist-Leninist ideology (as described by Bezmenov). This he revised and later renamed *Maoism*. Over his entire reign from 1949–1976, Mao Zedong is estimated to have conducted the greatest mass murder on Earth.

> While most scholars are reluctant to estimate a total number of "unnatural deaths" in China under Mao, evidence shows he was in some way responsible for at least 40 million deaths and perhaps 80 million or more. This includes deaths he was directly responsible for and deaths resulting from disastrous policies he refused to change.[11]

A fraction of those murdered belonged to one of the chief targets of Marxist-Leninist ideology: *religion*. But Mao didn't begin purging religion immediately upon the formation of the PRC. The only place he banned religion was within the CCP itself, just as Stalin did within the Communist Party of the Soviet Union.

The first step for Mao to eradicate religion was to prevent it from spreading. He did this by creating the Religious Affairs Bureau (RAB) in 1949 and declaring five official religions for China: Catholicism, Protestantism, Islamism, Buddhism, and Taoism. These five approved religions were given Mao Zedong and the CCP as their head. Each religion also had a "patriotic association" at the

---

[10] R. Fife and S. Chase, "Trudeau Condemns China's Encroachment on Hong Kong and Invites Expats to Return Home," *The Globe and Mail,* June 4, 2020, https://www.theglobeandmail.com/politics/article-trudeau-condemns-chinas-encroachment-on-hong-kong-and-invites-expats/.

[11] V. Strauss and D. Southerl, "How Many Died? New Evidence Suggests Far Higher Numbers for the Victims of Mao Zedong's Era," *Washington Post,* July 17, 1994, https://www.washingtonpost.com/archive/politics/1994/07/17/how-many-died-new-evidence-suggests-far-higher-numbers-for-the-victims-of-mao-zedongs-era/01044df5-03dd-49f4-a453-a033c5287bce/.

RAB, responsible for maintaining their adherence to state authority. All other religions were strictly forbidden.

Religious practice was tolerated to some degree in communist China until 1966, when Mao's Cultural Revolution began. During this period of violent cultural upheaval, there were no religious practices allowed at all. All temples, churches, and mosques were shuttered. Clergy were sent to re-education camps. Religion went underground throughout the Republic, as it was considered an enemy of the state.

> ... when he sensed that revolutionary fervor in China was waning, Mao proclaimed the Cultural Revolution. Gangs of Red Guards—young men and women between 14 and 21—roamed the cities targeting revisionists and other enemies of the state, especially teachers.
>
> Professors were dressed in grotesque clothes and dunce caps, their faces smeared with ink. They were then forced to get down on all fours and bark like dogs. Some were beaten to death, some even eaten—all for the promulgation of Maoism. A reluctant Mao finally called in the Red Army to put down the marauding Red Guards when they began attacking Communist Party members, but not before 1 million Chinese died.[12]

This persecution would last ten years, until 1976, when Mao died and the revolution ended. After this, it wasn't until 1982 that the CCP officially lifted the ban on religion. It enshrined some level of religious freedom under the *Constitution of the People's Republic of China*, Chapter II, Article 36, which reads:

> Citizens of the People's Republic of China enjoy freedom of religious belief. No state organ, public organization or individual may compel citizens to believe in, or not to believe in, any religion; nor may they discriminate against citizens who believe in, or do not believe in, any religion. The state protects normal religious activities. No one may make use of religion to engage in activities that disrupt public order, impair the health of citizens or interfere with the educational system of the state.

---

[12] L. Edwards, "The Legacy of Mao Zedong Is Mass Murder," The Heritage Foundation, February 2, 2010, https://www.heritage.org/asia/commentary/the-legacy-mao-zedong-mass-murder.

> Religious bodies and religious affairs are not subject to any foreign domination.[13]

The CCP had managed a conciliatory tone in the Constitution's Article 36, but despite its promise of freedom of religion, it firmly kept the power to control religious practice if it "disrupted public order," for example. The phrase "disrupted public order" is the kind of weakly defined argument that would allow arbitrary interpretations by law enforcement to shut down worship services, close churches, and imprison church members. The conciliatory tone would not last long, either.

In 1991, the CCP was horrified to witness the collapse of the Soviet Union. Their reaction was not to blame the Soviet's Marxist-Leninist ideology, which China also followed, but to seek out alternative reasons for such a collapse:

> The CCP dispatched researchers to Russia and Poland to determine what had gone wrong there. However, Party ideology prevented anyone from discussing the main problems, such as repression, economic stagnation and the horrors of the Soviet gulag. Instead, the conclusion was that religion was to blame. The impetus of revolution in Eastern Europe had nothing to do with flaws in the implementation of Marxism-Leninism, but rather lay in the persistence of religious faith. Consequently, the CCP's current religion policies are an extension of the lessons drawn from analysing China's own history and the demise of the ideologically aligned European Marxist states.[14]

Although it has allowed religious activity to be practised since 1982, beginning in 2018, the CCP has been recorded demolishing Christian churches and tearing down Christian symbols in mainland China.[15] The churches being destroyed include ones that don't belong to China's official five permitted faiths,

---

[13] "Constitution," The National Congress of the People's Republic of China, March 14, 2004, http://www.npc.gov.cn/zgrdw/englishnpc/Constitution/2007-11/15/content_1372964.htm.

[14] J. Powers, "China's Religion Problem: Why the Chinese Communist Party Views Religious Belief as a Threat," University of Nottingham: Asia Research Institute, October 17, 2019, retrieved July 13, 2023, from https://theasiadialogue.com/2019/10/17/chinas-religion-problem-why-the-chinese-communist-party-views-religious-belief-as-a-threat/.

[15] R. Goldman, "Chinese Police Dynamite Christian Megachurch," *The New York Times*, January 12, 2018, https://www.nytimes.com/2018/01/12/world/asia/china-church-dynamite.html#:.

typically Christian non-denominational churches that claim to strictly follow the Holy Bible. In China, such churches are known simply as "house churches," and their congregations can be quite large, with some having as many as fifty thousand members. *The Guardian* estimates the population of Chinese Christians at approximately 60 million.[16] In the meantime, the state continues to control all the five permitted religions with severe limitation:

> Religious believers, particularly leaders such as Buddhist monks and nuns or Muslim imams, are forced to participate in the ongoing propaganda indoctrination and to publicly endorse government-produced versions of their faiths. Chinese Christians, for example, are expected to reject salvation by faith and the Resurrection (because Marxist materialism denies the possibility of life after death). Buddhists are required to adopt a version of their religion created by non-Buddhists that fails to include most of the core principles and practices encoded in their scriptures.[17]

Xi Jinping has increased his persecution of religion over fear of a similar Soviet-style collapse. Although some scholars believed that collapse was due largely from failures in implementation of Marxist-Leninist ideology, it was likely a complex mix of factors. It's entirely likely the CCP's assessment of religion as a very serious contributor to the collapse of the Soviet Union was correct. The communist failure of the Soviets demonstrated European populations couldn't be controlled when they displayed resistance maintained through faith. Members of churches organized themselves into resistance cells on the level of both family and church (institutions of civil society!), which created an anti-communist bulwark. It allowed people to maintain their resolve in the face of a debilitating circumstance. They conducted underground worship services, meetings, and Bible studies to circumvent communist rule. By the time many of the network components were exposed, the membership was too great to be challenged.

---

[16] L. Kuo, "In China, They're Closing Churches, Jailing Pastors—and Even Rewriting Scripture," *The Guardian*, January 13, 2019, https://www.theguardian.com/world/2019/jan/13/china-christians-religious-persecution-translation-bible.

[17] J. Powers, "China's Religion Problem: Why the Chinese Communist Party Views Religious Belief as a Threat," University of Nottingham: Asia Research Institute, October 17, 2019, retrieved July 13, 2023, from https://theasiadialogue.com/2019/10/17/chinas-religion-problem-why-the-chinese-communist-party-views-religious-belief-as-a-threat/.

PART IV: THE WHEAT AND THE TARES

LIVE NOT BY LIES

In his book, *Live Not by Lies* (2020), American author Rod Dreher investigates specific examples of how the Europeans taken over by communism after WWII were able to resist. Such people fought tooth and nail against communism and its militant atheism, often ending up intimidated, wounded, imprisoned, tortured, or murdered for their efforts.

Live Not by Lies is a moving collection of accounts of the individual Christians who endured such persecution. Story after story of dissidents from Poland, Hungary, Czechoslovakia, and Romania comprise the reality of a faith in Christ that held people together in the most trying of times. There are also testimonials from families that lived within the Soviet Union itself, explaining how they survived the constant persecution, including night-time raids and executions of clergy members to terrorize others. The Russian Orthodox Church continued to bear the brunt of this evil. One priest that Dreher focuses on, who exemplifies courage in the face of evil, is Father Dmitry Dudko of the Russian Orthodox Church:

> In his 2014 book about Father Dmitry, The Last Man in Russia, journalist Oliver Bullough quotes an atheist saying that after hearing the priest preach, "the immorality of the Soviet society, its inhumanity and corruption, its lack of a moral code or credible ideals, means that Christ's teaching comes through to those who it reaches as a shining contrast. It stresses the value of the individual, of humanness, forgiveness, gentleness, love."
>
> Another witness said that "when Father Dmitry answered our questions publicly, it was like a mouthful of water." The priest stressed to his audiences that they needed to cultivate hope that tomorrow can be better, and that they must embrace the suffering and love them into healing. Bullough says that in 1973, when Father Dmitry's talks became known all over Moscow, the priest drew atheists, intellectuals, Christians of all denominations, and even Jews and Marxists.
>
> Why did they come? Because they lived in a total system that insisted that it had all the answers to life's questions. But the people, they were completely miserable, and lost, and in pain. They knew it was all a lie, because they were living within

that dark lie. They were drawn to people who looked like they were living the light of truth.[18]

When the leader of a free country, such as Prime Minister Justin Trudeau of Canada, has a record of believing and supporting a statist approach, it's a serious concern. When such a leader appoints government officers who seriously lack care for others, such as former Governor General Julie Payette, it's a stark sign the government is misaligned. Evidence of militant atheism is a dangerous signal that there are ideologues present with more aggressive and invasive beliefs in the woodwork, eager to eliminate Christianity. Currently, over 22 million Canadians claim to be Christians, but it's far from clear how many of them realize that their faith is in jeopardy under statist ideologies. Such statist approaches should be spotlighted and called out for the dark intentions they hide.

Of course, not every atheist is militant, so it would be far too simple to paint them together with the communists under Mao or Stalin. Other atheists, who didn't support their belief with force and lived within those communist systems, were often dissatisfied. They were offered the chance to feel the warmth of the light of those like Father Dmitry of the Russian Orthodox Church. If that sort of "friendly" atheism applies to you, then I offer that the community that allows atheism by choice is not the same community that forces atheism for all. Ask yourself which is which, and which community you would rather be a part of.

---

[18] R. Dreher, *Live Not by Lies: A Manual for Christian Dissidents* (New York, NY: Sentinel, 2020), 157.

CHAPTER FIFTEEN
MODERN MARXIST METHODOLOGY

THE MEDIA TODAY is incredibly sensationalist, whether mainstream or alternative. In contrast to the click-bait trend, it may be best to avoid writing or sharing inflammatory material. There's just no good result that occurs from posting such rubbish. All you end up proving is that there's an audience within which individuals share the same *emotional trigger*. While that's not an especially flattering accusation, we all have triggers to some extent. That may bring up images of fragile snowflakes whining for social justice, but the term "emotional trigger" doesn't necessarily imply something that makes you feel afraid. Emotional triggers can make you feel other emotions too, like anger. An emotional trigger can instantly change your emotional state, in part due to memory patterns and associations brought up each time the emotional trigger is experienced. That reaction is largely subconscious, so it's nearly impossible to control the moment it happens.

In this chapter, there are four key Marxist methodologies to remember: emotional triggers, emotional reasoning, dichotomous thinking, and direct action. Let's take a quick look at them here:

Emotional triggers are like thought buttons, pressed by an event to elicit an emotional response from memory. They can evoke the gamut of negative human emotions, including sadness, shame, anger, fear, panic, and defensiveness. Emotional triggers act fast because the brain processes emotion faster than it can process a rational response. Extremist groups use this to their advantage by promoting disinformation and memes that incite their members into action.

Emotional reasoning is the colouring or interpretation of events that first hits the brain before a rational thought process can be completed. It's so fast that it can't be addressed in the moment but instead must be dealt with retroactively. It sometimes elicits a response wholly inappropriate or entirely based on a perception instead of the reality of an event. This is especially dangerous because emotional reasoning can be abused by deception and the creation of false and inflammatory interpretations of events.

Like emotional reasoning, *dichotomous thinking* is a cognitive distortion, a thought process more associated with mental illness but also occurring in those with normal thought patterns. Dichotomous thinking is the grouping of all individuals into either "for" or "against" on a particular issue, with no exception allowed for individuals to abstain from participation. Dichotomous thinking is particularly divisive because it causes enmity between identity groups that may not necessarily be in conflict at all.

Direct action is a term used by extremist groups for engagement in physical actions designed to reflect and promote their ideology. It typically refers to protests but can also include more violent acts such as threatening, lynching, and damage to public property. The more unstable an individual is, the more likely they are to conduct the most violent forms of direct action possible, which may involve criminal acts up to and including murder. Extremist groups utilize their most unstable members to conduct the most dangerous forms of direct action, so as to retain the more stable group members to continue on the movement. They display a distinct lack of concern for the unstable members, who are abused to conduct criminal actions.

JUSTIN TRUDEAU MAKES HIMSELF AN EMOTIONAL TRIGGER

For many Canadians, Prime Minister Justin Trudeau has become an emotional trigger, and that's something he promulgates whenever possible. In a surprising way, it's to his advantage, because it often makes his opponents look like a bunch of buffoons foaming at the mouth when they snap back. A good example of this occurred when he purposefully called out people against vaccine mandates in December of 2021: "They don't believe in science/progress and are very often misogynistic and racist. It's a very small group of people, but that doesn't shy away from the fact that they take up some space," he goaded. "This leads us, as a leader and as a country, to make a choice: do we tolerate these people?"[19]

---

[19] Dave Naylor, "Trudeau Calls the Unvaccinated Racist and Misogynistic Extremists," *The Western Standard*, December 29, 2021, https://www.westernstandard.news/news/trudeau-calls-the-unvaccinated-racist-and-misogynistic-extremists/article_a3bacece-2e14-5b8c-bf37-eddd672205f3.html.

It was unabashedly inflammatory rhetoric, but it served its purpose. People noticed and were outraged. Trudeau was trying hard to emotionally trigger his opposition into over-reacting. The Freedom Convoy would begin its journey to Ottawa on January 22, 2022. Trudeau's inflammatory words from December had become catch phrases of ridicule among the truckers as they made their way to the nation's capital.

The results of Justin Trudeau becoming a widespread emotional trigger can be seen in the numerous ridiculous, more rarely criminal, over-reactions against him, which tend to make him look like a victim.

When Corey Hurren, a reservist with the Canadian Rangers, smashed through the gates at Rideau Hall, home to Canada's prime minister, on July 2, 2020, everyone lost. He jumped out of his black Dodge Ram and headed forward armed and on foot. The results could have been devastating, but Hurren was quickly subdued and arrested. It was, of course, a terrifying event for those who lived in Rideau Hall, such as the Trudeau family, though they weren't there at the time. Hurren, who didn't show remorse during court proceedings, was sentenced to six years in prison.

Suddenly, everyone who expressed a legitimate beef with the federal Liberals might end up conflated with Corey Hurren. Hurren helped subvert legitimate, non-violent claims against Trudeau and place them into a more easily assailable light: that the poor Prime Minister is a victim of a handful of vicious Canadians who promote conspiracy theories.

The Woken Promises Facebook page, which we discussed in Chapter Thirteen, has only a single post online that cracked the 100,000 views barrier.[20] It was a ten-minute critique of Trudeau's inflammatory speech to the European Parliament in March 2022, *and people loved it*. It provided sound, rational arguments against his conflation of the Russian invasion of Ukraine with the Freedom Convoy in Canada. Trudeau may have been the emotional trigger in that post, but the analysis provided didn't play along. He provided the views; Woken Promises provided the reality.

A funny or crude meme can rack up a thousand Facebook likes in short order, while a carefully written news story is fortunate to get a tenth of that action. And it does matter what gets the action, because social media algorithms preferentially disseminate stories that have higher engagement stats, such as likes, retweets, mentions, etc. You either get noticed, or you lurk in relative obscurity.

---

[20] Woken Promises, "Trudeau's Europe Speech Analyzed," Facebook, March 25, 2022, https://www.facebook.com/100070211810265/videos/507198257463301.

In the online world, people can use emotional triggers to ensure they get the action necessary to ultimately monetize their content, though I think that should be discouraged in the face of the enmity it causes.

We bring up emotional triggers for two important reasons.

EMOTIONAL REASONING

Almost all media outlets peddle such inflammatory material because they realize that we humans, as an audience, are rather unsophisticated in how we respond. That's because we're subject to something called emotional reasoning, which can be elicited from emotional triggers. Emotional reasoning occurs whenever you let your feelings dictate reality. If a story makes you feel suddenly angry or disgusted, then that event is horrible or disgusting, *even if it's not true.*

Emotional reasoning is the chief weapon of the Marxist ideology. It relates back to Karl Marx's first interpretations of suffering witnessed by Friedrich Engels in the factories in Manchester, England. When Engels related those stories of victimhood to Marx, the two used them as the basis to prove widespread suffering under the capitalist system. They relied on those stories to evoke emotional reasoning in their readership and to foment revolution against the state. No revolution is going to occur if people aren't *angry* enough.

The reality of industrial capitalism though, however many suffered along the way, is that it reduced worldwide poverty astronomically. That is an eventuality Marx could never anticipate with his emotional reasoning blinders on. In fact, it was already happening during his lifetime:

> It is estimated that 200 years ago some 20% of the inhabitants of England and France were unable to work at all. At most they had enough strength to walk slowly for a few hours each day, which condemned them to begging for the rest of their lives. Karl Marx foresaw the impoverishment of the proletariat, but when he died in 1883, the average Englishman was three times richer than in 1818, the year in which he was born.[21]

Emotional reasoning is the chief weapon of every Marxist ideologue, whether they are socialists, communists, the No Pride in Policing Coalition, BLM, Antifa, or the academics who fuel such movements. It's a weapon for Marxists because

---

[21] R. Zitelmann, "Anyone Who Doesn't Know the Following Facts about Capitalism Should Learn Them," *Forbes*, July 27, 2020, https://www.forbes.com/sites/rainerzitelmann/2020/07/27/anyone-who-doesnt-know-the-following-facts-about-capitalism-should-learn-them/?sh=3cf9d5fd3dc1.

CHAPTER FIFTEEN: MODERN MARXIST METHODOLOGY

it activates the collective anxieties of a group and mobilizes them into what they call direct action. Direct actions are measures such as blockades, protests, riots, and more extreme physical manifestations of emotion. These manifestations can lead to violence and death—the worst of consequences—for what are, very often, entirely artificial reasons. Lies can cost lives. For Marx, emotional reasoning was necessary to achieve the greatest direct action possible: a revolution.

The second reason we mention emotional triggers is because they're not confined by ideological boundaries. The same kind of emotional trigger might set off people on the left and the right. This is where anti-police sentiment rears its ugly head. Take for instance the "ACAB" slogan. This is a currently popular leftist acronym which stands for "All Cops Are Bastards." It's a particular favourite of Antifa militants, but also for rank-and-file radical leftists (tankies and trots).

However, there are a whole lot of people with a whole lot of other ideologies who also don't like police at all. Such individuals often automatically jump on board with angry slogans (like "ACAB," "defund the police," or even "*%# the police") without realizing the implications. This unchecked sentiment demonstrates the same emotional reasoning that leftists live by, and perhaps worse, it opens them up to other radical patterns of thinking that fall under the Marxist umbrella.

Emotional reasoning is a pattern of thinking belonging to a group of what are referred to as cognitive distortions. These are unfortunate patterns of perception generally associated with mental illness, but all humans conduct these types of subconscious reactions to some extent. Emotional reasoning is the instant reaction you feel from processing information, and it's so fast it occurs before you can rationally work through new data. The rational thought process is slower than emotional reasoning and only occurs after it. Once you begin to rationally process that information, it will now be very difficult to overcome the colouring of your interpretation from the strong initial feelings you first processed with emotional reasoning. That's one reason why it's important to not give in to immediate reactions, as they can commit you to actions not based on reason or reality but on an instantaneous feeling.

Let's say you want to do something nice for a friend and notice a large, uncut pile of firewood in their back yard. On a weekend with nice weather when you have free time, you decide to offer to help your friend split the wood. You even offer that he should sit down and have a beer and chat with you as you do it. He's that good a guy, and he's always helped you when you needed it. But your friend, despite your intent, instantly reacts to this gesture in an unreasonable manner. He gets angry and becomes defensive about how messy his back yard is. He sees your genuine offer of help as criticism, and he flies off the handle. In no time, a genuinely friendly offer has been turned into a sore point, and he tries to start a fistfight with you for making fun of him.

That is emotional reasoning, and it's one critical method Marxist groups use to mobilize their members. They feed them a steady diet of disinformation, memes, and video out of context that will elicit immediate, angry emotions, regardless of the truth of the matter. From there, people are often easy to manipulate into various actions, ranging widely from financial support (passive) all the way to extreme violence or even murder.

ANTIFA MANIPULATE THE SUFFERING

In his book *Unmasked: Inside Antifa's Radical Plan to Destroy Democracy* (2021), journalist Andy Ngo discusses how Antifa uses the most vulnerable of its members in such fashion. Those individuals often exist on the periphery of the organization, which affords Antifa some protection, as they don't lose key ideologues from arrests or other issues, but rather "disposable" foot soldiers.

> Antifa are often assumed to be upper-class spoiled brats by their detractors, but this isn't broadly true. I've looked through records and backgrounds of nearly a thousand people arrested at antifa riots to get a better sense of who they are. While some are indeed highly educated and in white-collar professions ranging from law to academia to health care, those who are involved in the street violence are disproportionately individuals dealing with housing insecurity, financial instability, and mental health issues like gender dysphoria. Antifa could not give a damn if those people end up injured, imprisoned, or dead in the furtherance of their political agenda.[22]

This is the paradox of the matter. Marxist organizations will rely on those hurting the most, suffering the most, to do the dirty work for the rest of them. Look at the Marxist professors in their ivory towers; they don't dirty their hands

---

[22] A. Ngo, *Unmasked: Inside Antifa's Radical Plan to Destroy Democracy* (New York, NY: Center Street, 2021), 239.

CHAPTER FIFTEEN: MODERN MARXIST METHODOLOGY

with the most dangerous physical aspects of their movement. They use the poor and suffering every bit as much as the capitalist system they target.

Antifa is but one Marxist organization that frequently uses cognitive distortions such as emotional reasoning to further its goals. Black Lives Matter is another.

BLM: FOUNDED ON LIES

Black Lives Matter was first formed on July 13, 2013, when George Zimmerman was acquitted for the shooting death of an unarmed Black teenager named Trayvon Martin. Zimmerman had shot and killed Martin on February 26, 2012, in Sanford, Florida. It's important to see how BLM members reacted to the news the night Zimmerman was acquitted:

> That night we watched the news as it broke. In our respective homes we scoured the Internet and digested think pieces, commentary, tweets, and spent the night taking in the collective shock felt across the globe. Flurries of texts were exchanged with our friends. Our people were in a state of shock. It was common knowledge that, historically, police were rarely, if ever, found guilty when they killed Black people. But surely, we all thought, this case would be different.[23]

Notice the highly evocative language, which demonstrates that emotional reasoning was in high gear that night and is still something the authors wish to elicit. Also notice that the authors are conflating George Zimmerman with the police. Zimmerman is not a police officer. Connecting Zimmerman to police officers is a way to connect to the emotion people feel when dealing with police officers. This is a false conflation.

The BLM account continues:

> This was never just about Trayvon Martin and Zimmerman. The fervour on both sides of the debate was indicative of a more complex system of issues impacting Black people in the United States, Canada, and throughout the African diaspora. Cultural commentators were making the links between Martin

---

[23] R. Diverlus, S. Hudson, and S. M. Ware, *Until We Are Free: Reflections on Black Lives Matter in Canada* (Regina, SK: University of Regina Press, 2020), location number 195.

and the legacy of North America's chattel slavery; Jim Crow laws in the United States continued investment in prison cages, disenfranchisement, and the "wars" on drugs, gangs, and guns—the accepted rhetoric for what is really a war on Black people. Zimmerman represented the deep-seated anti-Black attitudes enshrined in North American culture; he was the new face of white supremacy.[24]

The second BLM paragraph contains another false conflation, citing George Zimmerman as "the new face of white supremacy." George's mother is of Afro-Peruvian descent, and calling him "White" is unfortunately a sign of the clouded opinion of the authors as opposed to the reality of the situation. Zimmerman also had Black friends, including one he attempted to start an insurance business with. Linking Zimmerman's killing of Martin to chattel slavery and the African diaspora is equally bogus.

Why were BLM lying like this? The answer is two-fold. Firstly, stating the truth doesn't induce enough emotional reasoning, so it was necessary to evoke the memories of police and White supremacy in these passages, although they have nothing to do with George Zimmerman. The other reason is because they're aiming for a second cognitive distortion called "dichotomous thinking," a relative to emotional reasoning.

DICHOTOMOUS THINKING

Dichotomous thinking occurs when we lump people into two groups: for and against. Everyone we meet is therefore either for us or against us. There is no neutrality. There is no disinterest. You had better pick a side, or we will pick it for you. This fits in perfectly with BLM's constant conflation of White supremacy, the police, and ubiquitous racism. Importantly, this conflation is a tenet of critical race theory, the Marxist-based theory we looked at in Chapters ten and twelve. You are either in support of BLM, or you are part of the racist, cop-loving, White supremacist system everywhere that is against BLM. It's a ridiculous oversimplification and one that causes very serious division by not allowing people to avoid being involved.

The only thing BLM seem to have right in their book regarding Zimmerman is referring to him as a "cretin." Zimmerman is obviously a person of low moral character and a wannabe vigilante who uses state laws—Florida's "stand your

---

[24] Ibid., location number 208.

ground law"—to hide his stupidity behind. The law is the law, however, and it must bind everyone. That's why Zimmerman was acquitted. It had nothing to do with race or White supremacy. Such declarations are meant to propagate cognitive distortions, to keep people angry in the face of a rational outcome.

The author examined the Trayvon Martin case in as much detail as the Internet allowed, including many different angles and opinions. He listened to much of the trial testimony and the phone call recording. In none of these did it come out that Zimmerman had acted illegally under Florida law or that he was verifiably racist. And you don't have to take the author's word for it. After Zimmerman's acquittal, the US Department of Justice (DOJ) investigated him for a total of three years, looking for a reason to try this as a hate crime. The DOJ found that Zimmerman did not meet the necessary standard to be prosecuted for a federal hate crime, and the investigation was dropped.

What seems abundantly clear is that there was no acceptable reason for Zimmerman to pursue Martin (and earlier, Martin's girlfriend) that night. Zimmerman was neither qualified nor were his suspicions of criminal activity sufficient to justify stalking Martin. But that wasn't the issue being contested in the courts. Once Martin engaged Zimmerman in a fight, the legal circumstances governing their interaction changed. There was no eyewitness to the fight, and it had to be reconstructed from circumstantial evidence. Zimmerman fired one shot—that's it. In that fight, Trayvon seemed to dominate the squealing-for-his-life Zimmerman, and could possibly have harmed him to a significant extent if Zimmerman had not shot him first. That doesn't change the fact that Zimmerman shouldn't have followed Trayvon in the first place—the police even asked him to stop as he was calling them during the stalking.

The outrage spawned by the acquittal of Zimmerman was swift but not highly organized. Civil rights leader Jesse Jackson insisted the DOJ get involved immediately, and Rev. Al Sharpton said the result was a "slap in the face to the American people." Small scale protests of up to one hundred people popped up around the US, with some vandalism and minor property damage reported. The result of Zimmerman's acquittal turned out to be a minor tremor, caused largely by emotional reasoning. A year later, however, the US would be shaken to its very core from a major quake, from the very same kind of incident.

On August 9, 2014, White police officer Darren Wilson shot and killed unarmed Black teenager Michael Brown in Ferguson, Missouri.

Before any verified information could be released on the shooting, Marxist agitators launched into action. A disinformation campaign began, claiming that teenager Michael Brown had thrown his hands in the air and said, "Don't shoot!" immediately before he was gunned down by officer Wilson. The protest chant quickly became "Hands up! Don't shoot!" to signify police brutality and lawlessness had occurred in the face of submission.

People were incensed and violent protests erupted the day following Brown's killing. Several stores were broken into and looted. A gas station and a convenience store were burned down. Police came out with full riot gear and helicopter support to restore order in Ferguson. They failed, despite a militaristic approach.

If that doesn't prove that direct action was the goal of emotional reasoning, let's hear it from BLM themselves:

> The small town of Ferguson became ground zero for an uprising. With Trayvon Martin's murder still fresh in our collective memory, Black communities across North America reached their boiling point. At the time Black Lives Matter, a loose coalition of American freedom fighters, organized a Freedom Ride to Ferguson. Busloads of freedom fighters descended onto Ferguson to lend solidarity and support to the Black people of Ferguson, then engaged in continuous protests.[25]

There it is, by BLM's own admission: their Marxist organization using emotional reasoning ("boiling point") to fuel direct action ("Busloads... descended on Ferguson").

Things got worse as rioters poured in. The riots increased in scope and size, and on August 16, 2014, a State of Emergency was declared in Ferguson and a curfew implemented. The National Guard were called in two days later to aid Ferguson Police, and it took until August 24 before the protests significantly slowed.

In the meantime, a grand jury was called to decide on how to proceed with officer Darren Wilson. After hearing extensive evidence, they chose not to indict him on November 24, 2014. It turns out that after thorough investigation, all that "Hands up! Don't shoot!" chanting was nonsense. Multiple eyewitnesses helped paint a clear picture of what actually happened, which corroborated the existing evidence collection.

---

[25] Ibid, location number 237.

CHAPTER FIFTEEN: MODERN MARXIST METHODOLOGY

Michael Brown had initially assaulted the officer. Wilson was trying to question Brown from the position of being seated in his police vehicle. When Brown approached the vehicle, officer Wilson tried to exit it but was blocked by Brown. Brown then reached in and tried to grab Wilson's service pistol. Shots were fired inside the vehicle as the two struggled to control Wilson's firearm. Brown was injured, and he began to run down the street. Wilson got out from the vehicle and ran after him. Brown stopped running after a short distance, turned, and charged. Multiple witnesses, including Brown's friend Dorian Johnson, saw Michael shot down while charging the officer. It was nothing at all like the protesters had made it out to be (execution of a surrendering man). But those facts—the truth—didn't matter.

Following the grand jury decision, a new wave of protests erupted in Ferguson and across the US in 170 cities, and criminal acts boiled over. The National Guard was called in once again to restore order. This time, the people didn't care about the reality of the verdict; they cared about having their anger quenched with "justice." This was emotional reasoning.

The very foundation of BLM, which includes confessed "trained Marxist" co-founders Patrisse Cullors and Alicia Garza, was built under false pretenses.[26] BLM was founded on lies. Racial inequalities may exist to some degree in society, but what the Marxists did in these seminal incidents that gave BLM some initial level of legitimacy was to lie and cajole the populace into supporting them. They made people angry with their deception and then used that anger to mobilize people for their cause.

BLM has since had something of a crisis of falling out with its supporters, as more and more of its true intentions have come to light. This is especially disappointing for those concerned with legitimate social justice in view of the truly disturbing death of George Floyd, which was filmed in its entirety and would have made a much more valid case for BLM's formation. It was a direct, completely filmed example of excessive force and an inability to de-escalate.

---

[26] Y. Steinbuch, "Black Lives Matter Co-founder Describes Herself as 'Trained Marxist,'" *New York Post*, June 25, 2020, https://nypost.com/2020/06/25/blm-co-founder-describes-herself-as-trained-marxist/

CHAPTER SIXTEEN
POLICE AND IDENTITY POLITICS

NOW THAT WE'VE seen how emotional triggers, emotional reasoning, and dichotomous thinking were used to make local tragedies in Ferguson and Sanford into a national nightmare across the US, it's time to shift our focus back to Canada. In this chapter, we'll examine the effect of these and other Marxist techniques being used in Canada, and who exactly has been utilizing them. The answer might surprise you.

In this chapter, the key point is that Canadian police forces—municipal, provincial, and national—are being torn apart by identity politics. This is part of the Marxist-Leninist subversion of the law and relies on critical race theory (through identity politics focused on race) to undermine the role of police in both the state and civil society. While police services may clearly benefit from constructive criticism and related reform initiatives, that is not the goal of the extremist groups challenging them today. Such extremist groups include No Pride in Policing, Black Lives Matter, and Antifa. These groups want to defund and ultimately abolish police.

When police choose to engage the broader public by confessing to systemic racism, they are met with derision by extremist groups. Such apologies inevitably demoralize their officers. Despite the pain it causes the rank-and-file, there are certain high-ranking police officers amenable to what is known as confessor behaviour. Coercion of confessor behaviour is a Marxist tactic designed to reinforce self-loathing and shame, rendering the confessor pliable and easier to deconstruct.

The procession of police officers with post-law enforcement aspirations who confess to systemic racism is growing. Herein we look at former TPS chief Bill Blair, and how he has used identity politics to keep his position in the federal Liberals. We look at former RCMP commissioner Brenda Lucki, who was pressured from the media to define her stance on systemic racism in policing. Lucki appears to have been pushed into confessor behaviour by Blair. We will also look at former Ottawa Police Services (OPS) Chief Peter Sloly, who was already fighting internally with OPS officers after implying they were systemically racist, before he resigned due to issues surrounding the Freedom Convoy in 2022.

Just as in the US, Canada has also had BLM and Antifa protests, with the largest ones to date occurring in Vancouver, Edmonton, Montreal, and Toronto. These protests are public disturbances where some property damage has occurred, police and media have been assaulted, and agitators arrested. However, there is rarely seen, if ever, the type of burning and looting associated with BLM/Antifa riots in the US. Instead, BLM protesters in Canada have defaced several statues, including one of Canada's first prime minister, Sir John A. MacDonald. It was splashed with pink paint and graffiti in Toronto in July 2020.[1] Antifa, whose protests are rarely reported on in Canada, assembled in Edmonton in February 2021 to try and incite anti-lockdown protesters into violence.[2] Antifa had been witnessed attacking both police and journalists in Montreal in August 2017, as counter-protestors against *la Muete*, a far-right Québécois nationalist group. At that protest, it was clear Antifa was the greater immediate threat to society. Thankfully, the *National Post*, unlike many other media outlets that simply ignore radical left unlawful assemblies, had the courage to cover the violence Antifa engaged in:

> After some anti-fascist demonstrators aimed at least three smoking flares at a line of officers—one of which hit an officer's helmet—Quebec City police announced that the protest had been deemed illegal. Counter-protesters dispersed after throwing fireworks and a flare at police.

---

[1] T. Fraser, "Three Arrested after Demonstrators Splash Paint on Statues of John A. Macdonald and Egerton Ryerson," *Toronto Star*, July 18, 2020, https://www.thestar.com/news/gta/2020/07/18/demonstrators-splash-paint-on-toronto-statues-of-john-a-macdonald-and-egerton-ryerson.html

[2] A. Ahmed, "ANTIFA Attempts to Incite Violence at Alberta Leg with Anti-Lockdown Protestors," *Western Standard*, February 21, 2021, https://www.westernstandard.news/news/antifa-attempts-to-incite-violence-at-alberta-leg-with-anti-lockdown-protestors/article_df3c206c-69ac-572b-b91f-8491a7510fb2.html.

A dumpster on wheels was set on fire and pushed towards a police line on d'Artigny St. Glass bottles and plastic chairs were smashed on the floor.

Masked anti-fascists also targeted the media. Three photographers were aggressed by counter-protesters while trying to take a photo of the smoking dumpster. A Global News cameraman said his camera was taken and thrown to the ground, damaging it.[3]

Thus far, Canadian radical leftist groups present a somewhat reduced threat compared to their American and European equivalents. This may be for several reasons, including that the freedom to assemble peacefully, as granted in the Charter of Rights and Freedoms, does not protect certain actions during such events.

The government of Canada website explains from the Charter of Rights and Freedoms, Section 2:

> 2. Everyone has the following fundamental freedoms:
> c) freedom of peaceful assembly;
> Section 2(c) guarantees the right to peaceful assembly; it does not protect riots and gatherings that seriously disturb the peace: R. v. Lecompte, [2000]. It has been stated that the right to freedom of assembly, along with freedom of expression, does not include the right to physically impede or blockade lawful activities: Guelph (City) v. Soltys, [2009].[4]

It's interesting that the government of Canada has included warnings that Section 2 c) does not protect the right to physically impede or blockade lawful activities. One wonders if future interpretations of this Charter right to peaceful assembly (which, according to the government of Canada website, has so far received "limited judicial interpretation") will be dutifully filled in with more restrictions on protests. It's likely something like that will happen, and soon. It's an eventuality from all the litigation currently underway related to protests during the pandemic.

---

[3] C. Loewen, "Hundreds of Counter-Protesters Swarm Far-Right La Meute Protest in Quebec City,". *National Post*, August 20, 2017, https://nationalpost.com/news/canada/hundreds-of-counter-protesters-swarm-far-right-la-meute-protest-in-quebec-city.

[4] "Section 2(c)—Freedom of Peaceful Assembly," Government of Canada, July 31, 2021, retrieved July 13, 2023, from https://www.justice.gc.ca/eng/csj-sjc/rfc-dlc/ccrf-ccdl/check/art2c.html.

Canada's *Criminal Code* also contains several sections dealing with how protests are classified as unlawful assemblies and further declared as riots (see Part II, Offences Against Public Order, Sections 63-69).

In case you're wondering why the masked militants of Antifa rarely openly protest in Canada, one reason is section 66(2) of the Criminal Code:

> Punishment for unlawful assembly
> 66 (1) Every one who is a member of an unlawful assembly is guilty of an offence punishable on summary conviction.
> Concealment of identity
> (2) Every person who commits an offence under subsection (1) <u>while wearing a mask or other disguise to conceal their identity without lawful excuse</u> is guilty of
>   (a) an indictable offence and liable to imprisonment for a term not exceeding five years; or
>   (b) an offence punishable on summary conviction.[5]

This explains why Antifa had to disperse during their 2017 counterprotest in Montreal after it was declared an unlawful assembly. The charges under the Criminal Code would suddenly become very serious, leading up to five years of jail time. Small protests like that can be very violent, but what about large-scale protests? Canada's largest and most recent example of protest doesn't come from the radical left.

THE FREEDOM CONVOY

It comes rather from what is often referred to as right-wing or even far-right populist ideology. We're referring of course to the Freedom Convoy, a protest in Canada that saw truckers from across the country converge in downtown Ottawa from January 22 to February 23, 2022, to protest vaccine mandates. There were also associated highway blockades on both the Sweetgrass–Coutts Border Crossing, going from Alberta into Montana, and the Ambassador Bridge, connecting Ontario with Michigan. Because of the economic effect and pressure from the US, the blockades didn't last as long as the Ottawa protest.

---

[5] "PART II Offences Against Public Order (continued) Sedition (continued)," Government of Canada: Justice Laws Website, emphasis added, July 7, 2023, retrieved July 13, 2023, from https://laws-lois.justice.gc.ca/eng/acts/c-46/page-7.html.

CHAPTER SIXTEEN: POLICE AND IDENTITY POLITICS

OTTAWA CHIEF OF POLICE PETER SLOLY

In the early days of the Freedom Convoy taking over the streets of downtown Ottawa, the Ottawa Police Board held many emergency meetings to deal with the matter. During those meetings, Ottawa city councillors kept hounding Ottawa police chief Peter Sloly to end the protest. They requested he physically prevent protesters from entering the city on the weekends, when their numbers would surge from a couple of hundred into the thousands. The Board accused OPS officers of being complicit with the protesters. The councillors demonstrated massive frustration with the lack of control over what was happening.

Time and time again, Sloly repeated to the councillors that he was in discussion with his legal team about the possibility of physically preventing protesters from entering downtown Ottawa. The lawyers advised him that the Board's requests would violate the rights of the protesters, so Sloly reasonably decided that he couldn't proceed with them. It was clear Sloly was saying that he wasn't legally able to do what the Board was asking, but they kept blaming him for inaction anyway.

Sloly also said that he didn't have the manpower necessary to control the size of the protests in downtown Ottawa, which had reached a maximum of around 18,000 people. This would be pitted against some fraction of Ottawa's approximately 1,500 officers, who of course had their regular duties to cover as well. Sloly wanted the support of an additional 1,600 officers (plus civilians), more than doubling his own force. By the time he asked for such reinforcement, he had already received officers from the RCMP, Ontario Provincial Police, Durham Regional, and several other municipal police services. Ontario premier Doug Ford didn't believe further reinforcements were necessary, and Justin Trudeau said, "What is needed is being provided," in a press conference on February 11, 2022, suggesting Sloly already had the resources he needed.

One of the councillors bucked the trend of criticizing Sloly: Eli El-Chantiry was a former Ottawa Police Board Chair and had served for twelve years. He made it clear how he thought Sloly was treated:

> "Instead of us standing with the police service and supporting the service, the board was absent, councillors were trashing him publicly every opportunity," Coun. Eli El-Chantiry said in

an interview. "They want police to be in every building, every corner, and all that he had is limited resources."⁶

El-Chantiry also noticed that other police chiefs didn't support Sloly, saying:

> "I was surprised to hear it took us 16 days to establish joint command. Why was that?" he said.
> "This time they left the chief hanging out to dry."⁷

It's likely lawyers were advising Sloly that the OPS could run into potential issues with the Charter of Rights and Freedoms, as seen in the past. They no doubt wanted to avoid the 2010 debacle that occurred in Toronto under the supervision of then chief of police Bill Blair, who was the Minister of Emergency Preparedness at the time of the Freedom Convoy.

MINISTER OF EMERGENCY PREPAREDNESS BILL BLAIR

Blair was at the helm during the G20 summit protests in June of 2010 when bedlam erupted. Police were accused of using excessive force to quell the protests, including the tactic of kettling to conduct mass arrests, as well as the use of tear gas. A class action lawsuit for wrongful detentions and arrests ultimately cost the city of Toronto $16.5 million, and the ongoing litigation was a significant factor in Bill Blair's TPS contract not being renewed:

> The agreement comes after 10 years of court proceedings and negotiations between the Toronto Police Services Board and representatives for about 1,100 people who were arrested during the summit.
>
> Under the settlement, those arrested will each be entitled to compensation between $5,000 and $24,700, depending on their experiences.
>
> The deal also includes a public acknowledgement by police regarding the mass arrests and the conditions in which protestors [were] detained, as well as commitment to changing how protests are policed in the future.

---

⁶ J. Willing, "Sloly Was Left 'Hanging out to Dry' as Ottawa Police Struggled to Control Occupation, Former Board Chair Says," *Ottawa Citizen*, February 16, 2022, https://ottawacitizen.com/news/local-news/sloly-was-left-hanging-out-to-dry-as-ottawa-police-struggled-to-control-occupation-former-board-chair-says.

⁷ Ibid.

Those who were wrongfully arrested will also have their police records expunged.[8]

It's important to note here that the biggest problem during these protests were so-called *black bloc militants*—which were the proto-type for Antifa in North America before it had officially declared itself. These anarcho-communists were the people responsible for most of the property damage and violence during the G20 protests, and they were a very serious challenge compared to what the Freedom Convoy turned out to be.

The Freedom Convoy organizers were, despite what the CBC was letting on, making a reasonable effort to maintain a peaceful protest. As we saw above in both the Charter and the Criminal Code, that is essential to maintaining your right to assemble in Canada. They were in constant contact with the OPP as they entered Ontario. They aided the OPS on the street by alerting them to protesters who were violating the law in any way (such as improper storage of fireworks or fuel). The CBC was increasingly unfair in its evaluation of the protesters as the days went on, but it was also, surprisingly, happy to demonize OPS chief Sloly when he wasn't solving their problems and ended up resigning.

> Sloly's resignation comes as sources tell CBC News he's been accused of bullying and volatile behaviour that has damaged relations with senior leadership and compromised the force's ability to cope with the truck protest.
>
> Multiple sources have told CBC News that Sloly allegedly belittled and berated senior Ottawa Police Service officers in front of their colleagues, and has failed to put forward a solid operations plan to end the crisis.
>
> Sources say he allegedly has come into conflict with members of the OPP and RCMP tasked with assisting the city's law enforcement efforts during the crisis.[9]

---

[8] "$16.5M Settlement Reached in Class-Action Lawsuit over Mass Arrests During 2010 G20 Summit," CBC News, August 17, 2020, https://www.cbc.ca/news/canada/toronto/settlement-class-action-g20-summit-1.5689329.

[9] T. Dhanraj, S. Hoff, and P. Zimonjic, "Peter Sloly Resigns as Ottawa's Police Chief, Says Force Now 'Better Positioned to End This Occupation," CBC News, February 15. 2022, https://www.cbc.ca/news/politics/sloly-ottawa-resigns-behaviour-leadership-1.6352295.

While it's entirely possible Sloly conducted himself in such a manner, and was ultimately not up to the job, what's amazing is how quickly the CBC was willing to change their opinion of him.

Just over a year before this, the CBC was actively defending Sloly for implying there was systemic racism within the OPS. The presence of systemic racism in policing is an unproven social justice narrative the CBC often pushes without sufficient statistical back-up. The author spent time investigating them on this and found their work to be problematic, such as with their *Deadly Force* database we mentioned in Chapter Thirteen. Let's look at how the CBC was at first championing Sloly before they chose a different path.

OTTAWA POLICE ASSOCIATION PRESIDENT MATT SKOF

In an interview with Matt Skof, then head of Ottawa's Police Association (OPA), CBC anchor Adrian Harewood tried his best to show Sloly in a positive light back on September 10, 2020. Skof said the OPA was dissatisfied with Sloly's assertion that a rookie officer had conducted a traffic stop based on race when there was no evidence to support that claim. The CBC was championing Sloly, defending his social justice approach.

The honeymoon didn't last.

The CBC, which has many correspondents who work out of Ottawa, was very involved and very agitated by the Freedom Convoy. They were quite probably too close to that event to be reporting on it objectively.

This is a complicated story. Ugly circumstances suggest possible infighting between various police chiefs, services, and unions. Such problems included the aforementioned Matt Skof and charges against him for breach of trust and obstruction of justice, laid by the OPP in 2019. Skof's beef with Chief Sloly may also suggest a breaking of ranks within the OPS itself, as many officers felt betrayed by Sloly's assertion of systemic racism. It's very possible that assertion contributed to the reluctance other police chiefs showed toward his requests for reinforcements.

There are other takes on this too.

What the press doesn't say is that the police dragging their feet on reinforcements was effectively a passive, entirely legal opposition to the Liberal government of Canada. Sloly himself kept calling the protest a "national" issue and said that he saw there was "no policing solution" to it. This was a clear hint to the federal Liberals that they should deal with the protests in a non-violent way, most preferably by negotiating. Sloly has been credited as promoting less draconian measures since his early days as a cop in Toronto, beginning in the late 1980s. If he did believe in the presence of systemic racism, then he surely wouldn't want to set the precedent that protesters should be subdued by force. That might then happen to groups like No Pride in Policing, Antifa, and BLM, whose claims of systemic racism Sloly seems to have agreed with.

Police wouldn't admit to passive resistance to the federal Liberals if you paid them to. But it might be a good idea to look at the number of police officers across the country who have either resigned or been disciplined for their conduct during the imposition of vaccine mandates.

The police are very aware that a significant reason behind this unrest is the way the federal Liberals handled the pandemic. Like everyone else, they likely feel sympathetic to those who have suffered from lost jobs and the loss of rights and privileges. Worse still, to have a Prime Minister openly taunting his own citizens by calling them racists, misogynists, and science-deniers probably doesn't sit well with officers from a country known for its acceptance of all cultures and races. Given the set of unusual circumstances they had to deal with, the police ultimately did their job and cleaned up the mess Trudeau had made.

Can we see what's going on here?

Here is a suggestion all police officers and citizens should consider, one that they are likely to have already discovered, but it's worth repeating: *Identity politics are pulling the police apart.*

Whether that means Justin Trudeau contributing to inciting the occupation of Ottawa by taunting the protesters with name-calling, former OPS Chief Sloly claiming there is systemic racism and fighting with Skof and the OPA, or the CBC peddling poorly-founded accusations of systemic racism, it's all contributed to severely destabilizing the police across Canada.

The police need to combat these accusations by demonstrating that no systemic racism exists, and they need to maintain that throughout their police forces in unity. The qualifier "in unity" is essential, because right now there is evidence that police, especially the RCMP, are being pressured into becoming politicized under the current Liberal government.

RCMP COMMISSIONER BRENDA LUCKI

RCMP Commissioner Brenda Lucki is probably the best example of what such political pressure can do. While being interviewed by Global News' Mercedes Stephenson in 2020, Lucki dodged the question when asked if the RCMP was systematically racist: "… I have been struggling with the definition of systemic racism and when I think of unconscious bias, there is unconscious bias in the RCMP, most definitely."[10]

When Lucki witnessed the immediate fallout from not admitting the RCMP was systematically racist, she then had a discussion with Bill Blair, where she was pressured to correct herself.[11] Sure enough, she resolved her "struggle" within two days and issued the following statement on the RCMP website:

> During some recent interviews, I shared that I struggled with the definition of systemic racism, while trying to highlight the great work done by the overwhelming majority of our employees.
>
> I did acknowledge that we, like others, have racism in our organization, but I did not say definitively that systemic racism exists in the RCMP. I should have.[12]

What Commissioner Lucki did with this statement was effectively politicize her office and the entirety of the RCMP by submitting to an ideological statement. As the head of her organization, she set the precedent for every officer beneath her. Now other police service members will be evaluated as in conflict with their commanding officers if they don't repeat the same unproven social justice narrative.

Lucki is a careerist. She realizes that in order to keep her job, and more importantly to have a potential future in politics at all (like Bill Blair), she's going to have to sing a different tune. What's disturbing is how quickly she allowed the livelihoods of her fellow officers to be jeopardized so she could retain career possibilities.

Submitting to social justice narratives means police lose respect based on authority, and their work will likely become more difficult as a result of this, as it relies on daily public interaction from a standpoint of authority above all else. A public perception of diminished authority, which the law in Canada doesn't agree with, can contribute to very dangerous situations for both officers and the public.

---

[10] A. Connolly, "RCMP Head Says She's 'Struggling' with Definition of Systemic Racism for Force," Global News, June 10, 2020, https://globalnews.ca/news/7049595/brenda-lucki-rcmp-systemic-racism/

[11] R. Patel, "Public Safety Minister Broached Systemic Racism with RCMP Head before Course Reversal," CBC News: Politics, June 13, 2020, https://www.cbc.ca/news/politics/public-safety-minister-broached-systemic-racism-with-rcmp-head-before-course-reversal-1.5611339.

[12] "Statement by Commissioner Brenda Lucki," Royal Canadian Mounted Police, June 12, 2020, https://www.rcmp-grc.gc.ca/en/news/2020/statement-commissioner-brenda-lucki.

Seeing police as members of the community is important, but seeing them as mall-cops that you don't need to take too seriously is a deadly mistake. Police should also always understand their roles clearly according to law, and not allow self-doubt perpetuated by social justice narratives to cloud their judgement, so critical in emergency situations.

This careerist accusation might still read like it's unproven, but consider that Lucki was investigated by a House of Commons Committee on the RCMP's handling of the mass shooting in Nova Scotia on April 18–19, 2020. This was Canada's worst mass shooting of all time, leaving twenty-three dead, including the shooter. During the investigation, Lucki had three senior RCMP officers (Supt. Darren Campbell, Chief Supt. Chris Leather, and Communications Officer Lia Scanlan) offer their opinions that Commissioner Lucki pressured the RCMP to release data on the weapons involved in the massacre. She presumably did so that the Liberal Party might push for their upcoming assault weapons ban, which, according to Minister of Emergency Preparedness Bill Blair, was well underway by then. Lucki confessed she was indeed under pressure by the government to divulge the weapons used in the mass shooting:

> "Was there pressure from the federal government for information about this incident? Yes," she said, adding that it wasn't surprising given the gravity of the event.[13]

Although she never confessed to being directly pressured by Bill Blair to reveal the firearms involved in the Nova Scotia massacre, Lucki was probably hoping the pressure from the investigation would eventually fade. She probably also hoped that audio recordings of her conversations with other RCMP officers wouldn't suddenly materialize. However, on October 21, 2022, that is exactly what happened. It seems that just enough information from these audio files was released to prove Lucki's involvement, without explicitly naming the Liberal minister behind the scenes. Here's a summary of what she said, from the *National Post*:

> In recordings made on April 28, 2020—nine days after the killings—Lucki says she understands the police force can't

---

[13] R. Raycraft, "Lucki, Blair Tell Commons Committee They Didn't Meddle in N.S. Shooting Probe," CBC News, July 25, 2022, https://www.cbc.ca/news/politics/lucki-blair-ns-shooting-committee-testify-1.6530994.

release certain details about the investigation into how a lone gunman killed 22 people during a 13-hour rampage. But she goes on to say she felt frustrated when she learned the speaking notes used for an RCMP news conference earlier that day did not include basic information about the killer's weapons. Lucki said her desire to publicly share these basic facts was in response to a request she received from a minister's office, though she did not specify which minister or the exact nature of the request.[14]

Although the optics—or in this case *the acoustics*—on this story seem bad, they are in fact much worse than we might initially think. The revelation of Lucki being malleable under government pressure, specifically to facilitate the release of the types of firearms used in the Nova Scotia massacre, was a sign that she was politicizing her role as RCMP commissioner again. The Liberals were pressuring her to release information on the weapons used to promote their desired gun ban, which they had in the chamber for some time before loosing it on the Canadian public on May 1, 2020, just days after Lucki's critical phone calls pushing to release firearm information.[15]

Although many Liberal MPs during the Trudeau years have been associated with scandal, they have proved very difficult to hold accountable. While Liberal MPs like Gerald Butts and Bill Morneau would end up as casualties for the Trudeau administration's mistakes, Trudeau himself has proved to be a kind of Teflon don. Pressure began to mount on Lucki as she appeared to be in the Liberals' pocket, while ministers Bill Blair and Marco Mendicino seemed to entirely escape the limelight. It really pays to have the CBC in your corner too, especially since they control a significant portion of the narrative as it comes out of Ottawa. Despite all the focus being on Lucki, she initially resisted accountability.

> "I'm not going to step down from my position," Lucki said in an interview in Prince Edward Island on [November 23, 2022].

---

[14] "Full Text and Audio: The RCMP Meeting That Sparked Allegations of Political Interference in N.S.," *National Post*, October 21, 2022, https://nationalpost.com/news/politics/ns-mass-shooting-inquiry-full-text-audio-rcmp-commissioner-brenda-lucki-meeting.

[15] J. P. Tasker, "Trudeau Announces Ban on 1,500 Types of 'Assault-Style' Firearms—Effective Immediately," CBC News, May 1, 2020, https://www.cbc.ca/news/politics/trudeau-gun-control-measures-ban-1.5552131.

CHAPTER SIXTEEN: POLICE AND IDENTITY POLITICS

"I won't focus on whether people want me in this chair or not. I'm going to focus on keeping Canadians safe."[16]

Eventually, perhaps at a time when it could be said she wasn't stepping down as a reaction to public pressure, the Commissioner publicly stated she would retire in March 2023.[17] Lucki's appointment to the position of Commissioner was besmirched with the political influence of the Liberal Party of Canada, despite her honest intention of "keeping Canadians safe."

Authority Figures and identity politics. Now it's important to take stock of how all these separate stories of RCMP Commissioner Brenda Lucki, former OPS Chief Peter Sloly, former TPS Chief Bill Blair, and Prime Minister Justin Trudeau fit into those Marxist techniques we discussed beginning in the last chapter. It doesn't seem like they are all contributing to the problem of destabilization of civil society in the same manner, but they're all definitely contributors. Let's begin with looking back at the Prime Minister, continuing what we started in the last chapter.

From the examples we have looked at thus far, we see that Trudeau promotes himself as an emotional trigger for his opposition. He does this by literally taunting his opponents, in this case people opposed to vaccine mandates, by calling them names such as "racist," "sexist," and "science-deniers." What he's doing fits broadly into the category of identity politics.

The effect of this is two-fold.

As we discussed in the last chapter, the biggest effect is the emotional reasoning this taunting elicits. It makes people really angry, and they don't always act rationally in the face of that anger.

But Trudeau's name-calling also has a second effect.

Through promoting dichotomous thinking, Trudeau's name-calling helps create the illusion of "us" vs. "them." Think of how Trudeau named those opposed to vaccine mandates as a "small, fringe minority" against the rest of Canada. People who fear getting the coronavirus (and that is a very legitimate fear) eat this kind of talk up.

---

[16] W. Snowden, and J. French, "Alberta Justice Minister Calls for Firing of RCMP Commissioner Brenda Lucki," CBC News: Edmonton, November 3, 2022, https://www.cbc.ca/news/canada/edmonton/alberta-shandro-rcmp-lucki-removal-1.6661722.

[17] J. Bronskill, "'Not an Easy Decision': RCMP Commissioner Brenda Lucki Will Retire in March," *National Post*, February 15, 2023, https://nationalpost.com/news/canada/rcmp-commissioner-brenda-lucki-says-she-will-retire-in-march.

Much more problematic than those ruled by fear are radical leftists, who often think that anyone on the ideological right is liable to be a science-denier, among other things. Many leftists in Canada are university educated and consider themselves smarter than their ideological opposition, despite the fact that they're open to a host of anti-science ideologies such as social constructivism, postmodernism, Marxism, transgenderism, and radical feminism. When Trudeau accuses the Freedom Convoy of various forms of bigotry, radical leftists uncritically consume his disinformation, and it ultimately fuels their direct action.

We know what Trudeau is doing wrong.

How does the Prime Minister's divisive choice of identity politics reflect in RCMP Commissioner Brenda Lucki and former Chief of the OPS Peter Sloly? When they agreed to accuse their respective forces of systemic racism when there was anything but ample proof of that, they both may have caused lasting damage. What they both demonstrated was a product of Marxist subversion, and in both Lucki's and Sloly's case, there is a strong argument to be made for their subversion being catalyzed by careerist aspirations. Both individuals demonstrated a want to obtain a higher career path, and perhaps a high salary associated with that intoxicating level of power.

Sloly had desired to be the police chief in Toronto after twenty-seven years of service there but was passed over. He had a history of addressing issues of race within the police force, which is very likely the reason he was chosen for the Ottawa job in 2019, as well as becoming the first Black person to lead the OPS.

> [Former head of Toronto's Police Services Board, Alok] Mukherjee said Sloly has valuable experience that will help the force deal with its challenges—for instance, fighting internally with Toronto police to end the practice of random stops, or carding, which disproportionately affects people of colour.
>
> He also credited Sloly with bringing in experts to train officers to recognize unconscious bias, and said the former deputy chief believes in bringing officers from different units together in special teams to solve problems.[18]

Brenda Lucki was elected to her position, which might make it sound like she was chosen using an unbiased process. Unfortunately, there is evidence for

---

[18] L. Osman, and J. Trinh, "Peter Sloly Named Ottawa's New Police Chief," CBC News: Ottawa, August 25, 2019, https://www.cbc.ca/news/canada/ottawa/new-chief-peter-sloly-1.5255843.

significant bias pushing the RCMP into hiring a female Commissioner when the opportunity arose in 2018. The previous year had seen a landmark class action lawsuit against the RCMP in which female officers' historical claims of sexual harassment were vindicated. Each sexual harassment claimant was awarded between $10,000 to $220,000.

> An unprecedented settlement that will pay up to $220,000 to women who were sexually harassed while working for the RCMP over the past 40 years has been approved by a Federal Court judge, who called the agreement fair and reasonable.
>
> While as many as 20,000 women are believed eligible for compensation, the lawyers involved estimate more than 1,000 claimants will receive about $89 million. The government has set aside $100 million for the payouts, even though there is no total cap.[19]

This situation strongly suggests that the selection of Lucki was influenced by the class-action lawsuit and an attempt by the RCMP to save face after being slapped with a court ruling. It's important to note that neither the RCMP nor the federal government explicitly admitted to any wrongdoing.

This entire scenario is indicative of the type of selection process that is going on within police forces around Canada. Anyone reading these facts must legitimately ask if either Brenda Lucki or Peter Sloly would have been chosen were they not considered part of a marginalized community. This in turn suggests that the merit-based system of selecting the best candidate for the job may have been avoided in both these cases. To make up for Ottawa's racial tensions in Sloly's case, or to make up for the horrible RCMP sexual harassment scandal, in Lucki's case.

And what about Bill Blair, the White male former Toronto police chief from 2005–2015? Was he hired because of his Whiteness and maleness? Doubtful. It's much more likely that Bill Blair got as far as he did in the upper echelons of policing because of the same factors that promoted Sloly and Lucki. Blair was willing to succumb to social justice narratives, even as far back as 2005, when he was appointed Toronto's top cop:

---

[19] C. Perkel and Canadian Press, "Landmark Deal in RCMP Sexual-Harassment Class Action Wins Court Approval," CBC News: British Colombia, May 31, 2017, https://www.cbc.ca/news/canada/british-columbia/rcmp-sexual-harassment-class-action-1.4140138.

> "I believe racial profiling exists," [Toronto Chief of Police Bill Blair] told the Star on the day of his appointment. "If we deny that it exists, how can we deal with it?"
>
> He also made inroads with ethnic communities, and the city's LGBTQ community, becoming the first chief since 1981 to march in the annual pride parade.[20]

Considering the examples of these three "successful" careerist police officers, it's possible to see that instead of electing a candidate based primarily on effectiveness, social justice warriors with police badges were chosen. All these individuals understood that social justice was the key to success in government and industry, but they took a chance that it would finally come to the world of policing.

The question becomes: Did their bent for social justice affect their ability to do the job? It's telling that neither Bill Blair nor Peter Sloly will escape harsh, widespread criticism for their inability to handle major protests—which questions how effective they really were at their job. Brenda Lucki likely succumbed to political influence during the investigation of the Nova Scotia massacre to promote the Liberal gun ban in May of 2022.

CONFESSOR BEHAVIOUR OF CAREERIST OFFICERS

The ultimate question of what they did by claiming the existence of systemic racism in policing is whether such statements are the elicited Marxist goal called "confessor behaviour." While it's impossible to know the genuine state of the individual minds of Lucki, Sloly, or Blair, three obviously accomplished police service members, it's likely they have caused significant damage to the ability of police forces to operate successfully. Another question will be if that confessor behaviour will damage these officers in the long run. That was the original purpose of the Marxist tactic. This is well-explained by former US Space Force Commander Matthew Lohmeier:

> On November 13, 1956, three years after the [Korean] war ended, a report was presented at a combined meeting of the Section on Neurology and Psychiatry at the New York Academy of Medicine as part of a panel discussion on "Communist

---

[20] R. Mendelson, "G20 Proved a Turning Point for Bill Blair," *Toronto Star*. July 31, 2014, https://www.thestar.com/news/gta/2014/07/31/g20_proved_a_turning_point_for_bill_blair.html?rf

Methods of Interrogation and Indoctrination." The report focuses primarily on Chinese efforts to extort "false confessions" from American prisoners, something half of American POWs experience while in captivity. Rather than inflict physical violence, as the prisoners perhaps feared most, the communist captors would seek to manipulate the beliefs, statements, and conduct of prisoners by establishing controlled environments and through the extortion of false confessions.

Why coerce false confessions?

Because, at least for some prisoners, the repetition of false confessions of guilt over time convinced them they were actually guilty. Acquiescence to the idea of one's own actual guilt, in turn, bred self-loathing, self-resentment, generated an internal struggle that was more successful than even exogenously imposed torment of a captor. In the end, it was psychologically crippling, turning the captive into a compliant pawn.[21]

Whatever their reasons for acquiescing to the social justice narrative of systemic racism within policing, Sloly, Blair, and Lucki must internally face the consequences of their confessor behaviour. This in turn will render them increasingly less effective as leaders (in addition to the incalculable damage it does to the rank-and-file police officers that were under them) and will help destabilize policing in Canada. Their compliance, on the other hand, will only serve at making them more effective "pawns," as described by Lohmeier, which in this instance suggests furthering social justice as they advance through the remainder of their careers. Their contribution to policing in Canada is buried under this agenda and doesn't seem to have come to fruition in its effort to appease others to date.

How should we treat police? Should we judge them based on the actions of careerist cops like Lucki, Blair, or Sloly? Certainly not everyone aiming for the captain's chair is a careerist, but there are some concerning signs with these examples. OPA President Matt Skof was clearly exasperated trying to represent members of his union (OPS officers) when they had to deal with Sloly's implication of systemic racism. There is not sufficient evidence to support the claim that systemic racism exists in policing, and confessing to this for the

---

[21] M. Lohmeier, *Irresistible Revolution: Marxism's Goal of Conquest & the Unmaking of the American Military* (Self-Published, 2021), 87.

sake of one's career potentially leads to police officers whose work and lives are compromised.

It's important to treat police with respect, obey the law, and help encourage the ties between police and the community. As we will discuss shortly, although police must be considered as an arm of the state (they answer to the government), they have a unique link to the communities in which they operate. These are communities in which they often live and spend time, and this provides the opportunity to create a bond between peace officer and citizens that is resistant to unjust initiatives. This isn't the same as the military (the other arm of the state), who are detached in that sense and therefore are a much more dangerous choice to enforce laws.

Fighting against police, either individually or in protest, fits in well with radical leftist dogma. It joins in the chants and mimics the graffiti "ACAB" or "defund the police," as used by BLM and Antifa. It furthers the Marxist goal of tearing down society by pitting "us" against "cops," which forces police firmly on the side of the state and the law when they are among us citizens each and every day of our lives. Calling for police reform is another matter entirely, and a subject for perhaps another book. As things stand, in the highly unstable situation that was created by the pandemic and lockdowns, defunding the police would be one of the most foolish, anarchistic choices one could make.

PART V
THE HARVEST

CHAPTER SEVENTEEN

THE ATTACK ON CIVIL SOCIETY AND THE STATE

WE HAVE NOW covered two separate Marxist-based methodologies attacking Canada's free society. As we saw in Chapters Fifteen and Sixteen, radical groups seek to tear down society in the 1850s Orthodox Marxist tradition, while also pushing the woke ideology of today. We also covered the government's attempt to replace the institutions of civil society in Chapter Fourteen. Left-leaning politicians subscribe to this approach because they believe that big government is the best solution to the human condition.

Although many people compare the Marxist-based techniques used by Trudeau and the federal Liberals today to Stalin's militant push for the elimination of institutions of civil society, that push in modern times isn't likely to cause the same destruction it did in the twentieth Century. At least, not initially. It's hard to believe that Trudeau could conduct the acts necessary to place him among history's bloodiest tyrants. He's simply confessed to be an admirer of that approach.[1] He likely admires the power those dictators achieved and somehow believes it can be maintained without killing. For another example of such infatuation with despots, consider how enamoured with Fidel Castro the entire Trudeau family shamelessly was.[2]

In this chapter, everything you need to know is encapsulated in Figure 5 (see following pages). Figure 5 provides a model of the three Marxist-Leninist based attacks currently occurring against Canada.

---

[1] Toronto Sun, "ADMIRING A 'BASIC DICTATORSHIP': Trudeau's Bizarre Praise of China," YouTube video, 4:19, March 1, 2023, https://www.youtube.com/watch?v=sLTGbtfkh_s.

[2] M. Milke, "The Trudeau Family's Love of Tyrants," *Maclean's*, February 28, 2018, https://macleans.ca/opinion/the-trudeau-familys-love-of-tyrants/.

The first attack is lawfare from socialist political parties, including the NDP and Liberals. They are pressing for big government, high taxes, and heavy social controls (laws) to be put in place, regulating various aspects of human existence. The more government-controlled equivalents and regulations put in to replace institutions of civil society, the less it's represented by the Canadian people.

A second front of attack proceeds against both civil society and the state from extremist groups, led by academics from left-leaning universities and colleges. They aim to dismantle institutions of both the state (police and prisons) and civil society (schools and churches). Their goal is violent revolution to overturn the state and civil society together—the total collapse of Canada's free society.

A third form of attack, one we have not yet covered, has become clear within the past few years. The CCP has been revealed to be targeting Canadians, especially members of the Chinese diaspora, to use as infiltrators into Canadian society to increase China's worldwide soft power.

The result of these attacks is to accelerate movement toward a nation-wide crisis where the government can no longer function *for the benefit of Canadian citizens*. Other outcomes of crisis are even less desirable. Historical examples of the outcomes of Marxist-Leninist induced crises are examined herein.

CRISIS: THIRD STAGE OF MARXIST-LENINIST SUBVERSION

In his lectures, KGB-defector Yuri Bezmenov explained just where the real dictators stepped into the mix during the stages of Marxist-Leninist subversion. It wasn't during the initial stage of demoralization (fifteen to twenty years), or the more advanced, second stage of destabilization (see his lecture); it was during the third stage of the total collapse of society, which he called *crisis*.[3,4]

We can think of crisis (in terms explored by Karl Marx himself) as the simultaneous collapse of both the state and civil society in a revolution. This was Marx's goal, as he believed both the government and the business sector

---

[3] GBPPR2, "Yuri Bezmenov: Psychological Warfare Subversion & Control of Western Society," YouTube video, 1:03:15, February 23, 2011, https://www.youtube.com/watch?v=5gnpCqsXE8g&t=2915s.

[4] In Bezmenov's second stage of Marxist-Leninist subversion, called *destabilization*, the goal was radicalization of social interactions. This included radicalization of labour relations and bargaining processes, conflict resolution between neighbours forced into the court system, the media being alienated from the public at large, and the rise of minority group interests. Destabilization was not a long stage and quickly gave way to "crisis."

(civil society was equated with industrial business by Marx) were bourgeoisie controlled. What Marx described as wanting was a total and violent revolution that would destroy both the bourgeois state and the bourgeois civil society. Only then could the proletariat, the noble working class, be freed of the chains imposed on them by the ruling class.

Bezmenov described the stage of crisis not in abstract terms but with real world examples. It happened throughout the Cold War in countries including Iran, Afghanistan, Vietnam, Korea, Grenada, and others. It's important that this crisis not be confused with the type of "trouble" author William D. Gairdner is warning Canadians to avoid in his book *The Trouble with Canada ... Still!*

In Gairdner's understanding, civil society is the middle layer of the "political sandwich" model, comprised of institutions such as marriages, churches, clubs, corporations, etc., made of autonomous individuals (free people) below, not subject to direct control of the state above. It's that middle layer that critically keeps the state at bay and individuals free, in Gairdner's estimation. The concern in Gairdner's political sandwich model is that if civil society collapsed, the state would be directly in control over every aspect of an individual's life, and people would therefore no longer be autonomous.

What Gairdner describes in his model implies that there is an already existing Marxist state attempting to supplant civil society with government-equivalent institutions. He spends a good deal of time demonstrating that his concerns validly stem from the time of Pierre Elliot Trudeau as prime minister (1968–1979 and 1980–1984), when many socialist policies were first introduced in Canada. As we saw in the very first chapter, today's federal Liberals have created a ballooning state, almost doubling in size between 2015–2023. That's a sign that government regulation is greatly increasing in a myriad of sectors.

DIFFERENCES BETWEEN GAIRDNER/GRAMSCI AND BEZMENOV MODELS

In a construction of the overall framework of Marxist-Leninist subversion in Figure 5 below, what Gairdner is focused on is that the state is attempting to take totalitarian control of the people. This aim, in his view, can be achieved by the state replacing institutions of civil society with government-controlled equivalents (see stage 2 in Figure 5 below, top portion).

Figure 5: Violent and non-violent methods of transferring Marxist-Leninist ideology

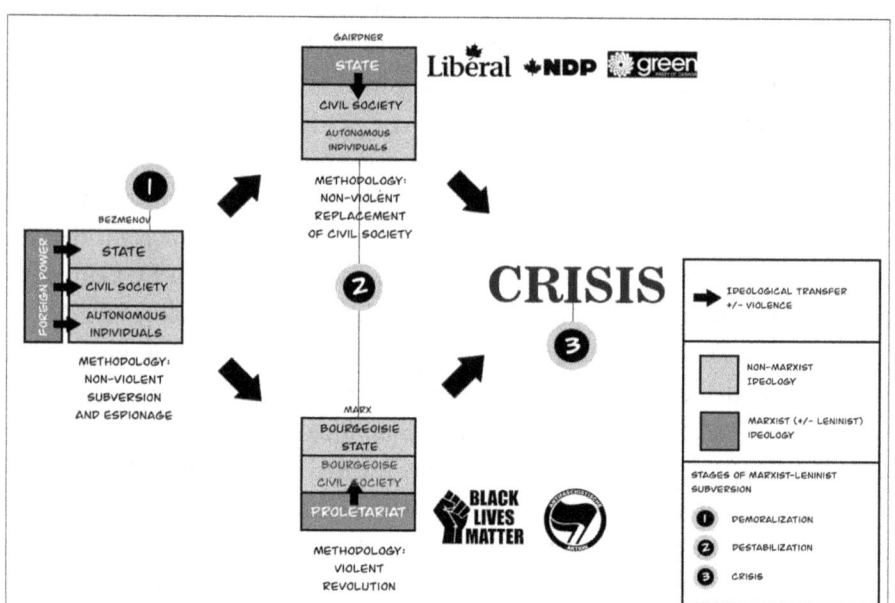

A good example of this push to replace an institution of civil society with a government-controlled equivalent is the federal Liberal initiative to deny grants to churches that didn't attest to abortion rights back in 2018. The Liberals did this in clandestine fashion by sneaking a clause into a grant application for church youth activities asking Christians to violate their beliefs. To receive funding, a church had to endorse the practice of abortion, heralded as "women's reproductive rights." The inclusion of this clause was so repugnant that a Liberal caucus member, Newfoundland MP Scott Simms, requested it be removed.[5] If a church had willingly attested on such a document, it would be very similar to the kind of government-controlled churches existing in communist China we saw in Chapter Fourteen. The clause was scrapped due to heavy backlash.[6]

---

[5] G. Barry, "Liberal MP Says Abortion Clause in Summer Jobs Program 'Not Right,'" CBC News: NL, January 22, 2018, https://www.cbc.ca/news/canada/newfoundland-labrador/scott-simms-abortion-clause-reproductive-rights-1.4498845.

[6] J. Press, "Liberals Drop Contentious Anti-Abortion Test for Summer Jobs Funding," CBC News: Politics, December 6, 2018, https://www.cbc.ca/news/politics/liberals-summer-jobs-program-changes-1.4934674.

Trudeau's motivation for allowing such a clause in the first place was unclear, but the desire to supplant the Church with a government-controlled equivalent was the goal. Trudeau admitted to having changed his stance on abortion back in 2019.[7] Although politicians frequently claim such changes of heart as based on conscience, it's much more likely to reflect what polling tells them will get the most votes and/or pressure from lobbyists and small-interest groups.

This is a critical part of the Gairdner/Gramsci understanding of civil society. You don't have to go about physically destroying and rebuilding the institutions of civil society; they can instead be ideologically subverted. A change in belief system can completely change the function of an institution and render it useless to the wants and needs of the citizenry who would normally have ideologically created it (in a free society). This demonstrates how Gramsci's powerful idea of attacking the cultural hegemony in civil society is an incredibly effective way to destroy those institutions, without breaking so much as a single brick or burning down a single building.

Of the two models presented here demonstrating subversive attacks on society—Gairdner's and Bezmenov's—Gairdner's neatly fits within Bezmenov's overall Marxist-Leninist schema, as demonstrated in Figure 5 above. In Bezmenov's model, there are indeed those who wish to break bricks and burn down buildings—in revolution.

It's clear that just as in the US, there is a devoted, subversive attack on Canada that aims to pit the marginalized communities in civil society against the state to collapse both. This Marxist-Leninist subversion is the goal of Marxist-affiliated groups like No Pride in Policing, Antifa, and Black Lives Matter, who aim to escalate a country as quickly as possible to the crisis stage described by Bezmenov (stage 3 in Figure 5 above). They attack the power of the state by defaming and demoralizing the police. They attack the institutions of civil society by subverting education and religion with ideologically divisive teachings based on critical race theory and intersectionality, which subvert teachers and turn educators into machines of indoctrination, to convert generations of students.

There's even evidence that during the Wet'suwet'en Pipeline Protest in the winter of 2020, non-indigenous, radical left agitators opportunistically joined to help blockade major railways, leading to billions of dollars lost for Canada,

---

[7] C. Tunney, "Trudeau Says His Personal Stance on Abortion Has 'Evolved,'" *CBC News: Politics*, October 4, 2019, https://www.cbc.ca/news/politics/trudeau-abortion-personal-beliefs-1.5308987.

potential train derailments, and defamation for the Wet'suwet'en people.[8,9] Although the CBC has proven unable to report on such radical left agitators, there was a story in *The Guardian* on July 29, 2021, exposing their terrorist tactics and the criminal convictions they led to.[10] We don't wish to include the Wet'suwet'en protest as an overall part of the Marxist-Leninist subversion of Canadian society, because it's unlikely that's why it occurred. It was abused for that purpose by non-indigenous anarchists (possibly including non-indigenous Antifa members), as reported in *The Guardian*: "According to anarchist blogs, the saboteurs were acting in solidarity with Indigenous people to stop construction of the Coastal Gaslink pipeline through Wet'suwet'en territory in northern British Columbia."[11]

Importantly, all these groups have an overlapping aim: to destroy civil society. That's the critical connection between the Gairdner/Gramsci and Bezmenov models. In both cases, civil society is a direct target for attack. The idea then is not to combine these two systems as some grand theory happening under one, incredibly elaborate plan. Let us instead focus on teleology, which will frustrate the ubiquitous approach of calling everything a conspiracy. The evidence suggests that two ideologically similar but clearly independent initiatives, one by political parties and one by extremist groups fueled by academe, both informed by dialectical leftism, compound pressure to collapse civil society.

There is no magic.

There is no hidden chamber with rich White men smoking cigars, planning the end of the world.

There is a Prime Minister who took a knee in solidarity with extremist groups, demonstrating the ideological overlap of two entirely separate forces that share some of the same goals.[12]

---

[8] "Rail Blockade Protesters 'Dragging Our Name through the Mud,' Says Wet'suwet'en Woman," CBC Radio, February 19, 2020, https://www.cbc.ca/radio/thecurrent/the-current-for-feb-19-2020-1.5468142/rail-blockade-protesters-dragging-our-name-through-the-mud-says-wet-suwet-en-woman-1.5468661.

[9] R. D'Amore, "CN Rail Layoffs Will 'Further Complicate' Tangled Supply Chain, Industries Say," Global News, February 19, 2020, https://globalnews.ca/news/6568323/cn-rail-layoffs-supply-chain-industries/

[10] H. Beaumont, "The Activists Sabotaging Railways in Solidarity with Indigenous People," *The Guardian*, July 29, 2021, https://www.theguardian.com/environment/2021/jul/29/activists-sabotaging-railways-indigenous-people.

[11] Ibid.

[12] J. P. Tasker, "Trudeau Takes a Knee at Anti-Racism Protest on Parliament Hill," CBC News: Politics, June 5, 2020, https://www.cbc.ca/news/politics/trudeau-anti-racism-parliament-hill-1.5600803.

But they may not realize nature abhors a vacuum, and that what comes in after that destruction will not be to their liking. The ultimate result of Marxist-Leninist subversion is to have a power come in and take control in place of the fallen state. The state will collapse because people will first protest and then fight against the destruction of their society. They won't be willing to accept unimpeded statism—just look at the growing populist movement in Canada as an example.[13]

As the Soviet Union no longer exists, and the Cold War has long since ended, it's unlikely Russia will significantly participate in the attempt to destabilize Canada, but there are other methods of waging war. There's also a very legitimate concern over communist China, a Marxist-Leninist regime, and what they would do in the wake of such a collapse.

Bezmenov explained the unwavering result of adherence to Marxist-Leninist ideology as "total societal collapse," and it's still difficult to wrap one's head around. All Marxism ever led to was failure, and the KGB knew this because they promoted the ideology in target nations for that very purpose. Despite what its academic proponents believed, all the ideology has ever led to is crisis, and from there, a secondary method—an injection of force—was used to determine the future of the country.

CRISIS: HISTORICAL EXAMPLES
Several historical examples demonstrate that injection of force after Marxist-Leninist subversion brought about a crisis. They fall under one of three categories: foreign military invasions, civil wars, or self-appointed saviours.

Military invasions by foreign countries include examples such as the Sino-Japanese War (1937–1945), the Soviet-Afghan War (1979–1989), and the numerous Eastern European countries occupied by the Soviets after WWII.

Civil wars within this framework include the Lebanese Civil War (1975–1990) and the Chinese Civil War (1927–1937 and 1945–1949). China's fight between Mao Zedong's communists and Chiang Kai-Shek's Kuomintang nationalists was interrupted by Japanese invasion, in which the nationalists and communists joined forces temporarily to fight against it. Chiang Kai-Shek was literally forced to co-operate after he was captured and held by the communists

---

[13] For example, an OPP intelligence report related to the Freedom Convoy warned of several anti-government groups, including Patriot Movement and Plaid Army. See: A. Boutilier, "Ontario Police Considered 'Covert' Surveillance of Anti-Government Group ahead of Freedom Convoy," Global News, October 21, 2022, https://globalnews.ca/news/9217463/opp-covert-surveillance-anti-government-group/.

until his capitulation. The communists believed, in accordance with Marxist-Leninist understanding, that Japan would have destroyed their country if it remained divided. They were likely correct, and the forced union of nationalists and communists probably saved China from, at the very least, a great loss of territory.

Self-appointed saviours include unelected committees that seize powers of the branches of government, turning it into an oligarchy or even a theocracy. They can also include Marxist political parties themselves, which can be viewed as having the strong policies necessary to combat a crisis. For this example, Bezmenov cites the Iranian Revolution (1978–1979). Many unelected "revolutionary committees" appeared out of nowhere to fight for power in Iran, even before there was any revolution. Let's have it in Bezmenov's own words:

> The process [of crisis] starts when the legitimate bodies of power—the social structure —collapses. It cannot function anymore. So instead, we have [an] artificial body injected into society such as non-elected committees. Remember, I was talking about them here? [points to demoralization stage] Social workers who are not elected by [the] people, media who are [the] self-appointed rulers of your opinion, [and] some strange groups which claim they know how to lead society forward. They don't, usually. All they care [about] is how to collect donations and sell their own concocted ideology—[a] mixture of religion and ideology. Here [points back to crisis stage] we have all these artificial bodies claiming power. If power is denied to them, they take it by force. In [the] case of Iran, for example, all of a sudden, we have [a] revolutionary committee. Who—or what—kind of revolution? There was no revolution yet, and yet they had a committee. They were taking power of judgement. They had the power of execution [executive branch]. They had the power of legislation [legislative branch] and they had the power of judicial [judiciary branch], all of them combined in one person who is [a] half-baked intellectual, sometimes graduated from Harvard University or Berkley. He comes back to his country, and he thinks he knows the answer to the social/economical problems.[14]

---

[14] GBPPR2, "Yuri Bezmenov: Psychological Warfare Subversion & Control of Western Society," YouTube video, 1:03:15, February 23, 2011, https://www.youtube.com/watch?v=5gnpCqsXE8g&t=2915s.

CHAPTER SEVENTEEN: THE ATTACK ON CIVIL SOCIETY AND THE STATE

Let's assume you can accept these ideas:

1. Canada has been ideologically influenced by (a) foreign power(s).
2. Canada's institutions of civil society are being replaced by the state.
3. Canada's government is preoccupied with identity politics.
4. Canada's academia is subverted by Marxism (see Woken Promises' video on this).[15]
5. Radical leftist groups in Canada, a product of academe, want violent revolution.

If so, you might then ask the question: What if Canadian society collapsed? The federal government didn't look especially competent during the Freedom Convoy, and that was a largely peaceful, cooperative group of citizens. The government refused to meet with protesters and had to bail themselves out with the *Emergencies Act*. A real threat might prove far more problematic.

CRISIS: WHAT IF IT OCCURRED IN CANADA?

Could Canada be invaded?

That doesn't seem remotely possible. Some might laugh at the suggestion. However, the servicemembers who work for the North American Aerospace Defense Command (NORAD) would find it *less* funny. Both China and Russia have escalated tensions with the US and Canada, and Russia's war with the Ukraine at the time of this writing is still ongoing. As we saw earlier, the director at CSIS saw the threat of China and Russia as significant enough to motivate the Canadian public into protecting themselves. The world is unstable—right now. Yet some people seem determined to test that instability.

Against the wishes of US President Biden and the American military, US Speaker of the House Nancy Pelosi, who demonstrates a preoccupation with woke ideology, suddenly made a stunning display of courage and visited Taiwan at the beginning of August 2022.[16] This was either the bravest or stupidest move since US Vice-President Kamala Harris decided it would be a good idea to discuss Ukraine's relationship with NATO shortly before the Russians invaded.[17] We live

---

[15] Woken Promises, "CBC: Marxist Mouthpiece," Vimeo video, 58:07, October 31, 2020 https://vimeo.com/474298118.

[16] R. Plummer, "Taiwan Braces as China Drills Follow Pelosi Visit," BBC News: Asia, August 4, 2022, https://www.bbc.com/news/world-asia-62416363?fbclid=IwAR22bU8l8rvcj_h2kgKJHtH5lASxuVjiyI8OsViJQb-r4yS_koZoYcAYvh8.

[17] "VP Harris Heralds NATO Unity as Ukraine Crisis Grows," WTTW: Politics, February 18, 2022, https://news.wttw.com/2022/02/18/vp-harris-heralds-nato-unity-ukraine-crisis-grows.

in extremely dangerous times, where the average citizen is disconnected from how close we are to war at any given moment.

A further development during the draft stages of writing this book, after already writing about the concerns NORAD *might* have, occurred when the Defense Command suddenly came under the public eye in the winter of 2022–2023. This was not because they wanted to be in the limelight, either.

A gigantic white balloon, flying at an altitude of sixty thousand feet (about eighteen thousand metres) and visible to the naked eye was spotted by numerous civilians. It was travelling on a course over both the US and Canada. The balloon really was huge—over sixty metres in diameter—and was carrying a correspondingly large payload. Therefore, an explanation to the public was indeed necessary, and NORAD would be the one to give it.

From January 28 to February 4, 2023, NORAD monitored what they identified and confirmed as a Chinese balloon floating surveillance equipment as it travelled over Alaska, Western Canada, and then the continental US. Its journey ended over the coastline of South Carolina when on February 4, US president Joe Biden ordered it shot down. After this, Biden tried to minimize the significance of the unusual incursion: "It's not a major breach … I mean, look, it's totally … it's a violation of international law. It's our airspace. And once it comes into our space, we can do what we want with it."[18]

Despite the inconsistent evaluation offered by Biden, no doubt to save China further international embarrassment, both the US and Canadian militaries publicly confirmed the balloon was equipped for surveillance. Biden, however, rationalized the action of shooting down the intrusive airbag as addressing the danger it posed both to commercial air travel and those on the ground.

Following the incident, the crashed balloon and its tech were retrieved to be studied. Since that time, another three separate objects have been shot down over North American airspace, including over Alaska, the Yukon, and Lake Huron. These three objects were shot down from February 10–12, 2023. Not all these subsequent objects shot down were retrieved, and the public has yet to learn the purposes of all these other objects and exactly why they are now being witnessed invading North American airspace.

This is hardly an invasion of North America in the traditional sense of the word, nor is it a crisis, but if the military is constantly trying to tell us we are under threat from communist China, then it's a message we ignore at our peril.

---

[18] S. Holland, "Biden Says Chinese Spy Balloon Not a Major Security Breach," Reuters, February 9, 2023, https://www.reuters.com/world/us/biden-says-chinese-spy-balloon-not-major-security-breach-2023-02-10/.

Some people believed this story to be a simple escalation in propaganda, and that could always be the real scenario, however unlikely.

Unfortunately, previous evidence demonstrated there was also Chinese communist infiltration occurring on the ground. On November 7, 2022, a blockbuster leak by CSIS, published by Global News, revealed there were a total of eleven candidates in the 2019 federal election who were subject to interference from Beijing. The most bothersome part about the leaks didn't end with China's interference, either. This was pointed out by Dennis Molinaro, a former senior CSIS analyst and expert on foreign interference:

> Molinaro said if the CSIS intelligence warnings sources say were provided to Trudeau are confirmed as accurate, they raise concerns about why the government hasn't yet responded by tabling new legislation to counter the threats.
>
> "The level of foreign interference activity you describe is serious and alarming," Molinaro said. "And if confirmed, the level of interference you describe says to me that foreign adversaries understand the legislative loopholes that exist in Canada and are taking full advantage of them."[19]

Only time will tell how badly Canada has been infiltrated by the CCP, if we can still eradicate such corruption by changing federal law, and if a subsequent invasion related to infiltration by the CCP is imminent. It's most likely this interference is focused on manipulating Canadian policy, however, and not a prelude to invasion of any sort.

CRISIS: VENEZUELA'S MODERN EXAMPLE

If Canada was really brought to crisis, it's unlikely it would be invaded, at least not for a long time. That's because if we look at the critical example of a resource-rich country that collapsed under Marxist-Leninist subversion in modern times, most notably Venezuela, there was no invasion during the long, ongoing crisis. What there was approached a civil war.[20]

---

[19] S. Cooper, "Canadian Intelligence Warned PM Trudeau That China Covertly Funded 2019 Election Candidates: Sources," Global News. November 7, 2022, https://globalnews.ca/news/9253386/canadian-intelligence-warned-pm-trudeau-that-china-covertly-funded-2019-election-candidates-sources/.

[20] "Venezuela Crisis: Maduro Warns of Civil War," BBC News: Latin America, February 4, 2019, https://www.bbc.com/news/world-latin-america-47112284.

PART V: THE HARVEST

The crisis began in 2010 under then President Hugo Chavez but has continued under his successor, Nicolas Maduro, to this day. After implementing increasingly unsustainable communist policies called *Chavismo*, including state ownership, social welfare programs, and price-fixing, Venezuela collapsed in traditional Marxist-Leninist fashion: with hyper-inflation and mass starvation. After some time, the US government decided to impose sanctions against Venezuela's oil exports to try and force out Maduro. The US released a summary of its concerns from the Department of State in March of 2022:

> Maduro, who was not re-elected via free and fair elections, clings to power through the subversion of democratic institutions, manipulation of elections, and force. His policies are marked by authoritarianism, intolerance for dissent, and violent and systematic repression of human rights and fundamental freedoms—including the use of torture, arbitrary detentions, extrajudicial killings, and the holding of more than 300 prisoners of conscience. The Office of Foreign Assets Control sanctioned Maduro in 2017, and in 2020 the Department of Justice charged him with offenses related to narco-terrorism and drug trafficking. The U.S. Department of State's Bureau of International Narcotics and Law Enforcement (INL) posted a $15-million reward for information to bring him to justice. The illegitimate Maduro regime has facilitated widespread corruption and stoked hyperinflation leading to negative economic growth, a humanitarian crisis, and widespread difficulty accessing basic goods and services including food, energy, and water shortages, in a country with the world's largest proven oil reserves.[21]

The situation in Venezuela today is reminiscent of times gone by when the US and the Soviet Union fought for influence in foreign nations. Communist subversion helped lead to a myriad of proxy wars during the Cold War. Those proxy wars famously included Vietnam and Korea, and it's a shocking truth that this kind of thing is still happening in countries like Venezuela in the form of economic warfare.

---

[21] "U.S. Relations with Venezuela. U.S. Department of State," June 27, 2023, https://2017-2021.state.gov/u-s-relations-with-venezuela/.

CHAPTER SEVENTEEN: THE ATTACK ON CIVIL SOCIETY AND THE STATE

Russia may have been targeting Venezuela for a long time. There is some evidence that Russian spies, possibly involved in the KGB's Marxist-Leninist subversion schema, were present in the country as early as 1952. This was well before communism became a serious threat in Venezuela and very near the start of the Cold War. Remember in Bezmenov's lectures that there is a period of indoctrination of fifteen to twenty years required to subvert one generation. Venezuela's massive historical instability would make it an easy target to reach crisis—it has spent most of its existence in political upheaval. The following is a report from *Time* magazine in 1952, revealing the presence of Soviet agents in Venezuela:

> Venezuelan security police intercepted two suspected Russian secret agents at Caracas' Maiquetia Airport a fortnight ago, and later deported them. Last week, after a bitter exchange of protests, Venezuela announced that it had broken off relations with Russia and recalled its chargé d'affairs from Moscow. In Latin America, only Argentina, Uruguay and Mexico still maintain diplomatic relations with the Soviet Union.[22]

In the aftermath of Venezuela's modern-day collapse, Maduro continues trying to suppress dissent. The "winners" of the subversion of Venezuela appear to be those who get Venezuelan oil at a discount, namely the Russians. They appear to have managed this by constructing stable joint-ventures with Maduro's government, which is incredible given Venezuela's history of nationalizing and removing foreign companies.

> The company, called Roszarubezhneft, holds 40% stakes in five joint ventures with the Venezuelan state-run oil giant PDVSA. Together, they produce nearly 120,000 barrels a day of crude, or 15% of the country's current output.[23]

So if Marxist subversion led to crisis in Canada too, what would that entail?

---

[22] "VENEZUELA: Broken Contact," TIME. June 23, 1952, https://content.time.com/time/subscriber/article/0,33009,859802,00.html.

[23] F. Zerpa and E. Fieser, "Russian Oil Rigs in Venezuela Complicate U.S. Talks with Maduro," Bloomberg. March 11, 2022, https://www.bloomberg.com/news/articles/2022-03-11/russian-oil-rigs-in-venezuela-complicate-u-s-talks-with-maduro#xj4y7vzkg.

Upon the collapse of the government and civil society, we would likely move into a situation where allied countries would be able to provide help, but such help wouldn't be able to assuage large economic and societal disadvantages to Canadians. There would likely be the same kind of problems with food supply, poverty, and health witnessed in Venezuela from 2010 onward. It might also cost Canada valuable resources to maintain relationships with foreign nations helping.

For instance, there has for a long time been a theory called the "Grand Canal Scheme," which assumed the United States would take advantage of Canada by taking water resources from Canada's Huron Bay by diverting it through a man-made canal into the Great Lakes, beginning in Georgian Bay. This possibility was taught in Canadian high schools in the 1990s, though it still seems far-fetched, most notably because the brackish water in James Bay is loaded with organic material and requires heavy treatment.[24] It could also mean the US might involve itself in fracking in Alberta (however unlikely in the wake of these green initiatives). It might mean the mining and forestry industries throughout Canada could be manipulated by US interest through joint ventures. It might entail greater military cooperation between our two countries to be able to protect Canada's landmass. That would be in the unlikely event Canada encountered societal collapse and the United States was the same as it is today.

But what would happen to us socially, economically, and ideologically? That's where it is possible that Canada's government, at least as revealed under the Trudeau Liberals, would allow what is called *technocracy* to come in full-force and take hold of the country.

TECHNOCRACY: THE BRIDE OF MARX

Technocracy is a regime type where the most skilled individuals are appointed to positions based on their scientific and technical merits. It's a form of government that occurred in both the Soviet Union under Leonid Brezhnev from 1964–1982 and communist China from the 1950s onward, during what political scientist Dr. Anders Esmark refers to as "the golden age of the engineer." During this time frame, engineers were lauded as the ultimate achievers in society and were required to promote gains associated with advanced industry. But things have changed since then. Technocracy is now much more about computers, communications, and control of sensitive data.

---

[24] J. Barrera, "Attawapiskat Declares State of Emergency over Water Quality," CBC News: Indigenous, June 9, 2019, https://www.cbc.ca/news/indigenous/attawapiskat-water-quality-emergency-1.5204652.

Modern technocratic governments are a new regime (remember computers and data, and less so engineers) that arise to combat economic crises, such as in Greece (2009–2018) and Italy (2009–2013). At those times, it was considered necessary to implement highly unpopular austerity measures. People often lovingly refer to these regimes as democratic technocracies because the people are able to vote them out (and that happens pretty fast). But the question becomes: What if that technocracy could not be removed and it was authoritarian, in other words, it combined with socialism?

A state of crisis in a geographically vast and resource-rich country like Canada would be very difficult to control in the absence of boots on the ground, but we live in a day and age where almost everything is technologically regulated. Few Canadians have substantial assets (1 per cent of Canadian families hold over 25 per cent of the wealth), and the Charter of Rights and Freedoms doesn't protect a right to own either property or firearms.[25] You can thank an agreement between Pierre Elliott Trudeau and Ed Broadbent for leaving property rights out of the Charter. If the Canadian government wanted to appropriate your land today, and they were able to construct a sufficient excuse for it, they could take it from you. They've done it to others; just ask the First Nations.

This all means that we are very close already to what the World Economic Forum (WEF), to which both Justin Trudeau and Chrystia Freeland belong as members, has promised: "You'll own nothing, and you'll be happy."[26] That's the techno-communist goal for the future, presumably to free us of the capitalist burden by replacing our needs with technologically-based equivalents. Technology will also critically grant military capability necessary to control the population, because people won't be willing to submit to this. We've already had the most infinitesimal taste of what that technocratic control might entail.

Although Prime Minister Trudeau was adamant that there was no use of the Canadian military during the Freedom Convoy in 2022, that ran smack into the fact that a military plane did fly over and monitor the convoy during the Ottawa protest.[27] The excuse given for this action by the military commanders was that they were using a third-party airplane to contain their surveillance equipment,

---

[25] "Canada's Wealthiest One Per Cent Hold 25.6 Per Cent of Riches, New PBO Report Says," CTV News: Business, June 17, 2020, https://www.ctvnews.ca/business/canada-s-wealthiest-one-per-cent-hold-25-6-per-cent-of-riches-new-pbo-report-says-1.4988207?cache=yes.

[26] Wikipedia, s.v., "You'll own nothing and be happy," March 15, 2024, https://en.wikipedia.org/wiki/You%27ll_own_nothing_and_be_happy.

[27] Cheryl Gallant, "Military Spy Planes Were Used during Freedom Convoy Demonstrations in February," Facebook, May 4, 2022, https://www.facebook.com/watch/?v=952965965343642.

and flying that third-party plane over the Freedom Convoy was therefore not restricted. It's the type of dishonest conduct that has ensured the Canadian military is struggling with its members and the public for a long time to come.

Whether we continue to be subverted by the efforts of the CCP, whether we receive a slow picking away of civil society by the state (as Gairdner has suggested and as there is ample proof for), or whether we are under a legitimate assault by Marxist-affiliates like BLM and Antifa, or all three, we will likely not be prepared for what comes in the wake of such disaster. The big trick up the sleeve of the next generation of tyrants is going to be dominantly technological, and the degree to which it invades our lives is impossible to predict.

CHAPTER EIGHTEEN
CONCLUSION

DIALECTICAL LEFTISM IS a chameleon of sorts. To be certain, its original form of Orthodox Marxism has in no way expired. The CCP, whose Party membership (almost 100 million) now approaches triple the size of Canada's entire population, is a serious threat. They hold many of the Orthodox Marxist teachings in a Chinese style as adapted through Maoism, an ideology in which President Xi Jinping and his Party are thoroughly indoctrinated. Just because they now engage in widespread crony-capitalism doesn't mean they have abandoned their communist social policies—which are, in fact, stricter than ever. The increasing risk of espionage, political interference, and the possibility of a new Cold War between the US and China for world supremacy make the threat posed by the CCP more of a reality than ever. We can be thankful efforts are being made by CSIS, the RCMP, and other courageous Canadians to expose the threat the CCP maintains against Canada.

While dialectical leftism remains a threat in its original form, it's also affecting Canada in its most modern form of the woke ideology. On Canadian soil, dialectical leftism is fading away from the deep red of the many Marxist-Leninist regimes of the past, with just a handful remaining today. It festers within the halls of universities and colleges, where select young students become a new wave of adherents. It passes in whispers and in coffee shops and on the streets among the disenfranchised and anxious, visceral types open to radical solutions. It's bandied back and forth between politician and activist, to leverage the newest woke ideology to direct social policy. It invaded Canada's left-leaning Christian church over a century ago, and continues to shift that institution as it evolves, dictating exactly what churchgoers must believe.

Despite purporting a scientific basis, dialectical leftism is technically a faith, because it presupposes that an absolute truth exists somewhere within the ideologies of today. That truth will be manifested in the greatest organization of government, ostensibly leading to the most equitable distribution of misery and suffering, spreading pain so paper-thin it might as well be considered a utopia. Of course, there's absolutely no proof such a utopia is hidden within the present iteration of dialectical leftism, a synthesis of Neo-Marxism and postmodernism. Neither is there proof any such perfection exists within any other ideology by which a state is run. Still, critical theorist and Marxist initiate alike wish to move the dialectic forward, looking for the next big contradiction to address.

But dialectical leftism has not been honest about its repeated failure to address the ultimate contradiction: reality itself. After dialectical leftism first definitively materialized in Orthodox Marxism, it was rebuffed by decades of empirical evidence. Marx's predictions of workers rising up to break the chains of their oppressors turned out to be fantasy. Industrial capitalist society, for good or for evil, did not move toward class warfare without a lot of pushing, and even then pushing was not enough. The closest an advanced industrial society came to Marxist revolution was arguably after the end of WWI, during the German Revolution of 1918–1919. Yet there were clearly many other factors involved in that instance, over and above class antagonism.

The next reality barrier would be met after extensive developments within Neo-Marxism. Herbert Marcuse and the other critical theorists at the Frankfurt School calculated that only through a false consciousness were the workers being held back from revolution. They rationalized the inability of the workers to understand capitalist oppression as one reason Orthodox Marxism failed. Another reason was Marx's narrow focus on the workers as the sole proletariat, when there could be added students, feminists, Black liberation movements, academics, critical theorists, and other disenfranchised groups that sought the destruction of society. Neo-Marxism got close to revolution in France 1968, but it still failed. The post-industrial society was able to adjust, pay workers fairer wages, and quell dissent. A democratic election process after that incident gave a landslide victory to the side of the so-called bourgeois oppressors, who had for months been labelled as "fascists" and "Nazis."

So when Neo-Marxism met with reality and failed, it attempted to co-opt the Civil Rights Movement as the next step forward in dialectical leftism. This was Marcuse's wish, as we saw in his *An Essay on Liberation* from 1969, but he wouldn't live long enough to see it through. The next advancement in dialectical leftism was conducted most clearly by lawyer and critical race theorist Kimberlé

Crenshaw in her work "Mapping the Margins," well-explained by Dr. James Lindsay in his book *Race Marxism*.[1]

According to Dr. Lindsay, the synthesis of Neo-Marxism and postmodernism by Crenshaw officially created the woke culture we have today, dominantly focused on identity politics of race, and that has promoted significant societal problems. Of course, such problems existed beforehand; that was why the Civil Rights Movement was appropriated by Marxism in the first place. That need to co-opt civil rights matters didn't end with the 1960s either, as evidenced, for example, by the timing of Crenshaw's "Mapping the Margins," released the same year as the Rodney King beating (1991). Following that incident, there was a prolonged period of reduced violence before tensions returned during the Obama administration.

Riots, burning, and looting began around the deaths of unarmed Black teenagers Trayvon Martin (2012) and then Michael Brown (2014), which led to the US being shaken to its very core. More recently, the death of George Floyd (2020) and related protests were an increasingly veridical sentiment of discontent reigniting a dwindling momentum. Still, even after the co-optation of the Civil Rights Movement and the inception of woke ideology using critical race theory and intersectionality, dialectical leftism has thankfully proven unable to overturn society.

If reality is such a powerful bulwark against the call for revolution, why can't we just sit back and realize that dialectical leftism is not a serious threat? It's an over-generalization to say that reality is standing in the way of revolution, because that doesn't address the aspects of reality that contribute to the inertia stopping that revolution. Apathy also doesn't address the potential threats in Marxist methodology, some of which have been realized through extremist groups. While violence is always part of the Marxist mindset, murder occasionally comes to the fore.

The resistance to revolution has been the largely non-violent product of the state and civil society in North America. It's generally more easily observed in the United States than in Canada because the US typically displays more dramatic swings in societal tension. When the state is functioning well and close to a democratic representation, the general sentiment of the population has not conceded to extremism or submitted to extremist measures to solve societal problems. Arguably, the state can only remain a voice of reason as long as it

---

[1] J. Lindsay, *Race Marxism: The Truth About Critical Race Theory and Praxis* (Independently Published, 2022).

continues to represent the will of the majority of the people. That is certainly the only way it remains democratic. This is becoming more problematic with time in both Canada and the US, where left-leaning governments are creating increasingly egalitarian regimes that have both woke and technocratic aspects that reinforce depoliticization.

The State

The power of Canada's parliamentary system, which is supposed to be top dog in a parliamentary sovereignty, has come under question with increasing methods of depoliticization, such as the use of the Emergency Act in 2022, the choice to reduce parliament during the coronavirus pandemic, and the back-door deal to prop up the federal Liberals with support of the NDP until 2025.[2,3,4] None of these examples are democratic decision-making but rather attempts to use existing power to keep decision-making from the people of Canada as long as possible.

The pushing of woke ideology in parliament, especially by the Trudeau Liberals, is of great concern because such an ideology ignores reality, as we have seen, and this has caused problems in the efficacy of education, policing, and the state itself. The ineffectual nature of a great deal of woke policy is not allowed to be discussed for fear of emotionally triggering groups or individuals with specific sensitivities. This fear of dealing with emotionally charged subjects has arguably led to the loss of lives, such as in the acceleration of police homicides between 2022–2023.[5] A weakened judicial system that does not adequately contain violent criminals is a serious problem that threatens all lives, not just police.

---

[2] C. Tunney, "Federal Government Invokes Emergencies Act for First Time Ever in Response to Protests, Blockades," CBC News. February 14, 2022, https://www.cbc.ca/news/politics/trudeau-premiers-cabinet-1.6350734.

[3] B. Curry, "Trudeau Liberals Limit Scrutiny with Fewer Sitting Days in the House," *The Globe and Mail*, October 18, 2021, https://www.theglobeandmail.com/politics/article-trudeau-liberals-continue-to-sideline-parliament-opposition-says/.

[4] R. Aiello, "Liberals' Deal with NDP Will Keep Trudeau Minority in Power for 3 More Years," CTV News: Politics, March 22, 2022, https://www.ctvnews.ca/politics/liberals-deal-with-ndp-will-keep-trudeau-minority-in-power-for-3-more-years-1.5829116.

[5] J. Laucius, "Nine Police Officers in Canada Have Been Slain Since Last September. The Big Question Is Why Now?" *Ottawa Citizen*, May 19, 2023, https://ottawacitizen.com/news/local-news/nine-police-officers-in-canada-have-been-slain-since-last-september-the-big-question-is-why-now.

CHAPTER EIGHTEEN: CONCLUSION

The Media

The Canadian Broadcasting Corporation, Canada's dominantly state-funded legacy media, is ideologically aligned closely with the federal Liberals. This is problematic because they exclusively promote that ideological view, increasingly at odds with many Canadians, despite receiving their paycheque from those same Canadians (though indirectly). The CBC represents a critical weakness in the state, in that without an unbiased or at least representative media, the population should not be forced to endorse exclusive ideological standpoints they don't agree with.

The popular initiative to "defund the CBC" might be too simplistic. A better solution may exist in reforming the CBC so that it necessarily *must* include a broader range of ideological standpoints, more representative of Canadian interests throughout the country. This includes interests that are represented by varying religions and cultures, but also could include more fairly represented geographically influenced differences. The alienation of Alberta in issues regarding oil and gas, for example, continues to be a sore point in Canadian politics and media, and that is not acceptable. A more balanced media would go a long way to providing a stable relationship between state and civil society, instead of creating division as witnessed, for example, during the Freedom Convoy in 2022.

The Police

As an arm of a just state, the police remain a critical contributor to the stability of a free society. Perhaps equally important to this, they are citizens within civil society itself, and so contribute to that society in a multitude of ways. Many officers are not disconnected from the communities in which they operate, and if they are, that should be remedied as much as possible. The extremist narratives to defund or abolish police are foolhardy solutions that rely on a radical conception of society and humanity. A thankfully small demonstration of the disaster that ensues from such anarchism was provided in the CHAZ/CHOP zone in Seattle 2020, which saw multiple murders during its brief existence and was ultimately shuttered as a fiasco.[6] The police are vital to state and civil society, and it is critical they remain supported by citizens and demonstrate responsibility to those same citizens through initiatives such as police reform.

---

[6] K. Johnson, "Another Fatal Shooting in Seattle's 'CHOP' Protest Zone," *The New York Times*, June 29, 2020, https://www.nytimes.com/2020/06/29/us/seattle-protests-CHOP-CHAZ-autonomous-zone.html.

PART V: THE HARVEST

The Church

As we looked at previously, education and religion have had a tumultuous relationship throughout the history of Western society, but they are a great deal more intertwined than most would care to admit. The biggest problems between the institutions of education and religion have occurred not when they operated as separate entities, however, but rather from when they were addressed dialectically to reconcile them. It was G.W.F. Hegel's dream to marry Christianity to rationality, and although he tried to synthesize the rationalism of Kant with Christ Jesus, he ended up hating what he made. The Hegelian dialectic was a second attempt to reconcile Christianity with philosophy. If Hegel could see where dialectical leftism was today, he would likely be incredibly dissatisfied or even outright revolted, but he opened the door to that descent. When he tried to appropriate God into his philosophical understanding—his dialectical method—he gave humanity a new, distinctly non-Christian faith to follow to paradise. Hegel would weep to think his ideas had been manipulated into Lenin's October Revolution or Mao's Cultural Revolution. The monistic vision he claimed to have received from God to inspire his philosophy has not borne out some dramatic ascent to heaven on earth, but has clearly shown a path wrought with destruction and death.

The institution of the Church has been the biggest scapegoat throughout history for society's ills, and while organized religion must certainly take the blame for some of these failures, we hope to have shown herein that it is not the ubiquitous failure many claim it to be. The Christian faith, written down in the Bible and not subject to drastic change in interpretation, can always be checked against the actions of self-identified Christians. If considered directly from scriptural instruction, the Bible clearly precludes wrongs such as papal indulgences and other abuses of power witnessed repeatedly throughout history. Even the punishment for disbelief in Christ, the unforgivable sin, is supposed to be in God's purview, and not humanity's to enact.

The Education System

The institution of Western education, beginning during the fall of Rome in monastic schools, was originally Christian. Only after it evolved into cathedral schools and then medieval universities did it approach the institutions we have today. For over a thousand years, Western education was beholden to the Christian faith that oversaw its expansion.

CHAPTER EIGHTEEN: CONCLUSION

All that changed in the 1800s. At that time, Christian affiliation in universities began to fall away in the belief that science, with its impartiality and rational basis, would fill the void. The truth seems to be that science couldn't fill that space for very long, as in the absence of Christianity, radical indoctrination flooded the halls of academe in a relatively short time. This is exactly when dialectical leftism first crept into universities. The values of the Age of Enlightenment provided little stable ideological basis for human beings, who have been spiritual throughout their existence and not just simple creatures of flesh and blood. While Christianity took over a thousand years to fall away from the education system, reason and science took less than a hundred. By the 1960s, the postmodern movement was in full swing, and the rejection of the values of reason and the scientific method were all the rage. A host of anti-science, irrational ideologies permeate education today.

The critical institutions of both the state and civil society we have examined here must be fought for in order for society to endure violent attempts at revolution. For the state, this means the police force, a target for radical left activists, must be supported and not constantly attacked and demoralized by politicians. Police must never be forced into confessor behaviour as former RCMP Commissioner Brenda Lucki was. The current state of affairs is predictable in light of the constant criticism and blaming of police for increasing societal problems. Continued attempts to increase gun laws have had no significant effect on this trend, either.

In civil society, both the existing educational and religious institutions are subject to subversion by dialectical leftism when they become preoccupied with social justice narratives. The system of education was traditionally a place to teach, experiment, and learn about the world around us to increase the body of knowledge available to us. More and more it tends to focus on class antagonisms, past and present, to reinforce the use of identity politics to create a new value system in society. This is a form of cultural subversion, and Canadian parents are just starting to realize the level of indoctrination their children are being exposed to. Solutions addressing such indoctrination must fall to the level of the parent or guardian, who should be involved with their child's education to a level where they understand what is being taught. The idea of letting the state educate children so that the parents could be free to do other things is as old as the Utopian socialists of the late 1700s. The Utopian socialists were lethargic examples of potential parents that couldn't be bothered to address the needs of their children. They wanted to do more "important" things, like write about philosophy.

As for the left-leaning church, its congregants have chosen a faith that is constantly evolving according to the precepts of dialectical leftism. There's no point in trying to forcefully overcome the indoctrination of such systems, as waves of the Social Gospel movement have clearly taken these churches far away from any form of Christianity the Bible might instruct. This is a reality of the effectiveness of the methodology of Cultural Marxism and the ability to ideologically subvert an organization without so much as lifting a finger. The best thing to do is to shake the dust off your feet and move along.

Dialectical leftism is a faith. It promises the answers to society's problems, but for almost two centuries has delivered little more than murder, riots, looting, and burning. It is used by virtue-signalling politicians to show they are worldly or caring, when in fact the heart of dialectical leftism is dominantly uncaring. Somehow, this ideology has become a threat to institutions of both the state and civil society. The efforts of each citizen to become involved in the goings-on of the Canadian government and police, the scope of the legacy media CBC, the orientation of their own church or religious institution, and to oversee the curriculum of the education system where their children participate are never wasted. Every single citizen who becomes involved on some level and contributes to the decisions and actions of these institutions is a contributor to establishing a stronger, more resilient civil society, and a stronger, better government.

BIBLIOGRAPHY

Dikötter, Frank. *Mao's Great Famine: The History of China's Most Devastating Catastrophe, 1958–1962*. New York: Bloomsbury USA, 2010.

Diverlus, Rodney, Sandy Hudson, and Syrus Marcus Ware. *Until We Are Free: Reflections on Black Lives Matter in Canada*. Regina, SK: University of Regina Press, 2020.

Dreher, Rod. *Live Not by Lies: A Manual for Christian Dissidents*. New York: Sentinel, 2020.

Esmark, Anders. *The New Technocracy*. Bristol, UK: Bristol University Press, 2020.

Gairdner, William D. *The Trouble with Canada ... Still!: A Citizen Speaks Out*. Toronto, ON: BPS Books, 2010.

Hicks, S. R. *Explaining Postmodernism: Skepticism and Socialism from Rousseau to Foucault*. Brisbane, AU: Connor Court Publishing, 2019.

Jenish, D. *The Making of the October Crisis: Canada's Long Nightmare of Terrorism at the Hands of the FLQ*. Toronto, ON: Anchor Canada, 2020.

Kengor, Paul. *The Devil and Karl Marx: Communism's Long March of Death, Deception, and Infiltration*. Gastonia, NC: TAN Books, 2020.

Landolt, Gwen, Patrick Redmond, and Douglas Alderson. *From Democracy to Judicial Dictatorship in Canada: The Untold Story of the Charter of Rights*. Independently Published, 2019.

Lawton, Andrew. *The Freedom Convoy: The Inside Story of Three Weeks that Shook the World*. Toronto, ON: Sutherland House, 2022.

Levant, Ezra. *The Libranos: What the media won't tell you about Justin Trudeau's corruption.* Toronto, ON: Rebel News Network Ltd., 2019.

Lindsay, James. *Race Marxism: The Truth about Critical Race Theory and Praxis.* Orlando, Florida: New Discourse LLC, 2022.

Lohmeier, Matthew L. *Irresistible Revolution: Marxism's Goal of Conquest & the Unmaking of the American Military.* Self-published, 2021.

Lukianoff, Greg and Jonathan Haidt. *The Coddling of the American Mind: How Good Intentions and Bad Ideas are Setting Up a Generation for Failure.* New York: Penguin Press, 2018.

Manthorpe, Jonathan. *Claws of the Panda: Beijing's Campaign of Influence and Intimidation in Canada.* Toronto, ON: Cormorant Books Inc., 2019.

Marx, Karl and Friedrich Engels. *Marx/Engels Selected Works, Vol. One: Manifesto of the Communist Party (1848).* Moscow, RUS: Progress Publishers.

Ngo, Andy. *Unmasked: Inside Antifa's Radical Plan to Destroy Democracy.* New York: Center Street Publishing, 2021.

Paul, Rand and Kelley Ashbey Paul. *The Case Against Socialism.* New York: Broadside Books, 2019.

Peterson, Jordan B. *12 Rules for Life: An Antidote to Chaos.* New York: Random House Canada, 2018.

Peterson, Jordan B. *Beyond Order: 12 More Rules for Life.* New York: Random House Canada, 2021.

Saad, Gad. *The Parasitic Mind: How Infectious Ideas Are Killing Common Sense.* Washington, DC: Regnery Publishing, 2020.

Schwab, Klaus and Thierry Malleret. *Covid-19: The Great Reset.* Geneva, Switzerland: World Economic Forum, 2020.

Wiker, Benjamin. *10 Books that Screwed Up the World: And Five Others That Didn't Help.* Washington, DC: Regnery Publishing Inc., 2008.

AUTHOR BIO

MAVROS WHISSELL IS the researcher, writer, and presenter for *Woken Promises*, which analyzes Canada's left-leaning political initiatives. He has spent the past six years researching leftist ideology and its direct effect on Canada's political sphere, while creating a discussion forum for all Canadians to participate in. Mavros has a B.Sc. (Hons) in Geology, and his extensive background in science allows him to challenge media narratives with analysis designed for everyday people like himself.

www.ingramcontent.com/pod-product-compliance
Lightning Source LLC
Chambersburg PA
CBHW060654100426
42734CB00047B/1669